AF521769

Political Representation in the Later Middle Ages

PETER LANG
New York • Washington, D.C./Baltimore • Bern
Frankfurt am Main • Berlin • Brussels • Vienna • Oxford

Hwa-Yong Lee

Political Representation in the Later Middle Ages

Marsilius in Context

PETER LANG
New York • Washington, D.C./Baltimore • Bern
Frankfurt am Main • Berlin • Brussels • Vienna • Oxford

Library of Congress Cataloging-in-Publication Data

Lee, Hwa-Yong.
Political representation in the later middle ages:
Marsilius in context / Hwa-Yong Lee.
p. cm.
Includes bibliographical references and index.
1. Marsilius, of Padua, d. 1342?—Political and social views.
2. Representative government and representation—Europe—
History—To 1500. 3. Philosophy, Medieval. I. Title.
JC121.M35L44 321.8092—dc22 2007030632
ISBN 978-0-8204-9531-6

Bibliographic information published by **Die Deutsche Bibliothek**.
Die Deutsche Bibliothek lists this publication in the "Deutsche
Nationalbibliografie"; detailed bibliographic data is available
on the Internet at http://dnb.ddb.de/.

The paper in this book meets the guidelines for permanence and durability
of the Committee on Production Guidelines for Book Longevity
of the Council of Library Resources.

Printed in Germany

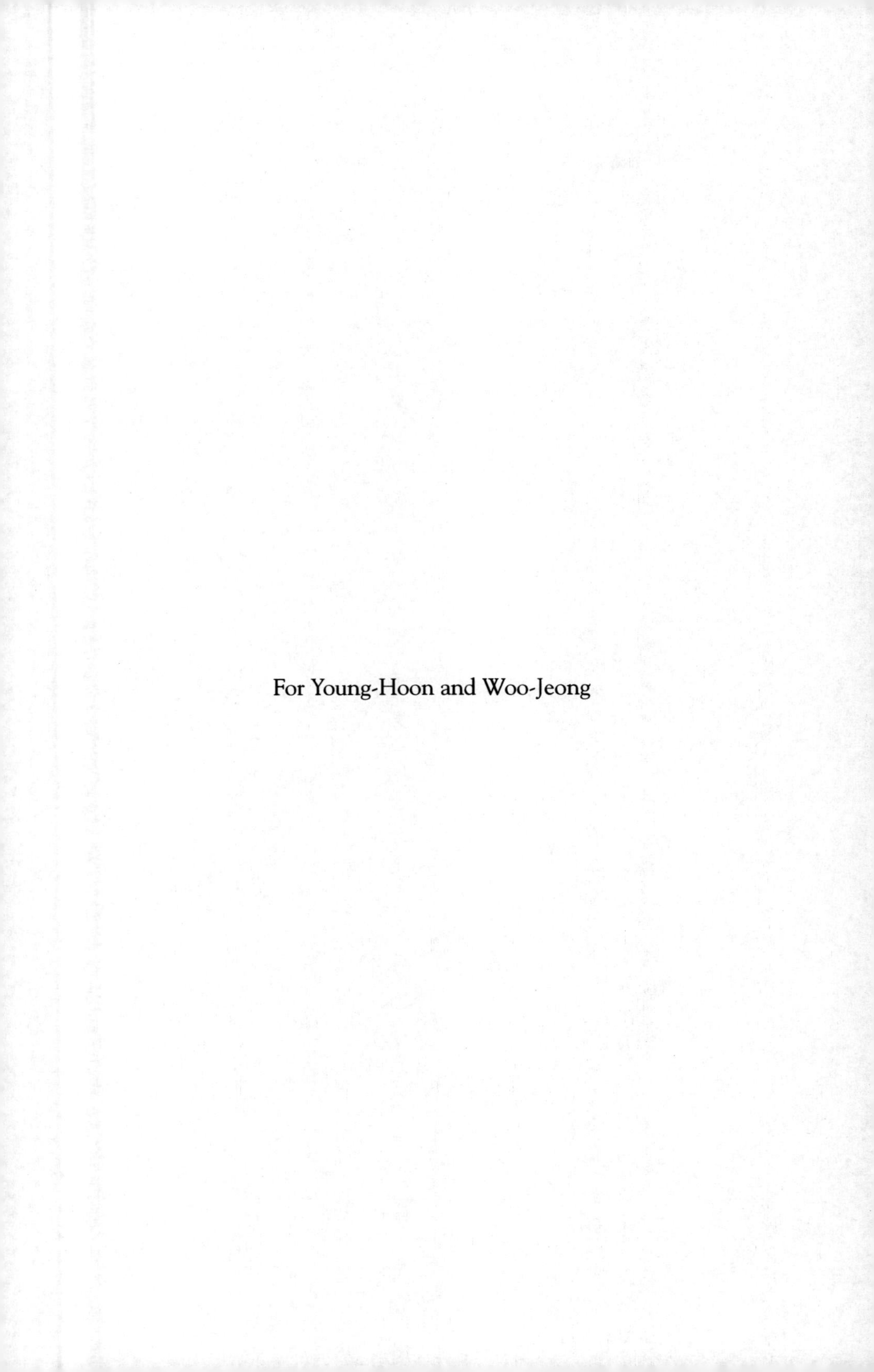

For Young-Hoon and Woo-Jeong

CONTENTS

ACKNOWLEDGMENTS

This book has its origins in my dissertation submitted for the degree of Doctor of Philosophy in the University of Cambridge. Both during the writing of the dissertation and subsequently I have incurred many debts to the numerous friends, colleagues and teachers who have helped and advised me. I am delighted to remember their names and have an opportunity to express my warm thanks to them.

First, I would like to pay tribute to the memory of the late Professor Robert Cook, who was to me a second father in Cambridge. I remember him with reverence and thanks. I am also deeply grateful to Dr. Annabel Brett, who was my supervisor at Cambridge and with whom it is still a pleasure to communicate. I am also thankful to Dr. John Coffey and in particular Dr. Timothy Duff, whose help and advice was very valuable. I should like to thank my teachers at Ewha, Seoul, especially Professor Seung-Tae Yang and Professor Duk-Kyu Jin, who instructed me in political theory and the history of political thought. I would also like to thank Kyung Hee University, which now provides me with the opportunity to teach and study in its stimulating and friendly atmosphere. My friends gave me comfort and laughter at the times of tension. I thank them all.

This list would not be complete if I did not express the special thanks due both to Professor Dunn and to my family. Without Professor Dunn's unfailing support and encouragement, I could not have completed my work. His conversation and precious comments enabled me to clarify and focus my arguments. My best wishes for him and his family are not sufficient repayment for the debt I owe to him. My parents have been generous and supportive of me in all situations. My husband and daughter, Young-Hoon and Woo-Jeong, whom I did not have during the time of my PhD, have been my new supporters and a great source of strength for me. I am very happy to express my love to them through this book.

ABBREVIATIONS

The following abbreviations have been used for frequently cited sources:

D.	Digest
C.	Codex
CHLMP	The Cambridge History of Later Medieval Philosophy: from the Rediscovery of Aristotle to the Disintegration of Scholasticism, 1100–1600
CHMPT	The Cambridge History of Medieval Political Thought, c.350–c.1450
CHRP	The Cambridge History of Renaissance Philosophy
CMH	The Cambridge Medieval History
EHR	English Historical Review
MGH	*Momunenta Germania Historica*
TRHS	Transactions of the Royal Historical Society

Unless otherwise stated, all translations in this book are mine.

INTRODUCTION: WHY MARSILIUS AND POLITICAL REPRESENTATION?

This book seeks to explore how the theory of political representation was articulated in Marsilius of Padua, a fourteenth-century Italian thinker. My concern is not to explicate the genesis of political representation today by tracing the long and complicated history of the theorisation of the practice of political representation. Rather this project is prompted by the judgement that we still need to think again about contemporary claims concerning representative democracy embodied in our political practice today.

Historians and political theorists, despite their agreement about the necessity of the history of political thought, have different approaches and different intentions. When a political idea is the subject of inquiry, political theorists tend to think about the relation of the concept to that of the modern period or of today. Historians, on the other hand, tend to find out when and how the idea started to have its initial shape rather than to pay attention to its relation to our contemporary issues. Each approach reflects one aspect of the debate on the methodology of the history of political thought. The question of which approach to take for our research is the basic issue which a political theorist or a historian must confront, if he or she is to think seriously about how and why they are doing the history of political thought.

In his brief article, "The Contribution of History,"[1] Richard Tuck gives us a concise summary of the methodological debate about the history of political thought which began in the 1960s. Tuck names two schools at the forefront of the debate. One is the 'old history of political thought,' of which the primary concern was with investigating the classics in search for the values expressed in the texts.[2] The other is the 'new' history which surveys political and other ideas in the history of their actual circumstances.[3]

Quentin Skinner's often-cited statements, which make an explicit proposition about the relationship between ideas and reality, constitute a provocative starting point when we want to contrast the character of these two approaches:

> I turn first to consider the methodology dictated by the claim that the text itself should form the self-sufficient object of inquiry and understanding. For it is this assumption which continues to govern the largest number of studies, to raise the widest philosophical issues, and to give rise to the largest number of confusions...... The whole point, it is characteristically said, of studying past works of philosophy (or literature) must be that they contain (in a favoured phrase) 'timeless elements', in the form of 'universal ideas,' even a 'dateless wisdom' with 'universal application'......The aim, in short, must be to provide 'a re-appraisal of the classic writings, quite apart from the context of historical development, as perennially important attempts to set down universal propositions about political reality.'[4]

According to Skinner, the traditional way of reading the classics,[5] that is the 'old' approach, presumes that the classical texts systematically connote elements of perennial interests and suggests a theory or doctrine which readers themselves expect to find but the author of the text did not elaborate. Contrarily, Skinner argues that because a text is not by itself fully intelligible to us, it cannot form the immediate object of inquiry and understanding without the knowledge of the context to which it was addressed. He, against the 'old' approach, presents an alternative methodology by which to understand a classic text properly, that is 'a contextual approach':

> The understanding of texts...... presupposes the grasp both of what they were intended to mean, and how this meaning was intended to be taken...... The essential question which we therefore confront, in studying any given text, is what its author, in writing at the time he did write for the audience he intended to address, could in practice have been intending to communicate by the utterance of this given utterance. It follows that the essential aim, in any attempt to understand the utterances themselves, must be to recover this complex intention on the part of the author...... The appropriate methodology for the history of ideas must be concerned, first of all, to delineate the

> whole range of communications which could have been conventionally performed on the given occasion by the utterance of the given utterance, and next, to trace the relations between the given utterance and this wider linguistic context as a means of decoding the actual intention of the given writer.[6]

The 'contextual approach' starts with the presumption that the appropriate focus of the study is essentially linguistic in the sense that the texts express very complicated and compound human actions. In particular, putting the emphasis on the constitutive role of an author's intention in writing a text, Skinner suggests that to understand a text we should focus on the preoccupations and purposes that made that author compose it. That is, the key to understanding every text is to grasp the fact that it was the complete product of a human author's intention.

For this approach an understanding of the intentions of an author can be supplemented by knowledge of the contexts in which a text was being written. In this respect, the 'contextual approach' includes the study of the social context of the given text, but it does so on the understanding that the social context too can constitute a part of this linguistic enterprise. The contextual method in a broader sense—that is the linguistic context—is a means of determining the *meaning* of the text.[7] This is because the linguistic context is an ultimate framework for helping to decide "what conventionally recognisable meanings, in a society of that kind, it might in principle have been possible for someone to have intended to communicate."[8] In this sense, together with consideration of an intention of an author, the social, political and economic conditions function as a context in which to understand the meaning of a text. But the social context does not have to be treated as the determinant of what is said.[9] Thus, the 'contextual approach' is differentiated from other approaches, which take historical context seriously but focus on a social and institutional rather than a linguistic context.[10] To put it simply, the 'contextual approach' seeks to comprehend the meaning of a text in terms of social and intellectual context and of the writer's intention incorporated in it.

With this method of the 'contextual approach,' we seek to understand the use of a given sentence by a particular author who had a particular intention of making a particular point. To take an example of a basic concept for political understanding, the 'state' was not a naturally given entity which connoted an original and independent reality. It was formed in part by the clear and distinct ideas of great philosophers, but it has also its own history formed by praxis. So to understand the meanings of the 'state,' we need, amongst other things, to uncover specifically what such thinkers as Hobbes, Locke and Hegel meant by the 'state,' that is what they intended to convey with their own language in their own contexts. The 'contextual approach' argues that by doing so, the study of the history of ideas can return to history, not to mythology.[11]

The extensive debate over which approach gives us a greater insight into the history of political ideas demands that we reflect carefully upon our own historical practice. But these reflections reach back to a more fundamental problem, which is considerably more difficult to answer: if we are still to tackle the history of political thought, why are we doing so and what is it precisely we are doing when we do so?[12]

Indeed, by identifying what was the intellectual context which pervaded and formulated ideas in the period when a text was being written, how the author of a text was intervening in the conflicts of the day, what he or she intended to do, what the text meant and why it meant that and not something else, we can attain the understanding of meaning of the text with historical accuracy. In this aspect, as Skinner insists, any statement embodies a particular intention, addressed to the solution of a particular problem in a specific circumstance.[13] However, I suggest that the particular issues of a historical context are not necessarily confined to those of the past because clearly much that was written in the classics of political theory is still relevant to our own political thinking today and forms the conceptual framework upon which this is based. That is, the philosophical reflections of the classic writers have been of great historical consistency and consequence, since they have been attended to uninterruptedly by the society in which we now live.[14] In this aspect, the particular issues are not only what concerned past authors but also what concerns us today. This does not mean that the historical understanding of past issues can directly give us a convincing solution or answer to the problems which we face now. But at least, through philosophical reflection as a historical activity, we need to try to learn more about what kinds of conflicts there were, why these conflicts arose and, more importantly, how we can derive from them a set of values which might enable us to live with confidence in our own world of conflicts. To this end, the values or merits of historical study can be considered in various ways. The contribution of the historical study of past ideas or thoughts does not need merely to lie in revealing their origin or their conceptual ramifications in later periods. Rather, seeing the texts in a richer setting, we will be better placed to question the present and future relevance of a set of human creations fashioned in the past: 'what do the great texts of the history of political theory mean today and give to us?'

My own assumption is that the 'old' and 'new' approaches are far from being incompatible. The reading of a classic text is not a repudiation of the methodology which the 'contextual approach' puts forward. It too offers an example of how to make an historical enquiry to resolve or at least illuminate a modern theoretical problem. Equally, to suggest that a knowledge of the context is a necessary condition for an understanding of the classic texts does not deny that they contain any elements of timeless and perennial interest, and does not remove the whole point of the 'old' approach. Indeed, the reasons why we study political thinkers, and the character of the attention we pay them, have continuously arisen in the course of our historical experience.[15] So the difference between the 'old' and the 'new' approach is not as great as may at first appear. It is hard to believe that analytical argument could best be understood without considering in the first instance what the person who composed it was attempting to argue. On the other hand, an understanding of what its author meant can never by itself be sufficient to assess the current significance of what a great text's arguments contribute.[16] The important point for these tasks is how comprehensively a researcher tackles both the historical and philosophical issues in order to understand the concept which he or she is investigating.

My concern with Marsilius of Padua begins with these methodological points in mind. I will combine two approaches—historical and philosophical —in my interpretation of Marsilius' approach to the issue of political representation. That is, what I attempt to do in my dissertation is to explore Marsilius' thought in relation to the concept of political representation by examining the context to which Marsilius' texts were addressed. At this point, the question could arise whether, and in what sense, the term 'political representation' can be useful for an understanding of Marsilius' thought. It is true that Marsilius did not mention our own term 'political representation' directly. But I believe that it is reasonable to interpret the political thought of Marsilius with this issue in view as long as we recognise the distinctions of his own vocabulary and the focus of his intellectual interests. I also suggest that if we understand political representation not as a technical concept concerned with the rational representation of particular interests, but as a comprehensive concept which provides insight into much of the complexity of political phenomena, the analysis of political representation can be a key point in establishing a coherent understanding of Marsilius' thought. In fact, as we shall see, Marsilius provides us with a rich body of normative discussions about the philosophical foundations of political representation, a body of material which can help us to think again about the nature and significance of political representation as we still practice this today. Through Marsilius' case for political representation, I will show that he offers a perspective upon political representation which, beyond the mechanical pursuit of material interests as envisaged in our contemporary analysis of political representation, is expected to work as a scheme for good government for the whole people.

Many authors have acclaimed Marsilius as the most important and original political thinker of the Middle Ages, often more because of his contribution to modern political thought than because of his role within the political discourse of his own time. That is, Marsilius has been regarded as the precursor of modern political theorists. H. Laski, R. L. Poole, and C. W. Previté-Orton all made this claim,[17] although they did not argue systematically for its validity. However, on the other hand, R. W. and A. J. Carlyle denied that Marsilius set out a new and revolutionary democratic doctrine, and insisted that he simply expressed the normal judgement and practice of the Middle Ages, in asserting traditional principles.[18] In a similar way, G. de Lagarde argued that with Marsilius emerged the lay spirit (*l'esprit laïque*).[19] However, by claiming that Marsilius' argument for it, which denied the possession of the political power by the church, was not based on the equality of individuals, Lagarde supposed that Marsilius was far from being a precursor of modern philosophy.[20]

Alan Gewirth's pioneering work enables us to gain an overall view of Marsilius' thought.[21] Gewirth puts forward a detailed philosophical-conceptual analysis of Marsilius' key concepts such as the state, peace, law, the legislator, government and the church. Gewirth's primary attention is centred upon the immediate characteristics of Marsilius' doctrines. This does not mean that Gewirth fails to consider them in relation to their concrete historical contexts, but his understanding of the historical context sometimes leads to an inadequate understanding of the historical sense of Marsilius' terminology.[22]

J. Quillet is more helpful in understanding Marsilius' thought in its social and institutional settings. According to Quillet, to understand the significance of Marsilius' thought, we need to examine the contexts of the relations of the empire with the Italian city-states without neglecting the relation between the empire and the pope.[23] Quillet argues that Marsilius understood the unity of the city-states or the provinces in terms of the concept of empire. She emphasises that the empire had the *jura reservata* over the city-states, in particular in northern Italy, and that the *regnum* was just a technical term of constitutionalism.[24] On this understanding, Quillet asserts that Marsilius considered the emperor or the princes as the expression of the human legislator, or the rule and measure of human actions.[25] Unlike Gewirth,[26] she maintains that the principle of popular sovereignty as the source of political authority, a key point in Marsilius' thought, did not imply acceptance of the republican principle of modern popular sovereignty, because the tyranny of *signori* in Italy did not make this possible. She suggests instead that to discover the implications of popular sovereignty in the period, it is necessary to analyse the relation between the church and the state.[27]

These scholars of Marsilius all offer some interpretations which permit us to view his thought in a clear light. They touch on a variety of themes which are fundamental to understanding Marsilius. We can rely upon them to make clear views on these issues, despite the variety of their concerns in approaching Marsilius. In comparison, the originality of my research on Marsilius lies in its focus on the issue of political representation as an overall problem through which we can hope to understand his analysis of political authority with historical accuracy and explore its relevance to contemporary interpretations of political representation.

In this respect, Cary Nederman's book *Community and Consent* is a useful attempt to get Marsilius' thought into clearer focus. In reading Marsilius, Nederman, one of the most prominent modern interpreters of Marsilius, employs the twin approaches of a historicized interpretation and a philosophical one. *Community and Consent* is successful in some measure, but Nederman's historical understanding of Marsilius is not wholly convincing, not least because Nederman himself does not have in mind a clear and compelling conception of political representation of his own. Moreover, Nederman's all but exclusive preoccupation with the secular aspects of Marsilius' thought excludes the issue of the governance of the church, on the assumption, first, that Marsilius distinguished the secular and the ecclesiastical in his thought and second, that Marsilian ecclesiology relies more directly on religious assumptions which do not fit well with modern secular principles of politics.[28] In brief, his position is that Marsilius' conception of the nature and standing of the temporal community is quite distinct from his account of how the church is governed. I believe that this discrimination between temporal and spiritual elements of Marsilius' argument is not only unhelpful for an understanding of his thought as a whole, but also importantly misrepresents it.

With these questions in mind, this book is, first, an attempt to combine the 'old' and the 'new' approaches which I have explained above, in order to understand Marsilius' thought. For this task, I am not concerned only with Marsilius' texts but also with the context to which these texts were addressed. To this end, before explicating the arguments which Marsilius himself developed in his texts, I will examine the historical context of his main arguments, with special reference to the concept of political representation. The understanding of this context provides us with a clearer and more exact understanding of the claims which he advanced.

Secondly, I intend to show that Marsilius' conception of political representation provides us with a more adequate understanding of the nature and significance of political representation than contemporary political science interpreters are in a position to supply. Our contemporary understanding of political representation views it essentially as a relationship between the represented and the representative. However, I will argue that without a fuller understanding of political representation, we cannot hope to capture its political character as a more or less coherent scheme for public action or good government. That is, as we shall see, if we regard political representation as a more or less effective scheme for good government, we must focus on the nature of the transfer of power between the represented and the representative, not on the full practical content of the relations between these two political actors. To approach such an understanding, we can start by asking the following questions: is the scheme of political representation, that is, the alienation of judgement or its substitution, really necessary? Is the alienation or the substitution fair and therefore trustworthy? What is the necessary consequence of transferring power to the representative, thereby subjugating the represented? In the end, how far does representative democracy, a dominant version of political representation today in many countries, retain the understanding of authoritative and binding public action on behalf of the whole people? In what respects and to what degree, is it a desirable alternative to direct democracy? Marsilius offers a perspective upon political representation which is broad enough to deepen our comprehension of the normative foundation of political representation and to help us to answer these questions for ourselves.

My analysis will begin by examining the significance of the modern terminology of political representation. For this, in Chapter 1, I will explore normative theories of political representation in the eighteenth and nineteenth centuries to see the political implications of their interpretations of the practice of political representation. The examination of the normative theories which constitute a philosophical foundation of our contemporary understanding of political representation will show the sources of the main issues in the modern agenda of political representation.

Chapter 2 examines discussions about political representation in the later Middle Ages in order to identify the characteristics of the medieval idea of political representation. These discussions centred on a variety of practices in many different contexts and many different normative and practical conceptions were deployed in the course of them. The conceptual components of political representation in the later Middle Ages—consent, *quod omnes tangit* and *plena potestas*—did not comprise a single clear and unified conception of representation but had a clear, if embryonic, relationship to modern conceptions. The examination of these seminal notions of political representation will enable us to set out a theoretical history of political representation as a map in which Marsilius' conception of political representation can be placed.

Part II (Chapters 3–6) discusses the historical context in which Marsilius' arguments for political representation were developed, and thus equips us to understand how and why Marsilius' thought developed as it did. It explores the main components of the issues associated with the theme of political representation in the medieval context: the conflict between the temporal power and the spiritual power, the so-called *lex regia* debate about the locus of legislative power, the *de facto* independence of Italian city-states, and the prevalence and nature of contemporary Aristotelianism in Italy.

Chapters 7–8 show how the concept of political representation is articulated in the thought of Marsilius himself. To this end, they analyse the meaning and importance of the concepts of peace, law, justice and the human legislator for demonstrating the necessity of the sovereignty of the people. I argue that Marsilius' conception of political representation with its unyielding focus on the transfer of power provides a clearer and more compelling view of what is required if political representation is to function as a normatively coherent scheme of public action than can be derived from the analysis of modern processes of representation in contemporary political science. Chapter 9 focuses on the issue of who Marsilius' real legislator who had the sovereign power, historically speaking, was. These chapters establish that, both in theoretical and in historical terms, Marsilius' legislator is nothing other than the whole body of citizens and that the people as legislator continues to be sovereign without the forfeiture of its power in any practice of political representation.

In conclusion, drawing on this study of Marsilius, I reconsider one key element of our contemporary practice of political representation: how far representative democracy, as an alternative to direct democracy, really remains the best scheme for public action on behalf of the people. I do so by juxtaposing Marsilius' case for political representation with our contemporary interest-based conceptions of how political representation does and can function.

PART I

THEORY: APPROACH TO MARSILIUS

· 1 ·

THE LANGUAGE OF POLITICAL REPRESENTATION

In *Considerations on Representative Government*, John S. Mill claimed that representative government meant that "the whole people, or some numerous portion of them, exercise through deputies periodically elected by themselves, the ultimate controlling power, which, in every constitution, must reside somewhere."[1] This century-old definition can still help us understand what political representation signifies. Today, in countries which choose representative democracy as a form of state, ordinary citizens have the right to one man-one vote and thus they, in regular elections, vote for a political candidate or a political party which they want to be their own representative. We name this form of state 'representative democracy' or 'modern constitutional representative government' or political representation in general.[2]

Today, the legitimacy and authority of the representative government is regarded as resulting from its being an expression of the will of the people. However, this expression as the source of the legitimate authorisation for public acts is indirect: citizens transfer it to their representatives as intermediaries. The representatives as intermediaries are those who make the people's will present on its behalf. Thus, political representation has as its theoretical scheme two political actors: the citizens or the people and the representative. This scheme of political representation which looks simple actually has many political implications for political actors and processes. This chapter is concerned with exploring what the modern terminology of political representation means and what implications it involves. To this end, I will in this chapter examine the normative theories of political representation developed in the eighteenth and nineteenth centuries. Our contemporary analysis of political representation is still based on these eighteenth- and nineteenth-century normative theories of political representation as a philosophical foundation to justify the working of representative government today. Therefore, the examination of these normative theories will not only demonstrate the sources of the main issues in the modern agenda of political representation, but also provide a conceptual reference point from which to approach Marsilius' conception of political representation.

According to the *Oxford English Dictionary*, 'represent' is used to mean "to bring into presence: esp. to represent oneself or another to or before a person," and 'representation' means "an image, likeness, or reproduction in some manner of a thing," or "the action of placing a fact, etc. before another or others by means of discourse: a statement or account, esp. one intended to convey a particular view or impression of a matter."[3] The literal meaning of 'represent' or 'representation' has been variously applied in art, psychology, philosophy and political science.

As Hanna F. Pitkin,[4] Allen P. Griffiths and Richard Wollheim[5] show, the conceptual analysis of the idea of representation, or the distinction between the several senses of representation, is very helpful for avoiding equivocations in the word 'representation.' Griffiths posits four senses of representation. The first, descriptive representation, in which one person represents another by being sufficiently like him.[6] The second is symbolic representation, in which persons can represent or embody traditions and spirits of things without having any particular personal qualities: so the flag represents the state, even though the flag itself does not connote the character of the state. Third, ascriptive representation, like the relation between the member of parliament and his or her constituents, means to represent in the sense that what the representative does or decides commits those he or she represents. Fourth, members of parliament may always concern themselves with the interests of their own electors against any other interests. This is representation of interests.[7]

The distinctions between these four senses of representation provide us with a starting point for understanding what representation means. There is a certain idea common to the various senses of the term representation: a reflection of something in place of that thing. The common idea of representation applies within the political sphere in the sense that the basic scheme of political representation is the notion of one person standing in place of another for the performance of public acts. Our interest in political representation, beyond the conceptual analysis of representation in general, is to establish its meaning as a political term and then to clarify how to interpret its political implications.

The eighteenth- and the nineteenth-century European thinkers, Edmund Burke, Jeremy Bentham and John Stuart Mill (amongst many others), contributed to the establishment of the theorisation of political representation as a dominant political practice. They, albeit with different emphases and arguments, were interested in how it is appropriate or possible for the people to pursue their interests in a society, and how representative government must work to be a government for the well-being of all people. To address these issues, they investigated who was to be the representative, who was to be the represented and how their relationship was to be established and maintained.

Edmund Burke (1729–97): Trust, Responsibility, and the Public Interest

In the discussion of the establishment of a theoretical shape for the practice of political representation, it is helpful to begin with Burke, who is the chronologically earliest among the three thinkers whom I have selected for emphasis. Burke's ideas in his earlier speeches are not always consistent with those to be found in his later writings—the main turning point is marked by his *Reflections on the Revolution in France* (1790).[8] Accordingly, it is not easy to infer that he possessed a coherent conception of political representation nor, insofar as he did, quite what it is. Despite these difficulties, I intend to explore what he meant by political representation.

Let me start with Burke's view of politics or government, a starting point from which to approach his conception of political representation. According to Burke, politics or government is basically a matter of trust. The essence of this trust lies in the exercise of power being for the ultimate benefit of those over whom it is exercised, and hence in being in the end accountable to them. When the exercise of political power is contrary to this initial purpose, it loses its legitimacy:

> That all political power which is set over men, and that all privilege claimed or exercised in exclusion of them, being wholly artificial, and for so much a derogation from the natural equality of mankind at large, ought to be some way or other exercised

> ultimately for their benefit...... If this is true with regard to every species of political dominion...... then such rights, or privileges, or whatever else you choose to call them, are all in the strictest sense a trust; and it is of the very essence of every trust to be rendered accountable; and even totally to cease, when it substantially varies from the purposes for which it alone could have a lawful existence.[9]

Burke's view of politics as trust provides an important clue to how to understand his idea of political representation. As viewed in this passage, for Burke all political power is exercised by someone to the exclusion of someone else. However, the exclusive exercise of power is not for the specific group which has the power but for the benefit of those who entrust that power to it. This act of trust is a result of the voluntary will of the people.[10] Here, the issue under discussion is why they should give the power and authority to anyone else? This question leads us to see how central political representation is to any coherent specification of what politics is.

According to Burke politics, and in particular the constitution of a state and the due distribution of its powers, requires a deep knowledge of human nature, human necessities and various elements necessary for the operation of the mechanism of civil institutions. Politics is a matter of the most delicate and complicated skill, not to be taught *a priori*.[11] Due to this inherently professional character of politics, Burke thought that only people with reason and judgement had the capacity to engage in politics to control the state for the benefit of all people.[12] He believed that this was the way to guarantee the true interests of people. To this end, in Burke's view the representative must be created to act on their behalf. Burke's argument for the necessity of political representation thus originates from his appreciation of the different capabilities or merits of individual men. Further, a detailed examination of his understanding of men explains his insistence on the necessity of political representation.

Burke is deeply ambivalent in his views of human nature. Whilst he insists emphatically on the need to create the representatives because of the professional nature of politics, he does not necessarily mean that the people—the represented—are inferior to their representatives in every respect. Rather, in his earlier speeches, he argues that even though the representative's duty is to give the people information, not to receive it from them, the people are in the last resort always entitled to prevail: "the people's wish ought to have great weight, their opinions high respect, their business unremitted attention, and their interest profound preference."[13] Recognising the importance of general opinion to some extent, Burke argues that the legislative authority of parliament should seldom or never be exercised against the opinions and feelings of the people. This is because without the backing of general opinion, there is no right direction for affairs of state to follow: "In effect, to follow, not to force the public inclination—to give a direction, a form, a technical dress and a specific sanction, to the general sense of the community, is the true end of legislature."[14] Thus, for Burke a free government is nothing other than one which people believe to be so: the people are the natural, lawful, and competent judge of matters.[15] On the other hand, however, in his *Speech on the State of Representation of the Commons in Parliament* (1782), Burke describes the individual as foolish, and argues that the multitude act without deliberation.[16] Accordingly, if this multitude was not governed by discipline, they would fall into a state of "rude nature."[17]

How are these conflicting concepts of the people accommodated in Burke's argument for political representation? Are they simply contradictory? Or is the difference of view related to a change of ideas over time? I maintain that this ambivalent characterisation of human beings is successfully accommodated by Burke. To show this, it is necessary to differentiate Burke's conceptions of human beings: while one is a mere aggregation of individuals—which I shall hereafter refer to as "men" -[18] the other is an organic unity of orderly ranks—hereafter "the public".[19] When human beings act with reason, judgement and responsibility, they become "the public." When human beings are constituted as "the public" in the latter sense, they can claim their right to establish a form of government. But in the state of nature in which there is merely a number of discrete "men," i.e. loose individuals, who therefore have no collective power, "the public" simply does not exist.[20] Only after a civil society is artificially generated by common agreement, do individual men or the whole mass have the potentiality to be "the public".[21]

According to Burke, the conservation and secure enjoyment of human natural rights (equity and utility) is the highest purpose of civil society. But, even in civil society, political power, authority and direction in the management of the state are not original rights which every individual has. These political rights can be enjoyed only by men who are equipped with the prerequisites for being "the public." In order to obtain justice and secure a measure of liberty, they make a surrender in trust of the whole of it.[22]

When Burke asserts the importance of general opinion in governing a state, he is referring to a civilized and enlightened "public." By contrast, when he says that men are nothing but floating individuals, what he has in mind is "men" or the whole mass. Burke observes the coexistence of two kinds of human beings in a civil society as follows:

> In England and Scotland I compute that those of adult age, not declining in life, of tolerable leisure for such discussions, and of some means of information, more, or less, and who are above menial dependence, (or what is virtually such) may amount to about four hundred thousand. There is such a thing as a natural representative of the people. This body is that representative; and on this body, more than on the legal constituent, the artificial depends. This is the British publick; and it is a publick very numerous. The rest, when feeble, are the objects of protection; when strong, the means of force.[23]

As this phrase shows, "the public" are those who have political capabilities of knowledge, reason and judgement and therefore potentially can be the representatives. By contrast, "men," clearly different from "the public," may be enlightened and thus become "the public;" but they are always the due object of protection, and fully entitled to have their preservation ensured in a civil society. However, Burke does not suppose that the difference between "men" in general and "the public" in particular, or the need for representation which results from "men's" lack of political capabilities, is simply a matter of personal choice or natural inclination for politics. At this point, he has no clear and explicit theoretical conception of what kind of human beings are able to, or entitled to, participate in politics. Here, he was something less than a political philosopher. Instead, he takes for granted convention and the established disciplines of society,[24] and simply presumes that some are "the public" and others remain "men" within a civil society: some are eligible for taking a "leading, guiding and governing part,"[25] that is for being representative in the widest sense, and others are not. Thus, all members of a society do not have an equal entitlement to power.

Burke's representatives, who are distinguished from "men" in general above all by being equipped to participate in public functions, have two main tasks to perform for their constituents: one is to act on behalf of "men" in general because of the latter's incapability, the other is to act on behalf of "the public" in order to defend the interests of both. Together with Burke's acceptance of the contrasting social roles of "men" and "the public" and their essentially conventional basis, this definition of the representatives' task lays him open to the criticism that those definitions of the roles and the tasks in practice simply strengthen the predominant class in society.[26] From Burke's own point of view, however, the individual may all too often be foolish but the species is wise and acts rightly.[27] Therefore, for Burke the species itself to which "men" and "the public" each belong both deserves and needs to be protected by the creation of the representatives. This is why he insists that a representative or parliament is necessary to act as a guardian of popular privilege. To defend individual interests within a civil society, a representative must not only be committed to their defence but also he must also be able to judge accurately what their interests really are. Here it is especially important that Burke is so often thinking of a political representative as a member of a deliberative assembly. This places special responsibilities on him and makes distinctive demands:

> Parliament is not a Congress of ambassadors from different and hostile interests, which interests each must maintain, as an agent and advocate, against other agents and advocates: but parliament is a deliberative assembly of one nation, with one interest, that of the whole—where not local purposes, not local prejudices, ought to guide, but the general good, resulting from the general reason of the whole.[28]

For Burke, a member of parliament is not a simple delegate for the electors but a representative authorised by his or her constituents to exercise his independent judgement on their behalf. Therefore, the representative does not necessarily reflect what his or her electors already think and want. Rather, the representative is someone who must be "trusted" to act for their interests by employing his or her unbiased opinion, mature judgement and enlightened conscience. Thus, for Burke the judgement of interests of the individual and the society is made not by the electors but by the representative who has knowledge, reason, moral insight and commitment which is not reducible to anyone's particular interests. More generally speaking, he believes that "no man should be judge in his own cause."[29] Accordingly, when representatives judge that what their electors in a constituency think and wish is contrary to public utility in a wider sense, they should be able to reject it and then lead these electors to move in a right direction.[30] In this sense, for Burke, a representative is not a member merely of a single constituency (for example, Bristol), but a member of the parliament of a whole country, the representative in the widest sense.[31] The role of a representative is not confined to expressing, and to acting for, the particular interests of his or her constituency, but must make independent decisions in consideration of the general interests of a state in order to act legitimately on their behalf.

In analysing political representation, even if Burke insists on the need for the creation of the representative by the reason of the ordinary man's lack of knowledge and practical ability for politics, he does not deny that the whole people is the supreme author of political power. In making representatives the members of a state must aim to secure their interests according to their portions in a society, which is, in Burke's view, simply a requirement of justice (fairness). At this point, Burke is concerned with the modern understanding of political representation: the scheme of political representation aims to strive for the public good. But Burke, unlike most other more recent major interpreters of political representation, is far from accepting the full equality of the represented when he sets out what is involved in the selection of the representative.

Jeremy Bentham (1748–1832): Equality, *Vox Populi*, and the General Interest

Burke's conception of political representation is developed in different ways by various thinkers after him. I will now explore how J. Bentham and J. S. Mill address these issues. Bentham's idea of political representation emanated directly from his general philosophical position. That is, just as Bentham's philosophy, politics and sociology are all based on 'the greatest happiness principle,'[32] so too can we trace his idea of political representation to the same fundamental source. Bentham's main ideas about political representation are most clearly expressed in the principal work of his later years, *Constitutional Code* (hereafter referred to as *Code*),[33] although most of the ideas in it had already been developed in different contexts many years earlier. In this section, I will examine Bentham's conception of political representation mainly with reference to the *Code*.

As is well known, for Bentham a society is the total assemblage of self-interested individuals, and the public interest in a society is nothing other than the sum of the interests of the individuals. Bentham's distinctive view of society, unlike Burke's, is founded on the assumption that an individual is the best judge concerning what his or her interest is.[34] Therefore, when they pursue their interests respectively without relying on exterior criteria such as the judgements of the more capable men whom Burke mentioned, society's general interest can and will be obtained.

Bentham's view, which interprets individuals as the best judge of their own interest, extends to the standing of the individual in the sphere of politics. According to Bentham, sovereignty in a state is exercised by the constitutive authority.[35] The constitutive authority, to which all other authorities in a state are subordinate, resides in the whole body of electors.[36] These individuals making up the whole body of citizens or the political community can not only know their individual interests best but also can judge best what the greatest happiness of the greatest number is in a society, in other words, what favours or threatens the greatest happiness in a society and what has to be done to obtain it. But these members of the constitutive authority elect some person to act in their place. Bentham names these persons the deputies.[37]

Even though the citizens have representatives to act in place of them in the public sphere, Bentham does not believe that the representative ever possesses greater political knowledge and judgement than the represented—the people. Bentham is convinced that ordinary men, insofar as they are not oppressed or misled by those in power, do not lose their appropriate aptitude.[38] In addition, the ordinary people are in no way inferior to their representatives in respect of their overall political capabilities. Here, we might ask if, as Bentham supposes, the ordinary people are as competent as or still better than the representative, why the creation of the representative is necessary at all? Bentham presumes that it is necessary. As examined earlier, Burke's argument for political representation says that representative government requires knowledge, sense and experience of public matters and therefore that the appropriate representative is the person who is equipped with such requirements. Bentham's representative, however, very much unlike Burke's, is a matter of mere convenience, a view which entails the assumption of personal and political equality. That is, even if politics is more or less a professional activity, for Bentham the job does not necessarily have to be done by the particular persons who come to be representatives. This follows from the presumption that the individuals as the best judge know better what should be done in politics or for the public utility than any other political actors can do. That is, the people is always better than its representative or at least it is always just as capable as the representative. Therefore, decisions on matters of state depend upon what the people themselves think and want: the representative is simply the delegate who acts on the behalf of the people by reflecting his or her constituents' views and wishes.[39]

Thus, Bentham sees that when public decisions are the expression of the thoughts and feelings of the public, the general interest in a state is not separated from the particular interest of its individual citizens. The general interest cannot be established without direct reference to individual interests. In the process, Bentham notices the occasional conflicts between the general interest and the individual interest. But we can assume that he would think that by relying on and being reduced to the interest of each member of the society, this problematic tension can be resolved.[40] For Bentham, representative government is a form of government through which this identification of the general interest with the particular interest, or the settlement of the possible conflicts between the two interests, is carried out. In this way, the representative government can promote the greatest happiness of the greatest number of the individuals in a state.

With his belief in the people, Bentham maintains that the success or failure of representative government depends not on the people but on the representative, because while the people have the moral and political capability to sustain their polity, the representatives tend to have 'sinister interests' which are harmful to representative democracy.[41] To the end of the successful working of the representative system, Bentham emphasises the power and importance of public opinion as follows:

> Public opinion may be considered as a system of law, emanating from the body of the people ...... To the pernicious exercise of the power of government it is the only check; to the beneficial, an indispensable supplement. Able rulers lead it; prudent rulers lead or follow it; foolish rulers disregard it.[42]

For Bentham, public opinions are formed by the aggregate of the opinions of the members of society, and are not a mere echo of government or professional politicians. Public opinion made in this way is not corruptible.[43] Bentham's trust in public opinion as the determinant factor in bringing matters to a conclusion is specifically shown in his proposal of the 'public opinion tribunal.' Presupposing that public opinions reflect and articulate the public interest, Bentham suggests an instrument through which public opinion is expressed and names it the public opinion tribunal (hereafter p.o.t.). The p.o.t. consists of all members of society and every one who has an interest in the society.[44] Bentham puts higher status on the p.o.t. than on the legislature, and thinks that making the p.o.t. work well is in practice the best way to fulfil the greatest happiness principle. Probably for Bentham, this p.o.t would be the real institution to act for the greatest interests of the greatest number of the individuals in a state.

Believing that the people's voice, not the capability of the representative, is the social force behind the successful operation of representative government, Bentham argues that the settlement of conflicts and disputes in a society can be done through continuous attention to what the people thinks and what it wants. To take an example, let us assume that there is disagreement between the constituents and their representatives over a proposal for the establishment of a factory. While the representatives wish the plan to be implemented, the constituents object to it for reasons of environmental protection or the possibility of the destruction of community life. In this case, Bentham would say that the representatives have to follow the opinion of the majority of their own constituents. This is because, if the majority of the constituents vote against the proposal of a policy, it means that the proposal is not in the general interest in the sense that the general interest is an aggregate of particular interests.[45]

However, Bentham's confidence in the rightness of the people's voice does not always entail complete disregard of the judgement of the representative. Bentham does not conceive the role of the representatives to be always to add up mechanically the interests of their constituency. Like other theorists of political representation, Bentham understands that the representative's aim is to act for the public in order to advance the general interest. For this purpose, the representatives' independent judgement may interpret what measures are in the general interest.[46] But, because it is never quite true for Bentham that the general interest is one thing and the interests of their specific constituents are another, the role of the representative is not defined as it is by Burke. Bentham's clear priority is placed on the prevalence of the people.

In consequence, Bentham thinks that problems and tensions in making the representative government work lie more with the rulers whose interests could not be always assumed to be identical with the interests of the people. Hence, he establishes many institutional devices to enable the representatives to perform their roles properly in the interests of the whole people. For example, Bentham's conception of secret suffrage as a method of voting aims to make it a safeguard against the abuse of power.[47] In addition, such devices include the 'temporary non-relocability system' of the legislature,[48] the 'p.o.t.' and the 'legislation penal judicatory.'[49]

Through these devices, Bentham tried to make the representatives accountable to the represented. By doing so, he sought to ensure that the represented—the people—remained as the political actor qualified to decide the matters in a state even after setting up representatives. For him, the importance of the representative system does not only lie in it being a great (and certainly convenient) security for good government but also in its placing sovereign power in the hands of the people continuously. This is the central point of his case for political representation as a machinery for good government for the greatest number of individuals in a state.[50]

John. S. Mill (1806–73): Participation, Competence, and the Good Government

Like Bentham's *Constitutional Code*, Mill's *Considerations on Representative Government* is a good guide to understanding his main idea of political representation. For Mill too, the object of good government is nothing less than the well-being of the people who compose the community.[51] For the creation of this good government, Mill argues that two elements are required: first, the virtue and intelligence of the people themselves, second, the quality of the machinery of government which can promote these faculties of the people. That is, when moral, intellectual and active qualities exist in the people the good management of the affairs of state can and will be attained. The leading force which makes the operation of the government successful springs from the good qualities of the individual members of the community.[52] However, these qualities do not necessarily belong to the people by nature and conversely, the machinery of government has to be able to advance these qualities in the people for them to be governed well.[53] Mill says that the good government which satisfies these requisites is the ideally perfect free government[54] and that this government can be constituted in a polity where sovereignty lies in the whole people and the citizens' participation is always active because each person is the sole ultimate guardian of his or her own rights and interests:

> There is no difficulty in showing that the ideally best form of government is that in which the sovereignty, or supreme controlling power in the last resort, is vested in the entire aggregate of the community: every citizen not only having a voice in the exercise of that ultimate sovereignty, but being, at least occasionally, called on to take an actual part in the government, by the personal discharge of some public function, local or general.[55]

Thus, Mill argues that when the whole people, the sovereign of the state, participates in public action, all the demands of a state can be fully met. In Mill's view, it is according to an inherent condition of human affairs that individuals should guard their own rights and interests, and these can be secured through their participation in a society.[56] This participation of the people for their interests leads to the general prosperity of society.[57] Mill's understanding of the relationship between the individual interest and the general interest appears to be very like Bentham's. However, Mill grasps that the well-being of all members of society cannot be achieved by simply reckoning the particular interests of all citizens.[58] He argues that there is a gap between the manifest individual interest and the real individual interest or the general interest,[59] and that the difference, though it is not as great as Burke's, can be filled by a representative who has superior knowledge and judgement. That is, for Mill, as regards the true interests of the individual and the society, more cultivated opinion led by the representative is necessary.[60] However, Mill, unlike Burke and Bentham, does not suppose that the best person to know the best interest is necessarily either the representative or the individual. It is in this that the identity of Mill's representative government lies: a balance between the people's sovereign power and the representative's ability.

Mill understands politics as a highly practical employment of scientific intellect requiring professional political knowledge and judgement.[61] He gives the reason:

> The capability of any given people for fulfilling the conditions of a given form of government, cannot be pronounced on by any sweeping rule. Knowledge of the particular people, and general practical judgement and sagacity, must be the guides.[62]

Mill contends that, even though the controlling power in a state lies with the people,[63] the management of the state needs to be guided by enlightened knowledge and principle. These guides for the good government of a state—concerning, for example, the moral concern for the general interest and the ability to reason about the means and ends of broad courses of governmental action—are not common characteristics with which every person is equipped. By this reasoning, the exercise of the power of the representative—the persons of superior qualification—over the people or over the whole community can be justified. In other words, the superiority of knowledge and capability of the representative is to be valued insofar as it works for the general interest.

For Mill, however, the representative's superior knowledge and judgement is not the sole element which makes representative government necessary. The mere size of a polity too constitutes the main cause of the existence of representative government.[64] But Mill does not see representative government as a second-best, which is necessarily chosen because of the superior competence of the representative and the non-possibility of direct participation in a large constituency. These reasons make the creation of the representative inevitable, but representative government itself, as Mill clearly states, is also in practice the best form of government. This is because, as the representative's competence well complements the people's participation for the well-being of the people, representative government can be a better regime than any other form of governments.[65] Thus, for Mill, when the people's participation and the representative's superior competence cooperate in order to satisfy the interests of the whole people, representative government is established as the ideal government.

Mill asserts that representative government thus constituted should represent all, and not be the government merely of a majority of the people, which it exclusively represents.[66] Noticing that the majoritarian electoral system may lead to the disregard of the real majority of the electorate composing various minority groups in a society, Mill contends that in representative government, except persons who cannot read, write and do basic arithmetic due to their own laziness and who do not pay taxes,[67] no part of the citizens should be excluded from procuring their interests; otherwise the general interest cannot be attained.[68] To secure the representation of all, the representative system has to be such as not to allow one part of a society to dominate the remaining parts.[69] Otherwise there is the high possibility of class legislation either on the part of the numerical majority or of the dominant class which is the holder of power. In either case, this is the real danger to the representation of all, that is true democracy.[70]

In this context, Mill points out the evils of the current idea of democracy: 'tyranny of the majority.' Criticising Bentham's idea of popular dismissal of judges and officials, Mill rejects the idea of putting absolute power in the majority which imposes its will, beliefs and values on society.[71] He argues that whereas (right) public opinion has the strength to take the government in a right direction, the formation of (wrong) public opinion fosters the collective mediocrity of representative government and a politics of a low level of intelligence, which result from the extensions of universal suffrage.[72] Thus, Mill, like Bentham, on balance advocates universal suffrage, but Mill is more insightful than Bentham in seeing its advantages and evils.

A more balanced perspective leads Mill back to dependence on the representative. To prevent a politics of mediocrity dominated by ordinary people with their lack of professional knowledge and experience, the instructed minority which has superior intellect, abilities and character (attained after the training of long meditation and practical discipline) should be attended to and heard. This is why the more competent should have more influence on a society than the less competent.[73] In this context, Mill proposes plural voting to establish the competent minority as a counter force to the ascendancy of the ordinary majority.[74] At this point, however, it is noteworthy that Mill does not go as far as Burke in emphasizing the leading role of the representative. Mill is not an elitist theorist of democracy. He is convinced that representatives ensure the proper working of government, but at the same time the public voice is the generative power to operate good government. Therefore, the representatives should not act in opposition to their constituents' "fundamental convictions" and should be able to express the people's interests, opinions and wishes.[75] Thus, in managing the affairs of state, Mill does not wholly align himself with either the representative or the people. What Mill embodies as the ideal form of state is a representative government in which persons of superior virtue and intellect lead politics but are surrounded by a virtuous and enlightened public opinion.[76]

Just as Bentham's constitutional arrangements for the working of representative government are the product of his attitude both to the people and the representative, Mill's approach to the design of the representative system is based on his view of the different tasks and capabilities of the political actors concerned. Even if Mill's case for representative government is justified by the positive aspects of both the people and the representative — participation and superior ability—he fully recognizes the dangers which both the representative and the people can pose: that they might pursue the sinister interests either of the majority of the people or of the representatives themselves and thus neglect the general welfare of the community.[77] In particular, as mentioned earlier, class legislation—whether it is on the part of the numerical majority or of the wealthy and powerful—is a characteristic example of such sinister interests. Accordingly, for Mill too, one of the most important questions in determining the best constitution for a representative government is how to provide effective securities against this evil. A large part of the *Considerations* is devoted to technical devices to secure the representative government from the dangers inherent in both the people and the representative.[78]

To sum up, as in the cases of Burke and Bentham, for Mill the representative government is nothing less than a form of government which aims to guarantee the real and general interest in impartial regard for the interest of all and in opposition to the immediate and the selfish interests of each particular group. But Mill's opinion of how to work the representative government focuses upon the balance between the people's participation and the representative's practical capability.

Conclusion

Believing that representative government would enable the people to pursue their public interests effectively and representative democracy would thus be a desirable form of state, Burke, Bentham and Mill tried to address the theoretical justifications of representative government and its practical problems in the eighteenth and nineteenth centuries. Burke's conception of political representation was essentially based on a conception of trusteeship. Distrusting the political capabilities of the people, Burke held that the way in which the people could appropriately pursue their own interests and enable the government to act for the people was through professional men with political knowledge and judgement engaging in the affairs of state. For Burke, parliament is an assembly in which people of professional capabilities discuss and make decisions in a concern for the general interest without clinging to particular or local interests. Thus, although Burke mentions the prevalence of the people in the ultimate resolution of major conflicts, his conception of a healthy and viable practice of political representation commits him to a politics of trust on which the people is compelled to depend.[79]

Bentham's validation of the idea of political representation is developed very differently from Burke's. By presuming every person's entitlement to power in a state, Bentham maintains that the people has the knowledge and ability to judge public affairs for themselves. Nevertheless, the people employs a representative to act on its behalf as a matter of convenience. Bentham does not believe that the representative can run the state better than the people can, because the representative does not possess moral and political capabilities superior to the people's. Accordingly, for Bentham, the representative is a delegate to express the public opinion, wishes and feeling, which is a way to promote the general interest in a state.

Mill's argument for political representation stands between Burke's elitism and Bentham's populism. Mill admits that appointing representatives is inevitable since politics is a professional activity and the people lack relevant abilities. However, for the working of representative government, Mill does not entirely rely upon the representative of superior abilities on the ground that without the people's own participation and their sound opinions the representative government cannot proceed effectively. Thus, by stressing the roles of both the people and the representative in the delineation of good management of state, Mill takes a more balanced view of political representation than Burke and Bentham.[80]

Burke, Bentham and Mill all believed that representative democracy was a substitute which must be adopted for the performance of public action to act for the people. In particular, for Bentham and Mill representative government is a desirable, or even the best form of, state to accommodate the well-being of the whole people or the general interest of a society. To establish this, they consider closely on what basis and by what justification political representation can be employed as the scheme for public acts. Burke did not accept equality of personal right as the basis of representative democracy to anything like the same degree as Bentham or Mill. Bentham and Mill more than Burke, provided a theoretical account of the role of political agency and political processes in the practice of modern political representation, because of their more systematic concern for the implementation of popular sovereignty. Burke's hostility to any concrete institutionalisation of popular sovereignty led him to concentrate by contrast on a much narrower range of issues within the process of political representation.

These three thinkers theorize political representation in rather different ways. But the core issue over which they differ is quite simple: ought a representative to do what his constituents want, or what he thinks best?[81] The former proposition, the delegate conception of representation, supposes that a representative, chosen for his views on important issues, is bound to carry out his constituents' wills or wishes. The latter, the trustee conception, holds that a representative, chosen for his greater political knowledge and superior character, should be free to act independently of his constituents' wills or wishes.[82] Whether they argue for the delegate conception or for the trustee, what our modern understandings of political representation have in common is the idea of political representation as a process of the authorisation of legitimate public acts and of the supremacy of the people's role in such authorisation. This normative analysis by Burke, Bentham and Mill of the necessity of the representative system as a constitutional expression of political equality—whilst less prominent in Burke than in Bentham and Mill—and of public action, is still a helpful approach to understanding the significance of the modern terminology of political representation. It highlights the importance of the correct relation between the represented and the representative in representative democracy and of the practical challenge to operate representative government for the benefit of the people. Their approaches to political representation yield an understanding of the main problems posed in the agenda of political representation today. Contemporary thinkers, like those of the eighteenth and nineteenth centuries, see the point of political representation as a responsiveness or relationship between the represented and the representative.[83] Even if the very comprehensive issues of political representation cannot be handled solely in terms of this relationship, it is true that, as we have seen in Burke's, Bentham's and Mill's approaches to political representation, the view of how to make a representative government work is determined by the attitudes of theorists to the people, the representative and the relationship between the two.

However, I maintain that to establish the correct relationship between the represented and the representative and to assess whether a representative system functions as a fully legitimate and adequate scheme for public action, we must be able to explain why the substitution of the will of the representatives for those of the represented, which constitutes the basic scheme of political representation, is required in the first place. Neither of the two conceptions of political representation—the delegate one and the trustee one—can be specified without the presumption of an alienation of power or judgement. That is, in as much as a representative is authorised to take public actions, the represented always gives up some of his or her rights. Here the problems with which we must deal are why the alienation of power happens or why it is necessary and, after such alienation has occurred, who has the sovereignty and exercises the supreme power of judgement, and how can the represented's power be maintained after the transfer. How far at this point does the alienated judgement still reflect the power of the represented? Insofar as it continues to do so, what does this imply for the reality of the transfer of the latter's power to their representative? In other words, does the transfer of power mean the deprivation of a citizen's right? Or is it an alternative authoritative power to act for it? These are the centuries-old issues about the transfer of power, as we shall see later on when we discuss the so-called medieval *lex regia* debate. Even though alienation is essential to the basic scheme of political representation, this does not necessarily mean that the represented have to confer all their authority upon their representatives. They may do so, or they may not.

In order to explore these issues, I suggest that political representation must be understood not so much in terms of a particular relationship based on the theoretical justification for viewing the people and the representative as the main political actors, but through a broader and more comprehensive conception of the political process. Today discussion of more fundamental elements in political representation seen as a scheme for public action is almost non-existent. The problem is not only that we have not posed the questions seriously, but also that we are quite unable to answer them convincingly. The theory of political representation is at present in a very feeble condition.

Despite intense interest in practical issues of political representation, the term political representation itself has been poorly and inadequately understood. Without a fuller understanding of political representation than we at present enjoy, the main emphasis of political representation narrows to technical issues of the rational pursuit and advancing of particular interests and of elections as a means of allotting of power.[84] I do not, of course, deny that in contemporary politics we need to analyse how interests are distributed among groups if we are to grasp what is actually happening. But in order to assess how and how far representative government can reasonably be expected to produce good government, we must recognize that there is more to political representation than the instrumental and fundamental pursuit of material interests. Otherwise, as is demonstrated by the way in which our contemporary discussions about political representation have in practice been carried on, representative democracy works less as a substitute for popular self-rule than as a mechanism through which a given population of a society can in practice pursue their interests effectively. This means that we must learn to understand political representation not in narrow terms of the responsiveness of the particular relationship between two political actors but more through a comprehensive conception of the political process as a whole.

· 2 ·

THE MEDIEVAL UNDERSTANDING OF THE IDEA OF POLITICAL REPRESENTATION

As we saw in the previous chapter, our modern understanding of political representation has two main aspects: one concerns political representation as a general process of the authorisation of legitimate public acts, the other concerns political representation as a mode of recognition of the supremacy of the people. They are interrelated in the sense that the first presumes the second.

In this chapter I attempt to examine the medieval understanding of political representation, exploring the ways in which the idea of political representation was understood in the twelfth and thirteenth centuries, that is before Marsilius was writing. Many scholars argue that the modern idea of representation took its initial shape in the late twelfth and the early thirteenth century and that the interpretations of political authorization in that period were nascent forms of modern political representation.[1] Contrary to this interpretation, however, I suggest that modern and medieval understandings of political representation are quite different: in particular, there is a decisive difference between them in the interpretation of the issues of who or what is entitled to represent the whole and who authorises the entitlement. In order to identify this difference between the two ideas of political representation, in this chapter I intend to clarify the medieval idea of political representation. In addition, to this end, I examine some instances of the use of the notions associated with the concept of political representation by medieval writers and actors. When we consider the range of notions of political representation employed in the medieval context, we can hope to place more accurately the theoretical development of the issues of representation in Marsilius' thought.

The Representative's Two Bodies: The Monarch or the Representative Assembly[2]

Walter Ullmann's simplified themes of governing authority and law-creating power provide us with a useful clue to how government and law operated and how the idea of political representation worked in the Middle Ages. According to Ullmann, the medieval conceptions of the working of government and law can be classified into two types: one is the ascending conception of government and law, the other is its descending counterpart. The former sees that power in a society, more specifically, the power to organize government and create law, was ascribed to the community or the people. Accordingly, in this ascending theme, although public offices were occupied by particular persons, their offices were determined by and were responsible to the community or the people who handed over this power to them. In contrast, the descending conception of government and law supposes that governmental authority and law-creating power were given by one supreme agent. This supreme agent to which the whole community or the people belonged was nothing other than God. He appointed a vice-gerent in this world, who possessed the actual power on earth given from God. This descending theme implies a God-given form of lordship as the source of the power of governing and making-laws. Ullmann argues that these themes of government and law in the Middle Ages are opposed to and exclusive of each other. In terms of chronology, while the descending theme exerted greater force from the fourth century onward, the ascending principle reappeared powerfully in the late thirteenth century.[3]

This ascending theme in the Middle Ages, as Ullmann points out, is pertinent to the recognition of the idea of political representation, that is the idea that public officers represent the community in order to act on its behalf.[4] This is because representation or making a representative is regarded as caused by the people's grant of power to the representative. Insofar as the people authorizes power to particular individuals, they can exercise power legitimately in place of the people, that is the original author of the power. But this argument, in which the ascending thesis is associated with the idea of political representation, is a modern understanding of political representation based on popular sovereignty. This modern understanding, however, does not apply in the medieval period. At least, the idea of political representation in the Middle Ages was not necessarily construed at all in this way.

First, medieval representation can be understood in the sense that the monarch or the crown was the representative of the whole body. In identifying how the monarch represented it, Otto Gierke's analysis, despite its brevity, is quite insightful. According to Gierke, the main object of public law must be to decide upon the apportionment of power, and therefore every power of a political kind must depend upon the constitutional competence of some part of the body politic to 'represent' the whole. On this understanding of the nature of public power, the monarch in the Middle Ages was given a representative character for the whole body. In other words, insofar as the role and standing of the monarch had a public personality, a public right and a public capacity to commit the whole body, the ruler was not regarded just as an individual who acted purely with his (or her) own right, but was objectified as the exerciser of public power.[5] That is, the monarch was to exercise the rights and discharge the duties of lordship and, by virtue of the powers constitutionally assigned to him, he, as head, represented the whole body that was subject to him.[6] Thus, the idea of 'representation' found in the monarch presumes that anybody performing the public power for the people can be their representative. On this view of representation, the issue of by whom or by what the representative is authorised, a main aspect of modern understanding of political representation, does not arise. In other words, as far as the monarch has a public personality to undertake action on behalf of the whole community or the people, the monarch is fully entitled to represent that community as a whole.

The second characteristic of the medieval idea of political representation, more obviously, can be seen in a constitutionally composed assembly, that is the medieval representative assembly. In contrast to the representative nature of the monarch, this assembly is said to act directly with the powers which were ascribed to the community of the people. The representative assembly stood in place of the community as a whole, sometimes against the exercise of the right of the ruler or the pope. This interpretation of representative assemblies indicates that, due to this representative assembly, the arbitrary power of the crown could be constrained, so that the public power was exercised for the people. We see clearly the representative assembly's contribution to limiting the power of the crown in R. H. Lord's words: "the power of the crown was then more or less extensively limited by that of assemblies, in part elective, whose members, though directly and immediately representing only the politically active classes, were also regarded as representing in a general way the whole population of the land." [7]

Thus, in the medieval ideas of political representation, the entities which represent the whole are two: one is the monarch, the other is the representative assembly. It is perfectly true that either the monarchical power or the representative assembly represented the whole body of the population by acting instead of and for the people in the exercise of public power. The medieval idea of representation is, thus, bound up more or less with both the descending and the ascending theme.

However, as we may notice, the medieval idea of political representation—whether in the monarch or the representative assembly—is of a limited kind or at least differs from the modern conception of political representation, in the sense that their representative power was never authorised by a recognition of the supremacy of the people. In other words, in the Middle Ages, that is the twelfth and thirteenth centuries, to speak generally, the community as a whole or the people, unlike today, was hardly recognised as the entity to authorise political power, and they were not entitled to have supreme power over the crown or the assembly. Modern and medieval ideas of political representation are common in character in the respect that the central notion of both interpretations is the idea that a person or body of persons stands for a political collectivity in order to undertake action on its behalf. However, even though the monarch or the assembly stood for the community as a collectivity, there did not exist any clear or coherent notion of the sovereignty of the people as the political subject. To sum up, concerning the idea of political representation in the Middle Ages, there were definite conceptions of substitution for the performance of public action—whether by a king or somebody else.[8] But these conceptions did not include a recognition of the supremacy of the people in the authorization of public acts. This aspect of medieval ideas of political representation differs decisively from our modern understanding. It constitutes a dominating factor in determining the nature of the medieval idea of political representation.

This striking difference between medieval and modern conceptions of political representation makes the roles of the medieval representative assembly in managing affairs of a state limited and supplementary. Insofar as the representative assembly had the crown as the true head and itself merely stood beside this monarchical head, that assembly could not be above or independent of the crown. The role of the representative assembly was not so much to sanction the arbitrary power of the crown, as to perform public functions for the well-being of the people by consenting to resolutions which were virtually initiated and decided by the crown alone. This is clear in the historical development of the medieval representative assemblies. As is known, in the early period of the representative assembly, the representatives (specifically the knights and burgesses in parliaments) were created as a matter of administrative and political convenience of the king.[9] Later, even when the representative assembly was summoned to deal with such public affairs as taxation, legislation, jurisdiction and foreign relations, it was for the purpose of consultation.[10] When the king as the head took the initiative of governance over the community as a whole, it was difficult for the representative assembly to be identified as the political agency entitled to act independently for the whole body of the people, although it must be said that the power of the medieval assemblies *vis-à-vis* the crown varied at different times.[11]

In this respect, the medieval representative assembly was not a complete substitute to stand for the whole community. As Gierke maintains, the medieval assembly could be seen as the first development of the principle that "every set of men which is a representation of an *universitas* (corporation) must itself be treated as an *universitas*. This substitute took the nature of that for which it stood."[12] On this interpretation, Gierke would say that, without the participation of the whole people, the representative assembly eventually stands for the people as a whole by representing the several particular communities. However, even though through the form of corporation the representative assemblies contributed to looking after the interests of the community as a whole, they were far from being inclusive, but basically rested on a narrow class basis.[13] Here, we meet the problem of whether the representatives as a corporation could really stand for the people as a whole and have the peculiar rights of a representative authorized to be the public power, unless the supremacy of the people as a whole was recognised in the process of authorisation of making a representative.

Due to the crown being the head of the whole body politic, to the absence of any recognition of the supremacy of the people, and to the exclusion of many elements in society from membership of the assemblies—which constitute the medieval features of political representation—the medieval representative assembly did not function as full representatives,[14] that is a political agency equipped to make the whole community present. Thus, political representation in the Middle Ages too was just as much conceived in terms of the notion of substitution for the performance of public action, but its scope was far more limited. To repeat, this is because a king was the political agent who exercised the power of the community in practice and the role and standing of the representative assembly was itself limited by the lack of recognition of any authorisation of public power initiated by the supremacy of the people. For these reasons, the medieval idea of political representation is not compatible with our modern understanding of political representation, which is deeply bound up with the derivation of the public power for public action and the authorisation of such power by the people.

Owing to these decisive differences between the medieval and the modern concepts of political representation, I maintain that to interpret the medieval version of political representation as a type of modern political representation is gravely misleading. More concretely, in the following section, I will give examples of the use by medieval writers and actors of the medieval idea of representation which bring out this distinctiveness. I will do so by examining the conceptual components of political representation in the twelfth and thirteenth century.

Consent, *'Quod Omnes Tangit'*, and *Plena Potestas*

In modern democratic representative theory the notion of political representation is closely associated with the element of consent. In modern democratic forms of government the people consent to confer their power on particular persons, who take the power to represent them in order to act on their behalf. As the result of the people's consent, which is the voluntary and explicit expression of their own will to be governed, representative government is regarded as legitimate government. That is, both the source of legitimate authority and the basis of political obligation originate from the consent of those who have the original power to create a government, but over whom according to their consent power is to be exercised. In this way, the notion of consent constitutes an important factor for the legitimacy of representative government.[15] However, this kind of consent in political representation has not always been the case throughout the history of the development of political systems. The nature of consent in the medieval idea of representation has much in common with the role of the medieval representative assembly in the sense that both are limited by the decisions of the crown.

Medieval society was characterised by consensual practices. To illustrate, mutual consent was a foundation of feudal contracts and corporate groups chose their leaders by consent. What assemblies were summoned was mainly to consent to taxation. The ecclesiastical polity, that is church government, was largely structured by elective offices (e.g. elections of bishops and cardinals). In addition, even though no major work on law and political theory written around 1300 discussed the issue of consent as its main subject, virtually all contained at least passing reference to consent.[16] In this context, first, what draws attention to our concern with consent comes from Gratian, who around the middle of the twelfth century dealt with the term consent in the most detailed and systematic way. In his *Decretum*, which is a systematic compilation of church law and the effective foundation of the medieval and subsequent canon law,[17] he mentioned the term 'consent' in the context of the episcopal election.[18] Even though the *Decretum* aimed to deal directly with the issues of ecclesiastical rather than temporal polity, Gratian's treatment of the notion of consent makes it clear how inclusive the notion of consent was in the medieval context. Canonical election of a bishop in the eleventh and early twelfth centuries required the consent of all members of the Christian community concerned: that is, the consent of the canons of the cathedral chapter, the cathedral and monastery clergy, the nobility, the ministers and the ordinary laity.[19] However, this requirement did not mean that consent itself was the source of an ecclesiastical decision which involved both clergy and people equally. In fact, what Gratian asserted was the non-exclusion of laymen to the extent that they gave consent to the decision of the election:[20] the role of the priests, he says, is to elect, and that of the faithful people is to consent humbly.[21] Here, point of attention is that the right to elect is to be distinguished from the right to consent. That is, while the former is the decisive factor in choosing a bishop, the latter is required for the ratification of the decision in a merely supplementary way. With this differentiation between election and consent, therefore, election is not necessarily the specific way to express consent or will. The right to consent, which belongs to the people, is basically only a right to acclaim. To put it simply, for Gratian, whereas the clergy has to play the dominant role in canonical election, the people (including the king) is not excluded completely from the election but their role is merely to express their consent to or approval of the outcome of the election by way of acclamation, which is of secondary importance and without decisive power.

The limited nature of medieval consent, that is a kind of acclamatory role, apparently also held good in temporal matters. Gaines Post, an expert on medieval legal theory, explores what the term consent implied in the temporal sphere. According to Post, any final consent in the medieval context was exercised through the initiative of the royal prerogative.[22] This does not mean that the arbitrary will and decision of the king dominated the management of the affairs of state. The Middle Ages was not, as some people maintain misleadingly, a time in which private rights were never recognised by the principles of law and justice.[23] However, despite the existence of individual and communal rights protected by law and custom, it was the king that had the highest role in judgement and administration in the monarchy.[24] That is, just as in the case of the medieval assemblies, the judgement of matters concerned depended on the crown, so the king's ultimate authority as monarch exerted a heavy influence upon the consent of those who were summoned to his parliaments to make decisions on public matters. Therefore, even though the king required the consent of the people, this consent was, for the king, only a form of consultation.[25] It was the king as the political agent standing in the place of the whole community that had an overall responsibility and right for the kingdom as a whole[26]—which brings us back to the medieval idea of political representation, that is that the crown was the representative of the people.

For a fuller understanding of the nature of consent in the medieval context, we need to pay attention to a generalised doctrine of consent, the principle that "what touches all must be approved by all" ("*quod omnes tangit ab omnibus tractari et approbari debet*"),[27] henceforth referred to as q.o.t for short. This principle was one of the most important elements with the longest history of use in the legal practice of consent or representation.[28] The principle q.o.t. was known to be of Roman origin: the *Justinian Code* of 531 mentioned the principle of q.o.t. as a maxim of private law in respect of joint interests in a single issue.[29] But after the rediscovery of Roman law in the twelfth century, this principle was used widely and seriously to apply to public matters in both civilian and canonical jurisprudence and texts.[30] Canonists and legists referred to it in considering all kinds of several-, joint-, and common-rights issues.[31]

For canonists, q.o.t. was dealt with in the context of the inclusiveness of episcopal election.[32] However, as was mentioned above, the scope of all who could in practice choose a bishop in the election was never comprehensive. To take Gratian again, when Gratian mentioned q.o.t., it was not to argue for the necessity of the popular consent in the procedure to select a bishop. When Gratian employed the principle q.o.t., it was with reference to issues of clerical concern, both administrative and jurisdictional.[33]

On the other hand, legists made a variety of specific applications of the principle q.o.t. They applied the classical meaning of q.o.t., which was used in the private law of joint rights, to the public law and the government of communities in the twelfth and thirteenth century.[34] By the late thirteenth century the use of q.o.t. was very frequent.[35] These applications of the principle q.o.t., despite the differences of the locus of application, were nothing but the development of the classical Roman law on common consent in order to defend joint rights in court.[36] That is, what q.o.t. in the classical Roman law connoted generally was that the rights and interests of all the individuals in a joint matter must always be considered consistently with their interests in the joint matter.[37] However, "what touches all must be approved by all" in Roman law did not necessarily indicate that any decision on a matter of joint or common interest had to entail the specific individual consent of all parties concerned. Likewise, the medieval q.o.t. did not suppose that, for the joint matter to be settled, there had to be consent by every single individual of each party involved in the matter. What the medieval principle of q.o.t. signified in practice was that all persons jointly concerned in a matter were to be summoned and informed of the issue. That is, all interested parties had to be given a hearing and to be offered an opportunity for defence of their rights and interests in the matter. Actually to take the decision, whether in court or elsewhere, was beyond what they could do.[38] What this kind of consent which individuals gave implies is that they were not the political locus of the sovereign will in the judgement of matters. As we noted earlier, consent, whether in individual or several or joint matters, was initiated by the crown to exercise its authority and enforce the law.[39]

Furthermore, subjects who could in practice give consent in the temporal sphere were confined within some limits. Medieval writers, canonists, and theologians normally distinguished between *populus* and *plebs*. In general the *populus* was constituted of the 'greater men,' that is *maior pars*, *sanior pars*, *maior et sanior pars*. The *plebs* was constituted of the common people and did not include any noble or privileged section of the community.[40] Q.o.t. did not include every unqualified man without differentiation, that is both the *plebs* and the *populus*.

Accordingly, to have recourse to the medieval q.o.t. principle in treatment of issues never implied the people's final and decisive approval of what the authorities had proposed. '*Omnes*' in the text of q.o.t were asked simply to consult and to acclaim, not to decide.[41] In this respect, q.o.t. in the thirteenth century did not connote a constitutional principle providing limitation on the royal authority. The principle q.o.t. was not so much an example of the decision in an active sense to put a brake on royal decisions for the interests of the community as the whole, as a specific example of the subjects' (or the governed's) consent in a passive sense to the judgements of the king as the holder of a public office for the public welfare.[42]

Together with the notions of consent and q.o.t., the notion of *plena potestas* (full powers) is associated with the concept of political representation. In a modern theory of representative government, the notion that someone is truly the representative signifies that he or she is given 'full powers.' The full powers originally belong to the represented—that is the people—but they are given to the representative after the represented have consented to be governed. Being authorised by the represented, the representatives can exercise fully the power which the represented had previously possessed. Thus, the concept of full powers implies that the power given to the representatives authorises them to act on behalf of the represented without special prior authorization in the case in question. How fully the power of the representative is delegated depends entirely on the extent to which the representative is authorised by the represented. However, as we shall notice, the medieval recognition of *plena potestas* was not necessarily contingent upon a power delegated by the whole community. Rather, the *plena potestas* too was an expression of consent to the decision of the king (his court and council), not of consent to a decision of the community as a whole.

The concept of *plena potestas* originated in Roman law, but the concept was widely applied and developed by theorists and authorities in both secular and canon laws in the twelfth and the thirteenth century.[43] The concept was first formulated as a principle of private law to define the role of a proctor acting for a corporation in a legal suit.[44] But its adaptation was extended to ordinary business transactions, courts, the ecclesiastical sphere and temporal politics.[45] Our attention to *plena potestas* concerns the full powers of members sent to representative assemblies.

Broadly speaking, interpretations of the nature of *plena potestas* in the medieval assemblies are divided into two. One interprets *plena potestas* as implying a political consent to limit the royal authority. The other interprets it as nothing more than a consent to the acts and decisions of the king.[46] The interpretation which views *plena potestas* as the sign of the judgement and consent of the people argues that the communities (individuals or corporations)—in accordance with the Roman principle of q.o.t.—sent representatives to defend their rights *vis-à-vis* the king's court and council. According to this interpretation, the *plena potestas* of the representatives indicates that the communities had given the representatives the power and initiative of judgement expressly for the purpose of defending the rights of the community as a whole before the king. As with medieval uses of consent and the principle of q.o.t., however, the concept of *plena potestas* in the history of the medieval representative assemblies demonstrates its limited character. In other words, the extent of the full powers of the representative more or less corresponds to the role and standing of the medieval representative limited by the crown.

History demonstrates that the crown demanded the representatives' full empowerment by their community largely in order to obtain consent to taxation on the part of the king, which was a more important factor than any other in the development of the representative system.[47] In effect, the 'full power' from the community with which consent was given consisted not of deciding, but merely of giving consultation, information and consent in royal assemblies.[48] That is, the full power was given to the representatives less for the sake of the communities themselves than for the purpose of consenting to what the king and his council wished. As remarked above, in such circumstances when the king possessed a superior right and the responsibility to further the common interests of the people as a whole, the full power of the representatives in an assembly cannot help being under the superior authority of the crown. Even though the king, on his own, could not manage public matters of significance, in particular the case of extraordinary and larger revenues, without consulting the communities concerned which would be bound by the decisions,[49] the right and power of summoning were greater than the privilege of being summoned. This was because the king, as a guarantor of law and justice, had a superior jurisdiction and therefore was not limited by the *plena potestas* of the representatives from the community as a whole. Thus, *plena potestas* implied full powers on the side of the king, not on the side of the representatives or the community.[50]

In this respect, the medieval representatives with delegated powers, who appeared in various medieval public assemblies and parliaments, differ from our contemporary representatives who are vested with power by the people through the latter's greater authority. The medieval assemblies in which representatives were delegated by the communities concerned appeared to defend their communities. Insofar as the king was the highest judge and administrator and presided over the assembly, however, the power of the representative was never sufficient to become the full power to act for the community as a whole. Therefore, even consent with full power from the community was consultative and judicial, never sovereign in making decisions on affairs of the state. The king, not the communities, was the interpreter and holder of *plena potestas* and could thereby ask and obtain consent to decisions on public matters. That is, the medieval *plena potestas*, like the notions of consent and q.o.t., was an expression of the medieval idea of representation in which the king is the representative in charge of the public good of the monarchy.

PART II
MARSILIUS IN CONTEXT

Just as the modern terminology of political representation has different aspects from the medieval understanding of political representation, so the context in which Marsilius' conception of political representation emerged is in contrast to that of modern political representation. For example, while modern political thinkers, as we examined in Chapter 1, are keen to address the issue of how the relationship between the represented and the representative should be established to secure effectively the interests of the whole community, Marsilius' immediate concern with political representation was initially concentrated on the issue of how the people's power or the secular power is assured against the pope in order to protect peace in a political association. This concern led Marsilius to discuss the following issues as central to the arguments on political representation: the notion of peace as the common good, the aims of political society, the people as the original holder of political power, the people as collective power and the transference of its original power. In Part II (Chapters 3–6), I attempt to elaborate the historical context which developed Marsilius' concern with these issues which form the main elements of normative discussion about political representation. That is, Part II aims to examine the linguistic context in which these themes were being discussed: for example, the relationship between the spiritual power and the temporal power, the locus of legislative power, the *de facto* independence of Italian city-states, and the understanding of contemporary Aristotelianism in Italy. The discussion of these issues, it is hoped, reconstructs the context to serve as a framework for understanding Marsilius' argument for political representation more clearly and more exactly in the 'languages' of his own period.

· 3 ·

THE STRUGGLE FOR PRIORITY

> Seeking the highest degree of secular power, contrary to the command or counsel of Christ and the apostles, these bishops have rushed forth to make laws distinct from those of the whole body of citizens, decreeing that all clergymen are exempt from the civil laws and thus bringing on civil schism and a plurality of supreme governments.[1]

This is one of the passages in which Marsilius points the finger at ecclesiastical despotism. It is quite easy to find such passages against the misuse of the spiritual power in the *Defensor Pacis*, in particular Discourse II. It is not too excessive to say that Discourse II is entirely occupied by Marsilius' argument to prove that the actions of these 'bishops of Rome' or the priesthood as its general name work against the peace of a political community and are the root and origin of the pestilence destroying the state of Italy. As we shall see later, Marsilius anticipated that, insofar as these bishops departed from their proper roles and intended to exercise all power in ecclesiastical and secular domains, civil discord in Italy would not stop.[2] For Marsilius, the abuse of the power of the priests or bishops beyond its proper boundaries, was the beginning of the cause of friction in Italy, or in a political society in general. Here, we may ask immediately the question of how the proper role and power of the priest or bishop was defined. This issue is crucial in order to set out the relationship between the spiritual power and the temporal power (the church-state relationship) and to understand the theoretical justification of actual conflicts between church and state. Both before Marsilius and in his period, the definition of the nature of the spiritual power and its relationship with the temporal power and *vice versa* was the subject of controversy and constituted one of his main concerns.

When Marsilius was writing, the conflict of the spiritual and the temporal powers was exemplified by the controversy between John XXII and Louis of Bavaria, the most far-reaching and explosive controversy between the spiritual and the temporal jurisdiction.[3] This conflict may have been the immediate cause of pushing Marsilius into completing *Defensor Pacis*: it is hardly a coincidence that this completion was in the same year, 1324, that John excommunicated Louis.

Let me explain briefly the circumstances which created the church-state debate and produced the political writings about this conflict in the later Middle Ages. The election of the successor to the Emperor Henry of Luxemburg (1308–13) resulted in the division between the church and the empire. Both Frederick of Austria, who had the support of John XXII, and Louis claimed respectively to be the emperor. After defeating Frederick at the field of Mühldorf (1322), Louis proclaimed again that he himself was the real emperor. But John still supported Frederick against Louis and refused to confirm Louis by crowning him, asking him instead to refrain from the exercise of royal power until his title could be examined at Avignon. Louis refused and was then excommunicated (1324).[4] Rejecting this decision, Louis later (1330) deposed John on the ground that he was a heretic. This battle was not waged simply by personal offence-defence. It reflects a long term struggle for political priority. In fact, this battle included nearly all practical issues of the conflicts which were emerging concerning the relationship between the spiritual power and the temporal power: the issues over the rights of election, confirmation, consecration, excommunication or deposition.[5] These 'hot' issues in the long history of conflict between the two authorities, could not be resolved simply in the settlement of the process of the ceremony. The nature of the conflict can neither be summarised in any one event nor the events of a single year. The broader conflicts between the spiritual power and the temporal power need to be kept in perspective, although the exact points and arguments of the conflict differed according to the specific issues which were posed in the controversies.

In this respect, Wilks' observation that "amidst the interminable permutations of pro and con in the debate between the church and the state, the publicists never lost sight of the fact that they were debating the fundamental question of the origin of political authority,"[6] gives us a penetrating insight into the nature of the conflict. That is, the principle behind the actual and violent conflicts between the spiritual power and the temporal power is the question of who possesses the supreme authority which has no superior in this world, that is, who has the jurisdiction in this world. In this chapter, I am concerned with examining the principles behind the actual conflict, the principles with which the two authorities justified their acts and drove forward to excommunicate or depose each other in the violent conflicts at the time when Marsilius was writing.[7] This examination is not to provide simply a textual context of the relationship between the spiritual and the temporal powers, but is aimed specifically at enabling us to have a historical understanding of the specific problems which Marsilius tackled and intended to solve.

Papa Est Judex Ordinarius?

It has been suggested that there are three different powers of order, office and jurisdiction in the papal-hierocractic theory to support the argument for the supremacy of the pope in the church.[8] The first is the sacramental power (*potestas ordinis*), which a priest or a bishop receives from the Holy Spirit: that is, after a priest or bishop is ordained, he has the power to confer sacraments. The second is the right to exercise the sacramental power (*potestas executionis*), that is the *officium*, which means the right to use it in a parish or a diocese for a limited time.[9] For the lawful use and exercise of the sacramental power, this *officium*, at this point, is connected with the administrative power (*potestas administrationis*) to decide in which parish or diocese and for how long priests work. Furthermore, this administrative power takes a jurisdictional form in relation to the whole government of the church. For example, when a priest or a bishop acts against the good management of the church, the determination about whether he is to be removed from his *officium* or even from Christian society as a whole is to be made by the jurisdictional power of the church. This is the third of the three powers.

This distinction of powers in papal-hierocratic theory was developed in particular in the context of the internal opposition between the bishop and the pope for supremacy within the church in the eleventh and the twelfth centuries. In the thirteenth and fourteenth centuries, papalists such as Augustinus Triumphus argued that only the pope possessed the jurisdictional power as the supreme power, because he was the sole vicar of Christ. Accordingly, without papal authorisation no power could be given to any priest or bishop. By contrast, for proponents of episcopalism against papal control over the church, the pope was no more than the bishop of the Rome, who did not have any greater authority than a priest or a bishop, because all bishops were equally given the Petrine commission as vicars of Christ.[10] Therefore, jurisdictional power never belonged solely to the pope.

This debate over who has the jurisdictional power between the papalist and the episcopalist is about who has the supreme power *within* the ranks of the church. This distinction between the three powers provides a good starting point from which to approach the conflict between the spiritual power (priest, bishop and pope) and the temporal power over who has jurisdiction—the power of judging what is just or unjust—*outside* the church, that is in this world. It does so because the debate over the relationship between the spiritual power and the secular power *outside* the church is made as an extension of the argument for the papal supremacy *within* the church. In this section, taking the differentiation of the powers as my frame of reference, I attempt to examine how the relationship between the spiritual and the temporal powers was justified by papalist and imperialist respectively, before Marsilius dealt with the problem.

According to John Watt, in the medieval discussion of the problem of the church and the state, whatever the period or type of writer or his personal loyalties, there were three facets of the matter to be considered: that the powers were divided, that they must cooperate with each other and that the spiritual power was the higher one.[11] The crucial Gelasian definition—Pope Gelasius I (492–6)—of the relation between the church and the emperor presented these various facets:

> There are two main authori ties by which the world is ruled, the sacred authority of the pontiffs and the royal power of kings. But the authority of the pontiffs is the more weighty in that they will have to be responsible for the kings themselves at the Divine judgement.[12]

That is, God gives this world the dual vicariate of Christ: one is the spiritual sword (the church), the other is the temporal one (the state). The two authorities, the church and the state, are reciprocally recognised. So, whereas the control of temporal matters should belong to the empire, that of spiritual matters remains with the church. But it does so on the presumption that the responsibility of the priest is greater than that of the king. This Gelasian principle remained the official lay doctrine in the later Middle Ages.[13]

However, this theoretical harmony between the two powers did not always in practice take place. For the papalists who believed in the papal supremacy in this world, the mutual recognition of powers or the implicit presupposition of the superiority of the spiritual power, never gave sufficient grounds to claim that only the pope had supreme jurisdiction over both ecclesiastical and temporal matters. It was Pope Innocent III (1198–1216) who transformed Gelasius' implicit thesis about the superiority of the spiritual power over the temporal power into a definite assertion. Innocent argued that the spiritual power was superior to the temporal one with the allegory of two lights:

> God has set in the firmament of the heaven, that is, in the universal church, two great lights, that is, two great dignities, the pontifical authority and the royal power. But the sun which presides over the day, that is the spiritual, is greater; the moon which presides over the carnal, is the lesser. So the difference between the pontiffs and the kings should be as great as that between the sun and the moon.[14]

Innocent thought that the two powers were distinct, but this did not mean that the powers were equal. For him, the authority of the pope was greater than that of the emperor.[15] Innocent did not disregard the lawfulness of the jurisdiction of secular rulers, but nevertheless he did not recognise the independence of the temporal power in its own sphere. The decretal *Novit* (1204) provides an example justifying his position:

> Let no one suppose that we wish to diminish or disturb the jurisdiction and power of the king of the Franks since he neither wants nor ought to impede or restrict our jurisdiction and power. Since we are insufficient to exercise all our own jurisdiction why should we want to usurp another's? But the Lord says in the Gospel[16]: "If thy brother shall offend against thee, go and rebuke him between thee and him alone. If he shall hear thee thou shalt gain thy brother...... if he will not hear them, tell the church."[17]

For Innocent, as long as the secular jurisdiction does not violate the ecclesiastical jurisdiction, the two authorities would not be in conflict. But, what Innocent's interpretation of the saying "tell the church" indicates clearly is that the spiritual power includes the ultimate judgement even in secular matters and therefore the secular power is under the control of the ecclesiastical power. Innocent gave a concrete example of a case in the same decretal with regard to the conflict between the king of England and the king of France, arguing that although he did not intend to judge an issue (e.g. a feudal dispute) which required judgement by a king, he could certainly judge any sin which Philip committed.[18] This sacerdotal supremacy in the spiritual and temporal spheres is shown more clearly in Innocent's earlier bulls *Venerabilem* (1202) and *Per Venerabilem* (1202).[19] In these decretals, which respectively deal with the issues of imperial coronation and of legitimising illegitimate children, what he maintains is that the pope has the full power to exercise authority in temporal matters as well as in ecclesiastical ones. Distinguishing three kinds of judgement about civil crimes, ecclesiastical crimes and the cases which include both kinds, Innocent claims that in the case of these matters, whenever anything difficult or ambiguous happens, recourse is to be had to the apostolic See.[20] That is, everything should be "said" to the church.

If this assertion is to be accepted, where did the sacerdotal supremacy over both the secular jurisdiction and the spiritual one come from? According to Innocent, the papal legitimation in temporal matters was the result of his position as vicar, not of Peter, but of Christ or of God, who gave the pope extraordinary powers.[21] The pope, being Christ's vicar, became therefore the temporal overlord in order to ensure the reign of justice on earth, whether in the church or in the temporal sphere. This argument that the pope was the sole vicar of Christ constituted the basis of the theory of papal supremacy.

Innocent IV developed Innocent III's theory of the relation between the two authorities further in favour of the papacy and advanced the doctrine of papal omnipotence.[22] The struggle with Frederick II, whom he deposed at the council of Lyons in 1245, was the major political event which made Innocent IV produce a strong statement of the principle on which the papacy had long been working.[23] For the Carlyles and J. Rivière, Innocent IV is the source from which developed the extremism among papalists at the end of the century.[24] Both Tierney and Watt[25] assert that it is Innocent IV who proclaimed papal absolutism in the temporal domain without any of the subtleties of his predecessor.

Innocent IV, like Innocent III, assumed that the pope's plenitude of *potestas* originated from his being vicar of Christ:

> We do certainly believe that the pope, who is vicar of Jesus Christ, has power not only over Christians but also over all infidels, for Christ had power over all ...... He would not seem to have been a careful father unless he had committed full power over all to his vicar whom he left on earth. Again he gave the keys of the kingdom of heaven to Peter and his successors ...... But all men, faithful and infidels, are Christ's sheep by creation even though they are not of the fold of the church and thus from the foregoing it is clear that the pope has jurisdiction and power over all *de jure* though not *de facto*.[26]

Christ appointed the pope as the vicar to look after this world including both the church and the secular part. To this end, the pope is given full power over the two spheres. The pope's jurisdiction over secular matters cannot be questioned.[27] On this understanding, while Innocent III declared that in secular cases appeal could be made to the pope when the throne of the empire was vacant,[28] for Innocent IV the pope not only succeeds to a secular right in the case of vacancy of the empire, but when necessary, he intervenes in the king's or prince's jurisdiction.[29] So, Innocent IV asserts that "*papa est judex ordinarius omnium*," but he does so more unequivocally than ever before:[30] the pope is the final superior or judge, even in temporal matters, of all secular authorities.

In a similar vein, Boniface VIII promulgated the bull *Unam Sanctam* (1302), the most famous of all the documents on church and state in the Middle Ages.[31] The bull is nothing other than a reassertion of Innocent IV's principle,[32] that is the extreme papalists' position: the temporal power belongs to the spiritual.[33] It is only God that can judge the pope if he is to make a mistake:

> If the earthly power errs, it shall be judged by the spiritual power, if a lesser spiritual power errs it shall be judged by its superior, but if the supreme spiritual power errs it can be judged only by God not by man...... We declare, state, define and pronounce that it is altogether necessary for salvation for every human creature to be subject to the Roman pontiff.[34]

For Innocent III, Innocent IV and Boniface VIII, the pope is the apex of the hierarchical order in the church. They never think that priest, bishop and pope are churchmen working in various places without any hierachy among them. The priesthood in general possesses the sacramental power, but it is only the pope that has the jurisdictional power as the supreme power within the church. More importantly, they believe that the pope's supreme power within the church can extend to temporal matters on the ground that he is the keeper of two swords as the sole vicar of Christ. Thus, for the papalists, the pope's ecclesiastical authority entails political authority superior to that of the secular rulers. Here, Gelasius' principles of the two powers' reciprocal cooperation does not work any more. Instead, there remains the doctrine of the papal supremacy in an extreme form both *within* and *outside* the church.

However, contrary to the assertion of the papal supremacy in which no one except God could take away the ecclesiastical and temporal authority of pope in this world, there persisted arguments for the relationship between the spiritual power and the temporal power in terms of the perspective of 'equal' cooperation of two powers. John of Paris (1250?–1306), who was a Dominican and was involved in the conflict of Philip IV with Boniface,[35] was a representative publicist of this 'equality.' In *De Potestate Regia et Papali* (*On Royal and Papal Power*), one of the greatest of all political works written in the course of the controversy between the church and the secular ruler,[36] John attempted to refute the extreme papalists' argument by arguing that the spiritual power is distinct from the temporal power.

According to John, there are two lives: one is the eternal life, the other the secular life. The eternal life is higher 'in dignity' than the secular life and can be secured only through divine virtue. For divine worship, there is a need to create ministers who confer the sacraments. The priesthood means "the spiritual power, given by Christ to ministers of his church, of administering the sacraments to the faithful."[37] The spiritual power in this definition of 'priesthood' includes priest, bishop and pope, that is high and low priests. John admits that the pope is the head of the church as a whole, but he argues that his role of being head is not as lord but as the general steward to administer ecclesiastical matters.[38] On this understanding, the calling to "feed my sheep" (John 21:17) which is given by Christ, applies to the pope, not to the priesthood in general.[39] However, John does not believe that the calling implies the sort of absolute power which the papalists claim and therefore that the power to judge involved in "tell the church" belongs only to the pope. The priest, the bishop and the pope have the duty to feed the sheep and the jurisdictional power to listen and judge in parish, diocese and Rome respectively.[40] Thus, John does not suppose a hierarchical order within the church in which authority is concentrated in the pope. John argues that although the pope is the head of the church, the ecclesiastical power is dispersed among priests, bishops and the faithful people.[41]

John's pluralism of authority *within* the church is reflected in his discussion of the relationship between the spiritual and the temporal power *outside* the church. John never sees the reason why the ecclesiastical authority or the pope's power has to be exercised in the secular sphere on the assumption that the former is higher than the latter. Rather, John claims the distinctive jurisdiction of the two powers on the ground that Christ as a man did not have temporal jurisdiction and therefore he did not give such power to the church. In addition, John argues that even if Christ had, he did not give the power to Peter or to the apostles.[42] For John, the powers which the spiritual authority has—the sacramental power, the administrative power and the jurisdictional power—are confined to the sphere of conscience.[43] The prime role of the priesthood—whether as priest, bishop or pope—is to confer the sacraments on the faithful. This sacramental or spiritual authority of the priesthood, in contrast to the papalists' argument, does not include superiority in political authority *outside* the church. Hence, John's understanding of the saying "tell the church" indicates that God gives to priests the authority to judge, but the power is that of the ecclesiastical judge in cases of sin, not for temporal cases.[44] Accordingly, the pope cannot judge temporal matters *outside* the church because this would go beyond the jurisdictional scope of the spiritual power and would be against the words of Christ.

Furthermore, John maintains that just as the spiritual power is the supreme jurisdictional power in ecclesiastical matters, so is the emperor in temporal ones. Therefore, the pope should not infringe on the jurisdictional authority of the secular ruler. Based on this principle of the distinction of powers, John presents a division of judgements by the two authorities. For example, first, when a secular ruler is guilty in spiritual matters, the jurisdiction belongs to the pope. So the pope can inflict spiritual penalties or in the worst case impose excommunication upon him, but he cannot issue secular penalties (i.e. a corporal or financial punishment). Second, if the secular ruler commits a crime in temporal matters, the judgement of him falls to the barons and peers of the kingdom. Third, when a pope offends in spiritual matters, action can be taken against him by the cardinals. Finally, if a pope commits a temporal offence, the judgement belongs to the emperor.[45]

As viewed in these cases of jurisdiction, for John the heaviest punishment which the priest can issue would be excommunication—the exclusion of a sinner from the sacraments and from the community of the faithful, that is the deprivation of the bliss of the eternal life. This implies that any intervention on the part of the pope in secular affairs, or the pope's jurisdiction over secular rulers, is wrong. Instead, John argues that the judgement to deprive someone of secular rulership belongs not to the pope but to the people. Likewise, when the pope becomes guilty, the emperor can impose secular, but not spiritual, penalties within his temporal jurisdiction, but he would not be able to judge the matter of the pope's excommunication and deposition.[46] This is because the emperor does not have spiritual jurisdiction.

In distinguishing between the ecclesiastical jurisdiction and the secular jurisdiction, however, John is not always clear about the line between the two jurisdictions. For example, on the question whether the pope has the power to judge affairs concerning the property of a church, generally speaking John would say that he does so insofar as the church has the property for the well-being of the community of the church. On the other hand, however, John also says that when the matter pertaining to the property of a church is related to temporal things, the pope cannot have the power of judging such matters.[47] At this point, the differentiation between ecclesiastical and temporal matters in John's thought is confusing and therefore in practice difficult to maintain, because he does not specify the cases where the ecclesiastical property is involved for a temporal purpose or for a spiritual one. More exactly, it is not clear whether John's distinction between the two powers' jurisdiction is in terms of the location in which a crime is committed, or in terms of the character of the crime committed, or in terms of whether the guilty person is a secular person or a spiritual one. This ambiguity or the difficulties in this distinction was, as events showed, easily open to the dangers of political exploitation by each side, regardless of John's purpose in making the distinction between the two jurisdictions—in order that the superior in respective power, that is the pope or the emperor, could not be exempt from the judgement and punishment of their crimes and that the independence of the two jurisdictions should be guaranteed.

Furthermore, this danger might be fostered by the fact that John does not rule out the possibility that there is an indirect effect of the one on the other.[48] Taking again the cases mentioned earlier, John says that for the further punishment of a person upon whom a penalty has already been imposed but is still incorrigible, the pope and the emperor respectively can interfere with the judgement of the other part, although John does not allow the pope or the emperor to judge directly the matters of the other part. So, when it is necessary to take further action than excommunication against the secular ruler who offends in an ecclesiastical matter, the pope can do it together with the people.[49] Moreover, when the secular ruler who commits a temporal crime needs to be further punished, the church, on the request of the peers of the realm, can help. Conversely, if after a penalty is imposed by the cardinals the pope is incorrigible, the case belongs to the emperor as a member of the church, at the request of the cardinals.

As noticed in this final action of the emperor against the pope, however, despite John's argument for a parallelism of the spiritual and temporal powers, he seems to be inclined to be in favour of the imperial censure. John argues that the ecclesiastical jurisdiction beyond the spiritual sanction is indirect and incidental.[50] But he shows inconsistency in his evaluation of secular jurisdiction by saying that "the emperor has the primary right to correct the pope without any intermediary for any crime."[51] Also, if John were faithful to his principle of the distinction between the spiritual and temporal jurisdictions, he would not have argued for the emperor's intervention in the election of a pope. Moreover, John does not see that jurisdiction in the church is reliable: he says, "while the power of order is permanent and supernatural, the jurisdictional power of the priest is temporary."[52] This is because while the former is imposed by God and therefore is perpetual, the latter is created and is taken away by human consent or election.[53] Thus, for John, the true power of the priesthood lies in helping the faithful to attain eternal life through performing sacraments and in nothing else. Therefore, its jurisdictional power is of secondary significance.

To sum up, both the papalists and John of Paris argue that the church has jurisdictional power. However, the decisive difference between them is the scope of the power which the ecclesiastical jurisdiction can reach. While for the papalists the jurisdiction of the church has omnipotent power to judge ecclesiastical and temporal matters, John maintains that the spiritual power is distinguished from the temporal power but decides in favour of the imperial jurisdiction. This contrast to the papalists' claim for absolute power with John's imperialist stance finds an echo in their interpretation of historical events. The next section aims to examine the application of the papalists' and the imperialists' theses about the relationship between the two powers to the actual incidents of history in order to see how consistent their struggle for priority was.

The 'Donation of Constantine' and the '*Translatio* of Empire'

In the light of the relationship between the spiritual and the temporal power the debate over how to interpret the 'Donation of Constantine' and the 'Translation of empire' as historical events[54] provides us with good illustrations of the papalists' and the imperialists' different positions on the relationship between the two authorities.[55] Applying their respective arguments about the relationship between the two powers to the historical events, the papalists and the imperialists ensure their positions. First, let me examine the debate over the 'Donation of Constantine.'

The 'Donation of Constantine' as a document about Constantine's conversion to Christianity, is now regarded universally as a fabrication produced about the middle of the eighth century.[56] Nevertheless, the medieval debate over the 'Donation of Constantine,' that is whether the donation of Constantine was a donation or simple restitution, suggests important implications for the relation between papacy and empire. For the papalists, it was simple restitution: the restitution of that which *de jure* already belonged to the vicar of Christ. The true monarch or emperor was the pope, the vicar of Christ: the reigning emperor was his delegate. For the imperialists, on the other hand, it was a concession of the empire to the pope that confirmed the subordination of the papacy to the empire and the human origins of the pontifical primacy. Thus, the papalists and the imperialists respectively made use of the 'Donation of Constantine' as a theoretical justification to attack their enemy or to confirm their own arguments for superiority.

Let me begin by citing the text of the 'Donation of Constantine':

> I (Constantine)—together with all our satraps and the whole senate and the nobles and all the Roman people, who are subject to the glory of our rule—considered it advisable that, as on earth he is seen to have been constituted vicar of the Son of God, so the pontiff, who are the representatives of that same chief of the apostles, should obtain from us and our empire the power of a supremacy greater than the earthly clemency of our imperial serenity is seen to have had conceded to it...... And to the extent of our earthly imperial power, we decree that his holy Roman church shall be honoured with veneration; and that, more than our empire and earthly throne, the most sacred seat of St. Peter shall be gloriously exalted; we giving to it the imperial power, and dignity of glory, and vigour and honour.[57]

Therefore,

> For He (Jesus Christ) is God in Heaven above and on earth below, who, visiting us through His holy apostles, made us worthy to receive the holy sacrament of baptism and health of body. In return for which, to those same holy apostles, my masters, St. Peter and St. Paul; and, through them, also to St. Sylvester, our father,—the chief pontiff and universal pope of the city of Rome,—and to all the pontiffs his successors, we concede and, by this present, do confer, our imperial Lateran palace, which is preferred to, and ranks above, all the palaces in the whole world.[58]

The 'Donation of Constantine' alleges that in the fourth century the lordship over all the lands within the empire was granted to the bishop of Rome by the first Christian emperor, Constantine I. In the document, Constantine is described as offering Pope Sylvester all the insignia which identified the emperor—the diadem, the tiara, the shoulder band, the purple mantle, crimson tunic, all the imperial raiment, the imperial sceptres, the spears and standards, the banners and imperial ornaments[59]—that is the entire imperial regalia. Moreover, the emperor yielded to Sylvester and his successors complete power and jurisdiction over the Lateran and over the city of Rome and the whole of Italy and the western regions.[60]

The assertion that Constantine granted the empire to Sylvester is accepted as a historical fact by both papalists and imperialists. But their interpretations of why Constantine did it are respectively different. According to Innocent IV, the donation of Constantine is not in the true sense of the word a donation.[61] Innocent explains that the fact is that Constantine did not grant the empire to the papacy but the pope recovered it, because it had been the inalienable gift of Christ to the papacy but had been violently usurped from its legitimate owner, the pope. That is, for Innocent the donation demonstrates that Constantine recognised that the empire (the temporal power) belonged to the church and that the emperor had exercised a usurped and unlawful power which he could not own.[62] Thus, he maintains that those who think the pope's imperial power originated from a grant from Constantine are wrong. Through the donation Constantine humbly submitted to the church a power which had not been granted (*concessa*) but permitted (*permissa*), because it was the church which originally bestowed on him the divinely ordered imperial power.[63]

Up to the period when Marsilius was writing, the conflicting claims regarding the donation continued. They are illustrated by the writings of two contemporaries of Marsilius; on the papal side, James of Viterbo, and on the imperial side, John of Paris. According to James, earthly kingship must be subject to heavenly, since the kingship is made by God. So the pope, the vicar of Christ, has both spiritual power and temporal power and thus the earthly kingship should be subject to the pope, who is distinguished by the marks of dignity. Seeing that the pope is superior to the secular king in every respect, James holds that the 'Donation of Constantine' confirms that the pope has temporal power not only by divine law but also by human law. For James, the grant of Constantine was an expression of submission and veneration which the secular power gave towards the spiritual power. And when Constantine granted to Sylvester the earthly kingship and the imperial insignia and offices, he did not confer authority, but just showed reverence,[64] because Constantine did not have the authority to confer. What Constantine's grant of the empire to the pope under human law suggests is that the pope already possessed it under divine law.[65] That is, James' assertion of the donation indicates that, because the temporal authority and power originally belonged to the pope, the contention that Constantine gave it to the pope is contradictory.

Contrary to the papalist interpretation, John is persistent in contending that both the spiritual power and the temporal power derive from God, but the two powers are not dependent one on the other and they are distinct. Relying on Scripture (Romans 13), John claims that a king and a prince is not minister of the pope but God's minister. In addition, historically speaking, royal power existed before papal power and there were kings before there were any Christians in France.[66] Therefore, as we saw earlier, the pope does not have any jurisdiction in temporal matters[67] except in cases where a secular ruler grants the right to the pope out of piety.[68]

The 'Donation of Constantine' offers useful material to John through which he can reconfirm his argument over the relation between the two powers, in particular between the church and the French kingdom. John, against Innocent IV, maintains that it is nonsense that Constantine gave to the church the kingdom of Italy with full temporal jurisdiction and that such a grant bore out the pre-existing power of the church.[69] John holds that it was Constantine who bestowed universal authority upon the pope[70] and that when the church accepted Constantine's donation it was no longer the true church of God and became Roman.[71] In addition, John suggests that what Constantine transferred to the pope is confined to a certain territory, that is to Italy, in which France is not included. The pope has therefore no political authority over the king of France.[72] Thus, through the 'Donation of Constantine,' John maintains not only that, on the basis of the historically prior existence of the royal power, the church's jurisdiction over the temporal is nonsense, but also that, even if the church gained the jurisdictional power over the secular domain, it was only over Italy.

These contrary interpretations of a historical event which are based on the different principles of the relationship between the spiritual and the temporal powers, emerge clearly in the debate over the 'Translation of the empire' (the *Translatio imperii*) from the Greeks to the Germans, that is over the historical origins of the empire. Historically speaking, Charlemagne was crowned as Roman emperor by Pope Leo III at the famous ceremony of Christmas day 800. To both papalists and imperialists the coronation of Charlemagne implies a mark of the '*Translatio* of the empire.' The general meaning of '*translatio*' indicates the passage of an institution or of an honour from one place to another.[73] However, the controversy over Charlemagne's coronation led to the term '*translatio*' being employed, beyond its general meaning, as significant for the historical origin of the empire. It was Innocent III who was involved in the political schism (Otto of Brunswick vs. Philip of Swabia) that stimulated the debate.[74] In Innocent's decree, *Venerabilem* in which he touched upon the debate about the imperial election, the issue of the 'Translation of the empire' was raised in clear terms.

In *Venerabilem* Innocent III acknowledges that the election of an emperor belongs to the seven princes. But he claims that this right is given to the princes by the pope, because it was the pope who made the imperial translation from the Greeks to the Germans—a transfer to which the German princes owed the right to elect a king who would become emperor when crowned by the pope. Therefore, the election by the princes produces a candidate for the imperial throne, but the authority to examine whether a person is fitted to be a king, a future emperor, belongs to the pope, who has the right to consecrate and crown the candidate chosen by the princes.[75] Innocent held that in virtue of this transfer the papacy had the ultimate authority in such elections and thus intended to settle the disputed election. In clear contrast, John asserts that what the pope translated from the Greeks to the Germans is merely the title without any authority. Moreover, by arguing that even the papal transfer of the title of the empire was done with the people making acclamation and concession,[76] John demonstrates that the pope does not have the superior and independent power to do it.

Thus, while the imperialists maintain that Charlemagne became the ruler of the empire as a result of his conquest, the papalists say that his coronation meant the pope's bestowal of the temporal honour on Charlemagne as the king of the Franks and therefore the pope has the power to transfer the imperial seat, that is the power to create the secular rulership. These different interpretations of the historical fact by the imperialists and the papalists are a reflection of their respective theses about the relationship between the two powers: while for imperialists the secular rulership has its own power distinct from that of the spiritual authority, for papalists the temporal power originates from the spiritual power.

These controversies concerning the 'Donation' and the 'Translation' in order to prove who has the superior power were still issues of importance in Marsilius' period. The struggle between John XXII and Louis in which Marsilius was deeply involved was a version of the historical conflict between the two powers. Earlier, concerning the relationship between the spiritual power and the temporal power, while papalists asserted the jurisdictional power *within* and *outside* the church, that is over this world, John argued that the priests' jurisdictional power was ecclesiastical and distinguished from the secular governance. What did Marsilius contribute?—we shall examine this in Chapter 9.

· 4 ·

LEX REGIA

It may sound exaggerated when Accursius asserts that everything can be found in the *Corpus Juris*,[1] but it was true in twelfth-century Italy, in particular in Bologna and other city-states of northern Italy.[2] The rediscovery of Roman legal texts (law books of Justinian) in eleventh-century Italy made the glossators of the twelfth and early thirteenth centuries regard the *Corpus Iuris Civilis*[3] as a reference for their argument which had almost absolute authority.[4] It was a *jus commune*, a common law for the *unum Imperium*, the empire of which all Italians were citizens whatever their city.[5] Whenever the glossators had legal problems which troubled them, they relied on Justinian's law to provide the answer for them. Peter Stein points out that for the glossators, what was important in a legal argument lay in whether it was supported by a text of the *Corpus Iuris Civilis* because Justinian had said that his compilation was a complete whole, with no contradictions.[6]

My interest in the *Corpus Iuris Civilis* is focused on the so-called *lex regia* as a way of viewing the relation between the emperor and the people with special reference to the origin of legislative power. The applications of the *lex regia* can be various: it may concern the human origin of imperial power, the source of papal temporal jurisdiction, the source of jurisdiction of empire or city-states, the right of the people in regard to their ruler and the general model for the origin of governmental authority. For example, the arguments of *lex regia* in Bartolus' and Baldus' theory are used to argue for the human origin of the imperial jurisdiction and the source of the validity of papal temporal jurisdiction.[7] By contrast, I intend to examine the medieval debate of the *lex regia* as a general formula to see thereby where the legislative power lay and to consider the ideas about the sources of law which prevailed before and in Marsilius' time. Our examination of *lex regia* in the medieval context, in particular in relation to the problem of the source of jurisdiction in Italian city-states, aims to take account of the questions of who has the original power to make law and what follows after the transfer of such power, which constitute prime components of Marsilius' conception of political representation.[8]

Despite Justinian's assertion that *Corpus Iuris Civilis* had complete unity as a text, it is apparent that some texts in Roman law express the idea of popular sovereignty, while others appear to justify the unlimited power of the emperor.[9] Not presenting a clear view of where legislative power lay, Justinian himself left the possibility of the contradictory views open.[10] In addition, as Joseph Canning argues, the fact that the commentaries had no general thesis either of the source of legislative power applicable to the political entities of the Roman people, kingdoms and city-republics reflects the lack of a unified view of the source of jurisdiction and legislation in Roman law.[11]

In D. 1.3.31 Ulpian says that "*princeps legibus solutus est*" ("the emperor is not bound by laws"). Likewise, D. 1.4.1.1 begins by saying that "*quod principi placuit, legis habet vigorem*" ("what pleases the prince shall have the force of a statute"). These phrases are cited most often to argue that the source of law is the emperor, the absolutist interpretation of the *lex regia*. However, this interpretation seems to miss what follows in the same passage: "*utpote cum lege regia, quae de imperio eius lata est, populus ei et in eum omne suum imperium et potestatem conferat*" ("this is because by the *lex regia* which conferred his *imperium*, the people conceded to him and conferred upon him all their authority and power").[12] The twofold possibilities of interpreting the *lex regia* as the basis of either popular sovereignty or royal absolutism may take as their starting point the two different halves of the phrase. Given that the *Corpus Iuris Civilis* does not say clearly whether the *lex regia* implies the people's full and permanent transfer of power to the emperor or only a limited and revocable concession to him, these different texts are enough to provoke the conflicting views concerning the source and locus of the legislative power in Italian city-states or a political society in general. Indeed, one of the major topics for debate amongst 'civilians' in the thirteenth and fourteenth centuries was the debate about who had jurisdiction: whether the *lex regia* had been a revocable grant and in consequence the Roman people retained the sovereign capacity to make laws generally valid throughout the empire, or whether by *lex regia* the emperor obtained its full power because the people had permanently conferred their rights on the emperor. For an examination of this debate, in this chapter I explore the glossators and post-glossators of the twelfth, thirteenth and fourteenth centuries—Irnerius, Placentinus, Azo, Cynus and the author of *Summa Trecensis*—, who were concerned with the question of the temporary delegation or the permanent abdication of the people's authority to the emperor.

We begin with Irnerius, a famous jurist of the late eleventh and the first decades of the twelfth century and the founder of the school of Bologna, who was the first to apply to the legal texts the technique of the gloss.[13] Irnerius' position about the *lex regia* is simple and obvious. Supposing that *jus* is constituted by law (*lex*), by custom and by the necessity of nature,[14] Irnerius, in his *Gloss on the Digest*, says that custom once had the force of law and the people had the power of making laws. But according to Irnerius, popular custom does not have such a power any more because this power has been transferred to the emperor.[15] That is, the alienation of the power from the people is permanent, once it has occurred.

The *Summa Trecensis*, which was once thought to be by Irnerius,[16] shows an account of the source of the legislative power more detailed than and different from his *Gloss*. According to the *Summa Trecensis*, the law is defined as the people's constitution, whether it is written or unwritten.[17] Insofar as what the people declares as its will - whether by a vote, or by habit and custom -[18] determines law, there is virtually no difference between written law and unwritten law, that is custom.[19] Thus, the power to make laws or the power to command depends on the authority of Roman people, or on the authority of the person to whom the legislative power is permitted by the people, that is the emperor:[20]

> Certainly he who has the power to command has the authority to make the law. Therefore the Roman people, or rather he to whom this was granted by the people [has the power]: for the emperors have this capacity. For this duty is incumbent on the people or the emperor, to provide for individual men as the sons or members of their own.[21]

In describing the law-making process, the *Summa Trecensis* reveals once again the source of the legislative power. It argues that the laws should be made according to the legitimate course of their constitution. So, when the reason for making a law needs to be discussed, the discussion has to be in a public place by the nobles, in particular by senators. For the reason to be accepted, their advice is required.[22] This may lead us to think that the law is made by a specific group of people. But we should not miss the phrase after this passage: "the law is nothing other than the people's constitution passed with the approval of prudent men" ("*et hoc recte, quia lex est constitutio populi cum uirorum prudentium consulto promulgata*").[23] That is, on the understanding that the basis of making laws should originate from what the whole people agree, the wisdom and prudence of some of the people are necessary in enacting laws.

If so, after the people concede the power to make law to the emperor, what is the relation between the people, which is the foundation of law, and the person who is given the power by the people? Is the people's legislative power still greater than the emperor's? Concerning this question, unlike Irnerius, the author of the *Summa Trecensis* says that custom is the best interpreter of laws and, moreover, custom can abrogate the laws themselves.[24] In this passage, then, the *Summa Trecensis* indicates the permanence of the people's power to make laws. That is, since legislative power lies with the people, even though one person is allowed to have the authority by the people, still, when necessary, that power can be returned to the original author—the people.

In contrast, Placentinus (died 1192) at the end of twelfth century maintains decisively that the concession of the people's power to legislate is irrevocable and that therefore actually the emperor has the power. This interpretation of *lex regia* is first hinted at in his glossary of law. Placentinus glosses on the title of '*De Legibus et Constitutionibus Principum & Edictis*' (C. 1. 14) that the law is distinguished into law in a strict sense, *censura*, and in a broad sense, *lectio*:

> In a strict sense law is properly said to be censura (judgement), in a broad sense law is called any selection, like *lex Iuliana*: in a more broad sense it is said to be whatever is established about Justice. According to this limitation, selection is sacred sanction, ordering respectable things, prohibiting the contrary, or law is communal command; *et cetera*.[25]

According to Placentinus, *lex* was specially named as *populi censura* (the judgement of the people) and the people initially had the power to establish the law.[26] However, now *lex* in its strictest sense is nothing other than imperial sanction ("*item strictissimo modo lex dicitur, sicut in hoc titulo, Imperialis sanctio*").[27] Laws are established because of two faults which should be counteracted, namely so that human boldness is restrained and human ignorance is driven out ("*ut humana refraenetur audacia, and ut expellatur ignorantia*").[28] The laws made for these purposes are the emperor's or his agent's creation:

> Concerning the making of laws, it is set out by whom they ought be made, and it is said that they are to be made by the emperor or only by someone whom the emperor has permitted.[29]

For Placentinus, the laws which aim to rectify the negative aspects of human nature are made for the people by the emperor. Accordingly, they ought to be understood and observed by the people. Given that the people is the object of laws and is not entitled to make laws, when the laws are obscure and need to be interpreted, they should be referred to the emperor. Only the emperor can interpret the cases which are intricate, making unfair fair, making darkness light, making injustice justice:

> Concerning the laws which are made, the discussion is threefold, that is, about understanding, interpreting and obeying the laws...... I stress that the laws ought be understood by all people, even by country men, even by females, by the clergy, by the knights, although at all times it ought to be obeyed by the aforementioned people: this being the case if the laws can be understood. Therefore if anything should be discovered in the laws which is said obscurely, it should be referred to the emperor so that he may explain it.[30]

However, despite these phrases, it is hardly exact to say that Placentinus gives an absolutist interpretation of *lex regia*. This is because the law made by the emperor is not meant to be the product of his arbitrary will. In the section under the same title, Placentinus argues that if the law is not pleasing to everybody or nearly everybody, then when everybody is collected together, it ought be reconsidered ("*si omnibus vel pene omnibus placuerit, tunc denuo collectis omnibus debebit recenseri*").[31] Furthermore, Placentinus says even that in the process of law-making the emperor ought not to command, but should advise and consult.[32]

Thus, Placentinus does not give us consistent explanations about the source and locus of the power to legislate. But he is more in favour of the imperial power than Irnerius since he considers that the people's legislative power is not revocable:

> Furthermore today only the emperor or he to whom the emperor has permitted it, has the power to make the laws and interpret them. Therefore today neither the Roman people, nor the Senate has the power.[33]

Furthermore, glossing the relation between the imperial law and local law. Placentinus gives us a more convincing explanation concerning the irrecoverable power of the people. He says that custom, which is unwritten law brought in by the continued custom of the people, is of nature and is of great authority. On this basis, the custom of the Roman people can abrogate law and *lex municipalis* cannot,[34] however, this does not signify that the Roman people's legislative power could be resumed. This is stated in a direct way in the following passage:

> To the emperor through the *lex regia* the Roman people transferred all power; and therefore the right to make law and abrogate it: and thus the people has not reserved such a right themselves.[35]

These sentences clearly show that for Placentinus the people initially had the legislative power, but are not the holder of that power any more. Now legislative power lies in the emperor or the person whom the emperor permits. But this is only true if we realise that Placentinus does not endorse an absolutist interpretation of *lex regia* in the respect that the law reflects what the emperor wants at his disposal. Placentinus mentions that it is in this context that the emperor applies *digna vox* (the emperor's observance of the laws).[36] While the people ought to observe laws from necessity, the emperor who makes laws is subject to the laws voluntarily.[37] For Placentinus too, "*quod principi placuit*" (D. 1.4.1) does not indicate the arbitrary will of the emperor for his own interest. In sum, Placentinus understands that the power originally belonged to the people but is permanently granted to the emperor. Now the emperor has the power to make and to interpret laws. But the emperor is also bound by the laws and is not to exercise his will without legal commitments.

Azo (died in 1220) expounds a view contrasting to that of Placentinus about *lex regia*, as shown first from his explanation of what *lex* is:

> Law is posited sometimes strictly, sometimes broadly. It is strictly posited when in place of the statute of the Roman people. And this is what it means. Law is what the Roman people constituted when they were asked by a senatorial magistrate, for example, the consul, that is, by somebody who was from a senatorial office ...... Sometimes it is posited in a broad way in place of any reasonable statute, from which law is also said to be holy sanction ordering honourable things and prohibiting the contrary. It is a rule of the just and the unjust ...... The constitution of the emperor and his edict are the fathers of law, insofar as law is to be understood in broad way and it can be said to be posited in the broad sense of the rubric.[38]

For Azo, the strict definition of *lex* means the statute of the Roman people. On the other hand, when it is stated in a broad way for every reasonable statute, it is the constitution of the emperor and his edict. But when *lex* is established by the emperor, or by the pretorian prefect[39] or by the men to whom the emperor has given permission, it is so under the condition that all people agree.[40] This definition of law, which is in contrast to Plancentinus', leads Azo to argue for the perpetuity of the people's legislative power—that the people conceded the power to legislate before but revoked it later:

> Even today perhaps law can be established by the Roman people, as is posited by the definition of law mentioned before, although the power is said to be transferred to the emperor...... For it is said to be transferred, that is to be conceded, not in the sense that the people totally gave up the power...... For the people had transferred it before as well, but nevertheless revoked it after.[41]

Denying the accepted interpretation of *lex regia*, which suggested that the emperor had permanently the people's authority by means of the *lex regia*, Azo argues that this is not true:

> Therefore if the people had it before, they will still have it. Say therefore that it is not the people that is here excluded, but single individuals from the people. It is similar to the example that Scipio alone liberated the city and the Roman *universitas*. Indeed the people are not excluded because it would be false. But individuals from the people are excluded, because he did more than any one else, therefore individuals are indeed excluded, but not the *universitas* or the people.[42]

For Azo, the people as *universitas* is the source of the power to make laws, but it does not indicate an individual as a single member of the whole. Azo believes that the people as a whole should continue to have the power since the people has greater power than the emperor, even though the emperor can be greater than any individual member of the people.[43] This is very much like an Aristotelian principle, 'the whole is greater than the part,' with which we will deal in a later chapter.

That is, even though through *lex regia* the people transferred *imperium* totally to the emperor, the people's power is essentially inalienable. In consequence, when it is required, the emperor returns the *imperium* to the people, because the emperor too should be bound by the law in its strict sense, that is the statute of the people:[44]

> Every soul should be subject to the emperor as superior and to the leaders sent by God...... But a particular emperor cannot give an order to his successor, but can only advise that the successor should keep the laws, and set forth the cause of that

> advice: that is, because the authority of the emperor depends on the law, that is the royal law. And because through it the people transferred totally the *imperium* to the emperor. Therefore rightly he himself should also return this to the law, so that he keeps it.[45]

While Placentinus maintains that *digna vox* depends on the voluntary will of the emperor, Azo argues that *digna vox* is based on the delegation of the people's *imperium* to the emperor and therefore the emperor should be bound by the laws. For Placentinus, law is imperial sanction and the people's original power cannot be resumed. By contrast, Azo thinks that, although the emperor establishes the law, his authority is not permanent, since the law in its real sense is always nothing other than the consensus of the people. What is of permanence is what the people think and agree. By arguing that "it is a greater thing for someone to observe the laws than to be emperor,"[46] Azo confirms again that the emperor is never superior to the power of the people.

Azo in the early part of the thirteenth century manifested the populist interpretation of *lex regia*. However, this thesis did not survive continuously into the next century. At the time when Marsilius was writing in the early fourteenth century, the dominant view of *lex regia* was still that the people's legislative power was original but not to be returned later.[47] We can see this if we look at Marsilius' contemporary, Cynus de Pistoia.

Cynus (1270–1336/7), a jurist and a poet, studied at Bologna and at Paris. Thereafter he worked for the Emperor Henry VII at Rome.[48] Cynus expresses the populist view of *lex regia* that the emperor's legislative power originates from the people: "*dico, quod Imperator a populo est, sed imperium, cuius presidatu Imperator dicitur, dicimus a Deo.*"[49] However, concerning the perpetuity of the original power of the people, Cynus does not go as far as Azo. Cynus agrees with Azo only in the respect that the source of the emperor's power is the people and therefore, by virtue of *lex regia*, the ruler receives his powers from the people through its consent.[50]

In fact, Cynus was a strong supporter of the imperialist cause. Cynus, like Placentinus, holds that the legislative power which the people had initially, but which it conceded to the ruler, cannot be returned to the people. In addition, Cynus says that after the concession, the ruler to whom the legislative power is entrusted is divine in the sense that the emperor is '*dominus mundi*' as God's agent.[51] Therefore, the ruler, the '*dominus*' on earth, does not have any temporal superior and enjoys a *de facto* independence in his own territory.[52]

This theme of the 'non-superior' in Italian city-states is a main concern through which Marsilius attempted to argue for the people's *imperium* and *potestas*. Before the fourteenth century, the glossators' and post-glossators' arguments about the source of jurisdiction were not associated with the theme of 'non-superior.' In other words, 'non-superior' was not given as a philosophical foundation to justify the locus of legislative power in the glossators' and post-glossators' theory. By contrast, in the fourteenth century discourse, we find the theme of 'non-superior' adapted to explain the theory of sovereignty. Cynus was not the first to do so. Earlier, Innocent III mentioned that the king of France recognised no superior at all in temporal affairs.[53] But Innocent III's statement of 'non-superior' is to argue for the superiority of the temporal power (French king) in the secular domain. It is Bartolus, Cynus' pupil, who develops this thesis of 'non-superior' and of the *de facto* independence in Italian city-states to elaborate the theory of the sovereignty of the people.

· 5 ·

BARTOLUS (1314–57): WE HAVE JUST BECOME INDEPENDENT

The controversial issue of who has the power to legislate or who has the sovereign power, which was a hotly debated issue for the commentators, arose specifically in the milieu of the independent Italian city-states.[1] The tension between the universalistic notion and the territorially limited one or, in other words, the conflict between the empire and the Italian city-states provides a crucial clue in understanding and interpreting Marsilius' thought, in particular concerning the issue of who is, historically speaking, the sovereign legislator, with which we will deal in a later chapter. About the historical setting, whereas Shelley Lockwood supposes that the territorial element is almost lacking in Marsilius' work,[2] Skinner understands Marsilius' thought from the point of view of the Italian city-states.[3] In contrast, the earlier work of Woolf writing on Italian civic ideology at the beginning of the century, warns that it would be a great mistake to think that in the Middle Ages there was a simple antagonism between the universal Roman empire and local particularism. The attitude of the Italian city-states toward the empire was quite flexible according to circumstances.[4] In order to understand these double references of institutional background when Marsilius was writing about which scholars do not always agree, we must also understand the context of the Italian city-states and the empire.

This chapter aims at elucidating a textual context which justified the independence of the Italian city-states, in which Marsilius' thought took a concrete shape. To this end, I will explore the thought of Bartolus of Saxoferrato (1314–1357), in order to show how the tension between the empire and the Italian city-states could be accommodated and how the city-states acquired their own civic ideology. Through this examination, I intend to argue that Bartolus' justification of the autonomy of city-states contributes to the understanding of the emergence of the people as the sovereign law-maker.

As we saw, since the revival of Roman law at the end of the eleventh century, the *Corpus Iuris Civilis* had come to be used as the basic framework of legal theory and practice throughout the holy Roman empire. The texts of ancient Roman law stated that the *princeps*, who for the jurists was identified with the emperor,[5] had to be regarded as the *dominus mundi*, the sole ruler of this world. While the emperor had the strongest possible legal support in his campaigns to subjugate the cities, the cities had difficulty in vindicating any *de jure* independence from the empire.[6] The main concern of glossators was not with the independence of the city-states from the imperial authority.[7] In fact, it was through the 'Peace of Constance,' the treaty made by the Emperor Frederick I with the Lombardy League in 1183, that the Italian cities actually got to achieve their rights.[8] Furthermore, by the first decade of the thirteenth century, a republican form of self-government, that is an elective government centred on an official, the so-called *podestà*,[9] became the universal institution throughout the main cities of northern Italy.[10] Gradually, these brought them a measure of *de facto* independence, even though the holy Roman emperor continued to be *de jure* their lord[11] and the tension between city-states and the empire did not disappear. By the beginning of the fourteenth century, however, a civic ideology of Italian city-states was finally developed. Bartolus was the first jurist to present a thoroughgoing and consistent idea of the sovereignty of the city-states.[12]

First of all, Bartolus' main achievement can be found in his civic ideology: '*civitas quae superiorem non recognoscit, sibi princeps*.' To put it simply, this signifies that the cities, which are governed by 'free people,' wield their own *imperium* and therefore they are in effect *sibi princeps*, a prince unto themselves, without any superior. Before exploring this ideology for the independence of the Italian city-states in detail it should be mentioned that Bartolus' achievement in formulating a civic ideology is somewhat limited. Despite M. H. Keen's insistence,[13] Bartolus was not very much concerned to support the universal authority of the emperor. But at the same time he did not mean to assign completely autonomous powers to the cities. To put Bartolus in the position of civic ideologist *par excellence* is to go far beyond what he intended to argue. Bartolus too was still one of the post-glossators who conceded that *de jure* the emperor was the sole *dominus mundi*:

> Therefore I say that the emperor is truly the lord (*dominus*) of the whole world. It is no obstacle that some people are particularly the lords, because the world is, as it were, a kind of *universitas*; hence somebody (the emperor) can have the aforementioned *universitas*, although individual things are not his own.[14]

The imperial claim to lordship of the world was not in practice very influential after the death of Frederick II. But throughout the fourteenth century it still to some extent held real force in northern Italy, where the emperor was in fact recognised as a form of overlord who had authority to legitimise republican and signorial regimes.[15] This is true of Bartolus too: the emperor is *dominus universalis*. However, for him, universal sovereignty, that is the emperor as *dominus mundi*, was in fact needed for the external sovereignty of territorial city-states. That is, while the emperor retained a genuine *de jure* sovereignty within the *terrae imperii*,[16] other powers, by being *de jure* subject to him, could in practice obtain a sovereignty on a *de facto* basis. This allowed cities to possess an actual sovereignty within their territories without denying the universal sovereignty of the emperor.[17] The following passage indicates the relationship between universal sovereignty and territorial sovereignty, that is *de jure* sovereignty and *de facto* independence:

> Trust can be left to the cities which are not the enemies of the empire, and they will be able to act through their own syndics. This means that some cities are not under the emperor...... Solution: I understand that all cities are *de jure* under the emperor, but not in fact. There are some, which also are not *de jure* under the emperor, like cities given to the church.[18]

Although the city is one of the territories of the emperor, it too appears to be an independent political unit which has jurisdiction. The fact is that while the emperor of a territory taken universally has the jurisdiction over the whole world, the leader of a city or a territory is its own judge.[19] With this difference, through the *de jure* relationship compatibility between the empire and the cities is maintained. That is, on the understanding that the emperor has *de jure* sovereignty, the cities have their own rights within their territorial boundaries.[20] In other instances, there is restriction on the local sovereignty of city-states. As the above passage makes clear, for Bartolus, the cities within the territory of the church (mainly in central Italy) are outside the emperor's *de jure* jurisdiction and neither have the emperor as their *de jure* superior nor ever enjoy independence free from a superior, that is the pope. With these two reservations, Bartolus' argument for the independent power of cities goes further: 'they do not recognise a superior.'

Bartolus' argument that the cities have sovereignty on a *de facto* basis is associated with the theory of 'non-superior' in the respect that the cities do not in practice recognise a *superior*, to whom they have to be obedient, which is Bartolus' contribution to the theory of the sovereignty of the Italian city-states or the people.

To understand Bartolus' theory of 'non-superior,' let me begin by examining what the Roman law (D. 2.1.3) says about *imperium*. In the *Digest*, Ulpian says:

> *Imperium* is simple or mixed. To have simple *imperium* is to have the power of the sword to punish the wicked and this is also called *potestas*. *Imperium* is mixed where it also carries jurisdiction to grant *bonorum possesio*. Such jurisdiction includes also the power to appoint a judge.[21]

That is, *imperium* in Roman law includes both coercive jurisdiction and ownership. But when Bartolus talks about civic independence, he does not seem to refer to the double meanings of *imperium*. Bartolus' conception of *imperium* in discussion of the *de facto* independence of city-states implies more or less limited jurisdiction. For Bartolus, the scope of jurisdiction depends on which kinds of *imperium* or *universitas* they have.[22] Depending on this, some cities did not recognise a superior and others did. Bartolus distinguishes between three kinds of city, *maximae civitates*, *magnae civitates*, and *parvae civitates*, as follows. First, the large *universitas* or *civitas* means a province or a kingdom. This *universitas* has simple and mixed *imperium*, that is the power to punish someone, to grant possession and to appoint a judge. The second kind of *universitas* is exemplified in such cities as Venice, Florence and ancient Rome. They do not have simple and mixed *imperium* but have jurisdiction to punish less important crimes. The third *universitas* applies to lesser towns like Siena, Pisa and Perugia, to which no jurisdiction belongs. Therefore, they are under the jurisdiction of another city.[23] In a strict sense, these cities which have no jurisdiction have neither *universitas* nor *imperium*, so they cannot be properly called cities.

On this basis, Bartolus offers this definition of city-states: "*quaelibet civitas, habens distinctum territorium, quae superiorem non recognoscit, potest dici provincia, ut notat glossa.*"[24] A city which does not have a superior is, within its own boundaries,[25] its own *princeps* (*sibi princeps*) and is in the position of an independent political unit.[26] According to this definition, the third *universitas* is outside the category of the *civitas*, because by being under a superior who has jurisdiction on their behalf, they cannot be free from a superior.[27] Now city-states as '*sibi princeps*' can legislate for themselves, have their own *fisc* (treasurer) and therefore are autonomous political powers.

At this point, Bartolus' acknowledgement of the non-recognition of a superior in a city-state entails the argument for the people's power to make laws. That is, the fact that the *civitas* has no superior for jurisdiction means that the people, who are its members, are free ('*populus liber*'). Not recognising *de facto* the superiority of the imperial authority, the free people itself becomes the agent of law-making.[28] That is, the people can make statutes as they please ('*prout sibi placet*'):[29]

> Today no city of Italy, in particular in Tuscany, recognises a superior. The city has in itself a free people and *merum imperium*. And it has as much power over the people, as the emperor in the world.[30]

For Bartolus, the city becomes the collective corporation, not the individual gathering, of the free people, which has no superior in making laws. In such a city, the imposition of new laws rests with the people. The city does not need any superior's authorisation to make laws except that of the people. The city or the people holds the position of prince; the *populus* is *princeps* to itself. '*Civitas sibi princeps*' implies the people as the political agent which has the sovereign power to make laws: the position of a free people, a *populus liber*, is that of the ultimate bearer of legislative power.[31]

Theoretically, the theme of non-recognition of a superior in a city is reinforced by the argument from the people's consent. For Bartolus, in terms of people's consent, the city can have the power to make laws and can be free from the emperor. This is because the *populus liber* acts upon its own will through tacit or express consent, which excludes any need to acknowledge a superior to act on its behalf:

> When the people have complete jurisdiction they can make a statute without waiting for the authority of a superior ...... That in this case the authority of a superior is not expected is clear from the example of custom, which is introduced by the tacit consent of the people and is equal to statute, in which it is clear that the authority of a superior is not required.[32]

Moreover, Bartolus' definitions of custom and statute too reinforce the assertion that the people do not have any superior except their own will or consent. According to Bartolus, custom and statute, unwritten and written law, originate from the people's consent. Both of them have legally equal force, simply because while the former is the product of the people's tacit consent, the latter is the product of its express consent.[33] Thus, the equal legal force of custom and statute which lie in the element of consent, whether it is tacit or explicit, gives the power to change an action into a rule with binding force.[34] The people does not in consequence require the authorisation of a superior in making laws for the authorisation of their statutes.[35]

The popular will through consent is concretely articulated in the *concilium* which is the people's assembly and the real embodiment of power in the city. Bartolus maintains that the *concilium* represents the will of the whole people and city[36] because it is elected by them and acts for them.[37] Here, the assertion that the city or the people is *sibi civitas* and has no superior extends to the discussion of forms of government. In his *Tractatus de Regimine Civitatis*, Bartolus explains 'rule by the people'—that is a '*regimen ad populum*' in his terms - which Aristotle called 'polity' or 'politics.' According to Bartolus, a '*regimen ad populum*' is the best form of government: through the rulers the common good of all people is considered principally according to their statutes[38] but rulers are elected by the popular council. The decision of the council is always right, even though sometimes the wise object to it.[39] For Bartolus, '*regimen ad populum*' does not necessarily mean that the government is managed directly by the people, but it always means that the *jurisdictio* or the sovereign power is with them.

Bartolus' argument for the theme of 'non-superior' is a crucial factor in justifying the full legitimacy of the city's *de facto* independence from the empire. Through this justification, we observe the idea that the community or the people is the political subject which is not obedient to any superior: the people itself is the prince (*civitas sibi princeps*). Bartolus' argument for non-recognition of a superior in a city, despite its reservations that the emperor is *de jure* sovereign to the city, and that the cities within the papal power are an exception, suggests the advent of the people as sovereign without a superior required for the authorisation of laws. In Bartolus' own period, the people as the sovereign to legislate was not a political reality either in theory or in practice. But the attempt to argue for the autonomous power of the independent city or the free people is to be taken further by another medieval thinker who argues for the people as the sovereign with an insistence hitherto unknown—Marsilius.

· 6 ·

CONTEMPORARY ARISTOTELIANISM

In his *Defensor Pacis* (I. i. 3), Marsilius points out that Aristotle had a penetrating insight into the fundamental causes of strife in a civil community. But nevertheless, Aristotle, according to Marsilius, could not have foreseen the new cause which troubled all cities and states, that is the papal claim to plenitude of power, because it did not exist in Aristotle's times. However, Marsilius' new perspective, from which to view the problems of a state and his immediate concern with the Italian city-states, relies very much in its formation on Aristotle.

Aristotelianism in the thirteenth century was a major factor in introducing Marsilius and his contemporaries to certain key concepts of political theory: the idea that political life is natural to human beings, that the common good is the aim of political life, the necessity of the rule of law and the people as collective wisdom. With these Aristotelian concepts, Marsilius establishes the philosophical foundations of political discourse, which allows him to move to a consideration of political issues. My concern in this chapter is with how such Aristotelian notions were being advanced in Italy before Marsilius developed his political principles. To this end, I will first discuss briefly the implications of the reemergence of Aristotelianism in the thirteenth century, in relation to Italian Aristotelianism, which constitutes a context in which Marsilius' philosophical discourse was shaped. Then I will attempt to examine Remigius de Girolami and Ptolemy of Lucca, thinkers contemporary with Marsilius, who were faithful in following the terms of Aristotelian politics. Just as in earlier chapters we have understood the contexts in which Marsilius' *political* concerns were being formed, the exploration of contemporary Aristotelianism in Marsilius' period may help us to comprehend the context of the *philosophical* discourse, on the basis of which Marsilius presents his theory of politics.

Introduction: Reception of Aristotelianism

After the recovery of Aristotelianism in the thirteenth century, it had formed a distinct political language which persisted throughout the later Middle Ages. Ullmann claims that Aristotelianism in the thirteenth century amounts to a conceptual revolution and marks the watershed between the Middle Ages and the modern period.[1] In less dramatic terms than Ullmann, but more concretely, Paul O. Kristeller says that with the rise of scholasticism and universities during the thirteenth century, Aristotle's *Nicomachean Ethics* and *Politics* became the basis on which moral philosophy as an academic discipline in the West was established.[2]

However, Aristotelianism was not the only moral and political discourse available to medieval theorists.[3] Cicero's thought, in particular his view of justice as the prime political virtue or the precondition for the existence of a community, was also employed during the Middle Ages and influenced the way in which medieval thinkers thought about the citizen and the nature of the city.[4] Nevertheless, an examination of various medieval thinkers justifies the claim that the basic doctrines and principles of Aristotle's social and political philosophy were difficult to escape in the Middle Ages.

The translations of Aristotle's writings enabled medieval scholars to turn an intellectual corner around the year 1250.[5] In particular, it was William of Moerbeke's translation of the *Politics* into Latin (1265) that popularized the recovery of Aristotle's political principles and became the immediate source of medieval scholars' knowledge of those principles. But, more significantly than the translation, some writers are worth mentioning for the contribution they made to the establishment of Aristotelianism as a contemporary political language in the period. Albert the Great (1200–80) is the first commentator on Aristotle's *Politics*. Through his commentary, Albert taught, as Aristotle did,[6] that the city was naturally created, designed to realise the human good.[7] As such his view—beyond the conventional Christian conception of political life, that is the Augustinian one—widened the horizon of the medieval understanding of politics.[8]

However, it was the contribution of Albert's pupil, St. Thomas Aquinas (1225–74) which enabled many political writers until the fifteenth century to be familiar with Aristotelian principles and to see how they could subsume this secularised Aristotelianism within a Christian framework heavily indebted to the writings of St. Augustine.[9] Aquinas, unlike St. Augustine (354–431) who interpreted the world of politics (the *saeculum*) as the corrupt outcome of sin,[10] asserted that grace and human nature were not incompatible. This accommodation of the natural order and the human political order (Aristotelianism) to the divine order is well manifested in Aquinas' conceptions of politics and law.[11] In order to see the implication of the reemergence of Aristotelianism, let us take a look at Aquinas' understanding of politics and law.

Aquinas believed that God was the final perfection and the complete good to which this world had to refer.[12] At the same time, he thought that through political life, which was natural to human beings, man could act virtuously and look after the common good.[13] For Aquinas, to procure the common good of peace and justice[14] is not incompatible with pursuing the heavenly good, because the 'true' common good of a political community is the common good regulated by divine justice and aims at the attainment of divine enjoyment.[15] Aquinas, like Aristotle, asserted that, in order for men to attain the common good in a political community, there was a need for the making of law, which meant a rational ordering of things.[16] For Aquinas, without rules for actions, men cannot be truly good and therefore it is impossible to achieve the common good.[17] Thus, law has to be ordained to the common good.[18]

In presenting the ontological accounts of the laws which concern the common good, Aquinas shows that the acceptance of the Aristotelian principle is never at odds with the Christian faith and that God, nature and man act in harmony. According to Aquinas, there are several types of law: the eternal law, the natural law, the human law and the divine law. The eternal law means the divine providence which governs the universe. Being measured and regulated by the eternal law of God, all things participate and share in the divine reason by way of inclination.[19] Hence, rational creatures (human beings) have inclinations to control their actions. However, rational creatures have more than simply an inclination to their good: they have reason which allows them to participate rationally in the divine reason. This participation by way of reason is called the natural law. That is, the natural law is nothing other than the imprint of the divine light in man. In this sense, Aquinas says, the natural law is "the participation in the eternal law by rational creatures."[20] Furthermore, from this natural law or the light of natural reason, man has human laws to regulate his own actions.[21] However, Aquinas argues, because of the uncertainty of human judgement, the insufficiency of human laws and the necessity of the overall and impartial punishment of all evils, 'true' or 'good' human laws concretely refer to a divinely given law. By doing so, again, the human order can progress toward the eternal life as the final end.[22]

However, Aquinas believes that even though law is ordained for the common good, if it is not made by the good intention of the legislator, it cannot be true law.[23] To this end, Aquinas argues for the necessity of having a ruler who directs man towards the common good within the overall direction of God.[24] More specifically, he suggests that the best form of political order is the rule of a king,[25] because political prudence exists in the king who is like an architect, that is one who designs the structure of the whole.[26] In addition Aquinas, who reconciles Aristotelianism and Christianity, finds another reason why the best form of political rule is monarchy in the likeness of God's direction over the universe: as the universe is governed by one person, so rule by one is the best form of government for the common good of political unity.[27] However, for Aquinas, although monarchy is the best form of government, it is only an ideal. This is because he supposes that kingship easily degenerates into tyranny, corrupted by private interests or desires,[28] and therefore cannot work for the common good of peace. Rather, for reasons of practical feasibility, Aquinas seems to be in favour of a mixed constitution of monarchy, aristocracy and popular rule: that is a form of government which is ruled, under the single virtuous head, by virtuous few and in which all participate.

Aquinas' understanding of laws and politics reveals the harmonious correspondence between the divine, the natural and the human in his thought. There is a hierarchy of the three orders, but it is not the Augustinian sort in which the corrupt man cannot dare to approach and touch the highest one. For Aquinas, the human order does not exist in isolation from the divine because nature—which includes in part both the divine reason and the human reason—functions as the mediator between the two. While God embraces man, who is a part of nature which derives from the divine reason, man, through nature, takes the image and likeness of God and can know the divine reason. In consequence, the human order is no more the reflection of the situation of corrupted mankind. Moreover, it is not necessarily demolished by the higher orders. Nature and man are fundamentally in harmony with God. Specifically, they are so when the common good is the ultimate end of a political order which is directed according to divine justice. Both law and political rule, when they are established for the common good of a civil community, are subsumed under the ultimate good of heavenly beatitude. Thus, Aquinas showed how the natural-human foundation of political community, the new discipline of Aristotelianism, was in tune with the omnipotent power of God.

However, just as in suggesting the rational justification of politics, it was not necessarily Aquinas' purpose to deliver exactly what Aristotle had said or to interpret Aristotelian principles as they were, so medieval writers did not regard Aristotle's writings as the perfect and inflexible mould in which to pour their own political theories. They did not pursue Aristotle without modification nor did they say the same thing as Aristotle did.[29] In fact, they often took Aristotle's original meanings out of context.[30] Medieval commentaries on the *Politics* have the *Politics* as a common source, but Aristotle's political ideas were applied selectively whenever such concepts were relevant to the questions which they had in mind.[31] Dunbabin points out that the reasons why they show diversity in their approach were "partly as a result of the needs of the readership for which they were written, partly because they follow different academic conventions, and partly because some show a genuine originality of mind."[32] Our aim too in reading medieval commentaries on the *Politics* is not confined only to finding out how closely and accurately these commentaries came to explain Aristotle's meaning. Rather, our intention is to understand what arguments these commentators had in glossing the *Politics* in various contexts. Indeed, Black's claim that they used 'Aristotelianism' as a language and not as a doctrine is extremely relevant.[33]

On this understanding, in the following sections, I intend to examine how Italian Aristotelianism was being addressed when Marsilius was writing. To this end, I will explore the thought of Remigius and Ptolemy. Although they did not discuss the whole range of Aristotelian issues, the examination of the thought of these two Italian Aristotelians will enable us to map out the discussion about the political principles of civil communities in Marsilius' time.

Remigius de Girolami

Remigius (died 1319), a Dominican and a Thomist, studied at Paris in the 1260s. After that, he went back to Florence and taught at S. Maria Novella.[34] Remigius' interest in Aristotle is centred on the notion of the common good. His discussion of the common good came out of the very urgent and unstable political situation of Florence in which he was living and was witnessing with his own eyes. Remigius opens his tract *De bono communi* by mentioning the political cacophony in Italy. He thought that factional rivalry would lead to the destruction of Florence. Thus, just as Marsilius' concern with the common good came from his love of Italy and his efforts to integrate a divided unity, Remigius' notion of the common good was the expression of his serious concern with Florence.

Let me begin with Remigius' notion of community. According to Remigius, the community (the *commune*) is not *totalitas universalis* but *totalitas integralis*. Remigius does not explain in detail what *totalitas universalis* is in comparison with *totalitas integralis*. But he says that *totalitas integralis* is composed of rational parts or the whole which is inclusive of the parts. It is not supposed to be just the numerical collectivity of the parts, but rather the collectivity of rational parts. For Remigius, the highest rational being is God. So his understanding of *totalitas integralis* implies that it eventually aims to arrive at the highest reason, namely God.[35]

In the scheme of integral totality, a part has no meaning without a relation to the whole. In other words, the part outside the whole is no longer a part, that is a component of the whole. Because the existence of a part depends upon the existence of the whole, the part cannot have its own value without relying on the whole.[36] It is just as a hand which is separated from the body is no longer a part of the body; in that case, the hand out of the body is no longer called a hand in the sense of 'hand' as a part of the body.[37] By this analogy, Remigius defines the relation of the citizens and the city:

> For the whole must exist before the part. If the whole is destroyed, it will not be a foot, nor a hand, except equivocally, if, for example, someone meant a hand made of stone: for such a thing will be corrupt. For everything is defined by its function and virtue ... Whence if the city is destroyed, a citizen remains made only of stone or painted, because indeed he lacks the virtue and function which he had before ... So anyone who was a Florentine citizen, through the destruction of Florence, should now be called an object for tears (*flerentinus*) rather than a Florentine. And if he is not a citizen he is not a human being, because "a human being is a naturally civil animal," according to the Philosopher in 8 *Ethics* and in 1 *Politics*.[38]

If the community (the whole) is corrupted, the individual life (the part) correspondingly deteriorates. In the city which is destroyed, the citizens cannot be human beings because there is no more virtue with which to make them citizens and to give them proper human life. According to Remigius, a man can be a citizen only when he is existent in a city (a political unit) and has his own functions in a city, and then become a perfect human being. This recalls Aristotle's notion of a citizen: "man is by nature a political animal. He who is without a city, by reason of his own nature and not of some accident, is either a poor sort of being, or a being higher than man.";[39] "The goodness of the good man, and that of the good citizen of the best city, must be one and the same."[40]

For Remigius, just as the hand has an organic relation to the body, the citizen is nothing without relying upon the city. Remigius therefore claims that, when the citizen of Florence is impoverished and loses his virtue and functions in the city, he is as if made of stone and then *flerentinus* (an object for tears). If he is not a citizen, he is no more a man, because a human being, who is by nature a civil animal, lacks that nature and therefore cannot be a human being.

Moreover, Remigius argues that the making of a community is natural because the part's love for the whole is natural, and therefore a man or a citizen (a part) naturally loves the community (the whole) which has its own good. By forming a community, human beings are more virtuous and can attain perfect happiness:

> It has to be said that the part naturally loves the whole with the love of friendship, but because in the good of a naturally loved thing is also included the good of the thing naturally loving it, therefore the part is also said to love the whole because of its own good, not because the part arranges the good of the whole to its own good, but rather on the contrary it arranges its own good to the good of the whole.[41]

As is mentioned above, Remigius' concern with the *bonum commune* (common good) came out of his love of Florence:

> Make a judgement and decide together what should be done (Judges 19: 50); this saying urges you to four things very necessary for your office...... Third, to the advance of Commune, because 'what should be done in common' for the good of the Commune, that is the pleasant, the honorable and the useful, not for the good of this or that person or house, neither for the good of these or those groups of people, but just as you have been created and put in office through the Commune, so you should work for the common good.[42]

That is, for Remigius, the *bonum commune* as the highest good is not differentiated from the *bonum* of a city. What is really necessary in a community is a common good which can embrace the common benefit of the entire multitude.

Just to look for the interests of a particular house or person without any regard to the common good is inimical to the good of a community and eventually of the individual. In this sense, the *bonum commune* or *bonum Communis* is the same as the *summum bonum* of a political unity in general. In his tract *De Bono Communi*, it is not by accident that Remigius used the term *bonum commune* together with *bonum Communis*. Remigius paid close attention to the collective political virtue of the citizenry to make and maintain a community.[43]

In this context, Aristotle's theme that the common good of the greater number is better, for example the passage in *Nicomachean Ethics*, I. ii (1094b9–10)—"*amabile quidem enim et uni soli, melius vero et divinius genti et civitatibus*"—is supported by Remigius. He gives the following commentary on the passage:

> Evidently to many people as is said—the more the good is in common, the more it has to be loved—, evidently the good of a city is more than the good of a citizen and the good of a province which holds many cities more than the good of a city. Whereof consequently the good of the kingdom has to be loved more than the good of a single province and the good of the universal church more than the good of a kingdom.[44]

Concerning the common good, the good of a city is better, the good of a province is even better, the good of the kingdom is still better again than that of a city. This is because the greater the number of beneficiaries, the greater is the common good. Remigius says that *bonum commune* is better than a particular good: "*bonum commune indubitanter preferendum est bono particulari, et bonum multitudinis bono unius singularis persone.*"[45] However, while in the context of a particular city, e.g. Florence, the *bonum Communis* coincides with *bonum commune*, in the hierarchy of the common good the *bonum Communis* figures as a particular good. If one thing is said to be better than another, this assumes that it is the same quality in virtue of which the comparison is being made. Likewise, that the good of a kingdom is better than that of a province demonstrates that in number and in quality the *bonum commune* is superior to the *bonum Communis*. Further, just as with the individual citizen in regard to the city, the *bonum Communis* has an organic relation with the higher *bonum commune*. In this context, Remigius, in his *De Bono Communi*, claims that the good of the individual is less than that of the city and therefore the former should be subordinate to the latter to obtain the higher good. But it still remains uncertain what kind of political units Remigius had in mind. That is, is it a city, like Florence, or a larger unit, like the empire? As we shall see in the case of Marsilius, this uncertainty about the political unit is true also of Remigius. But whatever it means historically, Remigius has no doubt that the concept of *bonum commune* is like the interrelated relation of a part to a whole and it should be put on first priority in any political unit.

Realising that the common good is absolutely necessary for a community, Remigius tells us about what the common good is in more detail. According to Remigius, the *summum bonum* of the political association consists in *concordia*, which is nothing other than the harmony of all wills in wishing the same end.[46] Without *concordia* no city can be good. However, despite our knowledge of the definition of common good, we do not necessarily have the *concordia*, the highest good of a city. Why? In other words, in the context of Italian city-states, what caused the discord in Florence?

Remigius agrees that in order to achieve the harmony of a city or a political association, power and terror, namely compulsory forces, are inevitable.[47] It is a necessary condition for ruling a political association well. Apart from these physical conditions, what is of paramount importance for a city to maintain itself well is a voluntary will to keep justice. Remigius does not give a detailed definition of justice, but for him justice is the indispensable condition of harmony and good government in a political association. Remigius observes that justice is more concretely expressed through laws in a political unit.[48]

Aristotle argued that the rule of law ('legislative wisdom'), proceeding from moral prudence and understanding,[49] was the ultimate sovereign of the political association[50] and that it was intended to make men good and righteous.[51] Like Aristotle, Remigius conceives that without justice or laws there is no political association. However, justice or law is not naturally given. In the tract *De Bono Pacis*,[52] Remigius asserts that to maintain law and rightness in our political association there should be peace. If a political association cannot keep the peace, there is no justice, law and rightness in a civil community. Non-existence of justice indicates non-existence of a political unit.[53] Is, then, peace for Remigius the means of maintaining law or the goal of making law? On this matter, Remigius does not seem to clarify the sequence. What concerns him is the fact that peace is the first and absolute condition of human life in the sense that to live well in this world depends upon a community attaining peace.[54] As we will see, this is akin to Marsilius' notion of peace which is the prime requirement of a moral and physical self-sufficiency in a civil community. Let us take a more detailed look at Remigius' conception of peace.

Remigius says that there are two kinds of peace which we have to obtain and two methods to achieve them respectively. While one is the heavenly one, the other is that of this world. Remigius differentiates God's good from Caesar's good, but he does so on the understanding that the good of God is preferred to the good of his creature. For Remigius, ultimate peace signifies *bonum Dei* (the good of God):[55]

> The good of God is preferred to the good of every creature. But peace is the good of God and belongs to God. Temporal things, however, of this sort are the good belonging to human beings. Therefore, for the sake of pursuing the good of peace, losses of temporal things have to be endured.[56]

In addition, Remigius suggests the method of obtaining the good of God, the ultimate peace, as follows:

> It has to be said that the aforementioned words of God have to be understood when the prelates of the church are in harmony with Christ, especially with regard to intention, just as he who listens to the messenger listens to the lord who sends him, and he who listens to the vicar listens to the chief master, where the messenger and vicar are in harmony with the lord and the principal who send them. For where they are at odds with him, those who listen to them would not hear God.[57]

In other words, harmony with the church is to listen to the sermons of God through his messengers, and this is the way to acquire peace. At the same time, Remigius argues that the other way by which we can keep peace is to submit to the good and the order of this world:

> It has to be said that peace can be received properly and truly, and that it, like order, is always obtained in good because peace includes order within itself, as Augustine says in Book 19 in *De Civitate Dei*.[58]

But when we consider that good and order in the Middle Ages, as seen in Aquinas' thought, were very strongly dominated by God, the worldly peace cannot be imagined without the heavenly one. Therefore, it follows that in Remigius' thought peace is eventually through devotion to God. Putting more weight on the good of God than that of this world, Remigius talks about a method of procuring peace in this world.

Corresponding to his argument for the common good, Remigius asserts that the highest good of a civil society, peace, should be for the whole people and therefore that to keep peace in a community a part which is not helpful for the whole is to be cut off. Otherwise, peace itself will be on the brink of destruction:

> The Philosopher says in Book I of the *Ethics* that the good of a people and of a city and of the multitude has to be preferred as more divine and better than the good of only one person. But the highest good of the multitude and its purpose is peace, just

> as the Philosopher says in Book III of *Ethics*, just as health is the highest good of the whole body, as he says. Therefore, just as because of the health of body, the good of a member, which is sometimes even cut off, is neglected, so because of the peace of a city, the good of a particular person has to be neglected.[59]

Thus, the organic relation between the part and the whole, which is crucial for maintaining physical health,[60] applies to the concept of peace. Remigius maintains that in order to get peace from which to attain the good, a community is to remain in tranquillity. This tranquillity is made possible when all parts of this world are coordinated:

> The good of this world consists in peace, that is in a mutually regulated tranquillity, just as Augustine says in Book 19 in *De Civitate Dei*: peace of the body is a regulated harmony of parts, and the peace of all things is tranquillity of order. And in this order consists the good of this world, according to the Philosopher in 12 *Metaphysics*. There he says that everything is coordinated in some way. But the good of the whole is preferred to the good of a part. Therefore for the good of peace the temporal good of particular persons has to be passed over.[61]

As seen in this passage, Remigius shares Augustine's conception of peace. For Augustine, the mutual relation of body and soul brings an ordered harmony of life and health in the earthly city. The peace which is thus attained in this world is subject to the peace in the heavenly city, that is the supreme good.[62] Likewise, Remigius' notion of peace in this world is heavily founded on the heavenly good. Concerning the literal definition of peace or tranquillity, Remigius does not appear to differ from his contemporary Aristotelian thinkers, Ptolemy and Marsilius. As we shall see, all of them think that peace lies in the good disposition of all parts in a whole. But they differ from Remigius in the method of obtaining peace. As far as Remigius is concerned, he seems to rely more on the theological element than on the political (secular) one for achieving it.

Remigius' political principle shows an Aristotelian basis, the existence of a citizen being identified with that of a man, the natural and not divine institution of political society and a trust in the common good of the whole. Obviously, these are elements of Aristotelian teaching from which to understand human-based politics mixed with the Christian notions of men and society in the Middle Ages. But the Aristotelian principles in Remigius' thought are still ontologically limited by the existence of God as the highest reason. That is the way in which the two approaches—secular or natural and Christian—are integrated in Remigius' thought.

Ptolemy of Lucca

Ptolemy of Lucca (1236–1327), a Dominican, studied at Paris in the 1260s and became Bishop of Torcello in 1318. He completed around 1300–05 the *De Regimine Principum* (hereafter *De Regimine*)[63] which had been left unfinished by Aquinas after his death in 1274. Ptolemy, like Remigius, followed the same line of intellectual development in many respects, that is of Aristotelian political theory.

First of all, Ptolemy confirms Aristotle's account of the necessity of political life for human beings. According to Ptolemy, human beings form a society because it is their nature to be social and political beings and therefore human beings are naturally miserable when they are without community.[64] The aggregate being gathered together is the political association, whose chief concern is to ensure for its members, the citizens, the common good, the highest good, which is greater and more perfect than that of the individual. By being virtuous in a political association, man can have real happiness together with virtue.[65] Ptolemy thought that political life was a necessary condition for men's material and moral life, a real sufficient life. Without the city, men could not have a proper life.[66]

However, for the political association to be the community in which to achieve the common good, it should be well-ordered. For Ptolemy, order in a political association means nothing other than "disposition of equal and unequal parts, which gives each person his due" ("*parium dispariumque sua cuique tribuens dispositio*").[67] This is exactly what he means by peace. In other words, if all the different parts of the political community have their own proper place, the polity will be stable, so that men can have a perfect and a happy life. Ptolemy's thoughts concerning the natural necessity of political life and his definition of peace do not constitute any major difference from Remigius.' Our interest in Ptolemy with special reference to the contemporary Aristotelianism of Marsilius makes us pay more attention to Ptolemy's discussion about political rule.

Aristotle discussed the type of political rule (constitution) which was essential for attaining the common good in a political association. For Aristotle, without the right constitution, which is directed to the common good, it is impossible to have human life in a *polis*. Aristotle said that a constitution (or polity) meant "the organisation of a city (or *polis*), in respect of its offices generally, but especially in respect of that particular office which is sovereign in all issues."[68] In Book III of his *Politics*, Aristotle classified the types of political rule.

For Aristotle, the true goal of a state is to guarantee the good life, and when the government is ruled by laws the common good can be achieved. Aristotle therefore thought that the distinction between a right polity and a perverted polity depended upon whether the common interest was exercised in a state or not.[69] To ask who has dominant authority in the state or who is sovereign leads to the question of who makes laws and who controls the constitution. When the ruling authority is one and is exercised for the common interest it is called 'kingship.' The rule of more than one man but only a few is 'aristocracy' and political control exercised by the mass of the populace in the common interest is 'polity.'[70]

Ptolemy, like Aristotle, was equally occupied by the question of political rule. Ptolemy's categorisation of the types of political regime is little different from that of Aristotle: that is, monarchy is the rule of one, aristocracy is the rule by a few virtuous people, and political rule is rule by many people.[71] However, Ptolemy has a different view of kingship from Aristotle's, and from Aquinas' as well. For Aristotle, kingship is a good government for the common good, although it is rule by one person. For Aquinas, as seen above, monarchy is ideally the best form of government. However, Ptolemy argues that kingly rule, despite its care of the governed, is a kind of would-be despotic rule. According to Ptolemy in monarchies the laws are 'hidden in kings' breasts,' so that 'the will of the prince has the power of law.'[72] Because the law is the individual's will, not the will of the many, Ptolemy thinks that regal rule involves the possibility of becoming despotic rule. Thus Ptolemy, in contrast to other Aristotelians' preference for monarchy, has serious doubts about kingly rule as the good government.[73] For him, political rule in its true sense is the form of government in which sovereign power lies with the multitude as opposed to a single man and in which the governors, the rectors, are restricted by the laws of the city.[74] Arguing that this political rule exists in cities in which the people are governed in a political way,[75] Ptolemy names it 'political rule' and describes the rule of the multitude as '*quod est pluralitas, sive civitas*.'[76] He provides two illustrations from history: first, Athens after the death of Codrus, and second, the Italian city-states.[77]

Here, what is noteworthy is that Ptolemy developed a specific form of political rule (*principatus politicus*). For Ptolemy, 'political rule' is not simply a general term in the wider sense to describe a political scheme for political life as a necessary condition for men's sufficient life. For Ptolemy the form of government most suitable to preserve political life is 'political rule' itself. 'Political rule,' that is the rule of the people, is the best of the forms of government to enable us to have a well-ordered political association. On this basis, Ptolemy says that the '*dominium plurium*' ('the rule of the many') is not simply a type of political regime, but it means "what we call by its usual name political" ("*quod communi nomine politicum appellamus*") or politics itself.[78] It is specifically at this point that Ptolemy's thought commands attention in relation to Marsilius'. That is, Ptolemy's conception of 'political rule' provides us with a philosophical justification for the sovereign power lying with the people, a major theme in Marsilius' conception of political representation.

Ptolemy, unlike other contemporary Aristotelians who "separated political life from political regime and used Aristotle's text to mount an ideological attack against republican government,"[79] believed that in order to sustain the political life necessary for human beings, 'political rule' or the rule of the many was the most expedient form of government. According to Ptolemy, the rule of law and elective magistrates are the distinctive features of 'political rule.' In 'political rule' the rectors owe their power to the people which elects them for limited terms of office, so that in the polity the governors must be appointed in turn.[80] Further, elective magistrates are bound by the laws, the regime is stable. In this respect, as Skinner argues, Ptolemy shows preference for republicanism.[81] In particular, Ptolemy admired the Roman republic but was suspicious of the empire which superseded it.[82] In consequence, he has a marked hostility towards Julius Caesar, who, according to Ptolemy, usurped the supreme power and converted a genuinely 'political' regime into a despotic one.[83] Differentiating political rule from despotic rule, Ptolemy maintains that the rule of the many is to be preferred to any other forms of rule. While in kingly rule a prince regards the interests of his subjects, despotic rule means that the king or the prince governs in accordance with his own advantage and then perverts the common good.[84] In despotic government, which is in its nature like the relation of the master to the slave, arbitrary will prevails and therefore the law, that is the king's judgement, is not based on reason. By contrast, in a polity, the rulers govern by laws which the people make. 'Political rule' ('*regimen politicum*') is well adapted to the state of innocence or to the rule of men, like the ancient Romans, who are thought to be wise and virtuous. Despotic rule, on the other hand, is attached to the government of those who are perverse and foolish, and 'the number of the foolish is infinite.' Ptolemy claims that it is according to nature to say that 'political rule' in which the people is ruled well by the laws of justice is better, although he concedes that given the perverse and the foolish, royal rule is preferable in the sense of being more effective.[85]

In an absorption of Aristotelianism, both Remigius and Ptolemy demonstrate that the justification of the relationship between a man and political society is to be looked for on a human and natural basis, not exclusively on a divine one. Remigius' Aristotelian understanding is focused on philosophical discussions such as the relation of citizens and human beings, the natural cause of a city, the necessity of law and the common good. Likewise, Ptolemy's treatment of man, society and the common good too demonstrates its Aristotelian basis. In particular, Ptolemy's discussion about the types of political rule is of importance. While Aquinas, who combines Aristotelianism with a Christian understanding of political community, believes that rule by a king is ideally the best form of government for the common good, Ptolemy argues that the best regime is the rule of the multitude in correspondence with his Aristotelian understanding of the common good of the whole.

As we shall see, in arguing for the political principles of a civil community Marsilius echoes the Aristotelian principles of Remigius and Ptolemy. These three Aristotelians agree that the common good of peace is achieved in a political community where peace or order lies in the good disposition of all parts in a whole. However, concerning how to obtain the common good, they present rather different views. Remigius and Ptolemy suggested the secular merits of civil society through their respective understanding of Aristotle, without being involved in the intellectual conflict between Christian ideas and Aristotelianism. However, Remigius' and Ptolemy's acknowledgement of Aristotelian principles would still rest on a profoundly theological foundation (Ptolemy less so than Remigius). In particular, their notion of the common good includes peace as a virtuous order directed towards the heavenly good. That is, both were still Dominicans and they shared the same fundamental perspective, although in a different way. Their treatment of political issues remains within the framework set out by Aquinas. By contrast, Marsilius puts more stress upon the merits (virtue) of secular life on a human and natural basis than his two contemporary Aristotelians. For Marsilius, the common good, peace, is discussed as a socially and politically practical condition for the establishment of political unity, and could be achieved entirely through devotion to a civil society. It is high time to explore Marsilius' thought.

PART III
POLITICAL REPRESENTATION IN MARSILIUS

In Part III, I attempt to analyse Marsilius' own thought with special reference to the concept of political representation. In the Introduction and Ch. 1, I explained that a concept of political representation must involve, beyond the notion of responsiveness between political actors, the understanding of more fundamental political phenomena and political principles, if it is to explain the necessity of the scheme of political representation which it endorses—that is the necessity of the transfer of power to someone in particular. Here, by examining how the theory of political representation is articulated in Marsilius' thought, I intend to show that Marsilius offers a broad perspective upon political representation which sees it as far more than a simple matter of responsiveness between the represented and the representative.

In reading Marsilius, Cary Nederman, in a series of impressive and influential studies, has provided us with a more integrated and focused interpretation of political representation in Marsilius' thought than have other writers. Supposing that the modern idea of political representation is very much indebted to medieval practices, Nederman argues that in particular Marsilius' contribution to modern political representation lies in enabling us to see a fundamental conceptual conflict between representation and a substantive conception of citizenship.[1] According to Nederman, Marsilius perceived that political representation or the making of a representative threatened the central principles of communal organisation—for example, participation as a basic value of the citizen.[2] Nederman maintains that Marsilius understood that from political representation—that is delegation through a representative—would ensure the deprivation of individuals' civil freedom or power, the most crucial features of citizenship.[3]

Nederman's interpretation of Marsilius' conception of political representation transcends the narrow idea of political representation as a legal term[4] or the anachronistic view of Marsilius' understanding as containing explicitly modern political connotations.[5] Nevertheless, it appears that Nederman's understanding of the role of political representation within Marsilius' thought still defines it much too narrowly. That is, Nederman too, like the modern theorists on political representation discussed previously, sees the core of the concept of political representation as the relation between what people desire and what their broader interests are. Consequently, representatives are arbitrators with the task of balancing out and mediating between the dual factors of interests and wishes.[6] On this understanding, Nederman maintains that Marsilius is led to argue that the framing of legislation is not a representative matter, if one includes in the definition of 'representation' the notion of responsiveness to the mere private wishes of a constituency.[7] However, I claim that Marsilius' conception of representation integrates not only the notion of responsiveness, but also that of law-making in general. Indeed, for Marsilius, the concept of legislation has at its core the necessity of creating political representation.

Moreover, Nederman's interpretation of Marsilius' conception of political representation is caused by his inappropriate understanding of political representation itself. Nederman supposes that in Marsilius' view politics has meaning only because of and through political participation. Hence, according to Nederman's interpretation, Marsilius must believe that the fact that the people has its representatives is against the proper nature of politics. In contrast, I shall show that Marsilius argues for appointing representatives precisely in order to bring politics back to a political community. I maintain, rather, that Marsilius' understanding of representation provides resources which could enable us to understand political representation in broader terms—not in terms merely of the delegate conception or the trustee conception, but in terms of an integration of legislation and participation in which the sovereign power of the people is never lost.

Marsilius raises the fundamental normative issue of the philosophical foundations of political representation in a way which is still instructive today. He does so not by inquiring specifically into the relationship between the real wishes of people and their immediate wishes or into the capacity of the representative to serve as mediator, a main focus of our contemporary conception of political representation. Rather, he correlates a range of ideas—peace, justice, law, the role of the human legislator as lawmaker, the people as the sovereign and the representative as delegate—which together form the crux for understanding the normative character of political representation and which we still need to view in relation to one another, if we are to understand political representation in its full political significance and not as a narrow technical term for analysing the articulation of particular interests. Our task in Part III is to explore how Marsilius' theory of political representation is developed.

· 7 ·

POLITICAL UNITY

The Political Association, Self-Sufficiency, and Peace

As the title of his book *Defensor Pacis* indicates, the defence of the tranquillity or peace of civil regimes[1] is the most important issue with which Marsilius is concerned. For Marsilius, like contemporary Italian Aristotelians such as Remigius and Ptolemy, peace is the first and the last word in discussing political principles. It would not be excessive to say that he was entirely occupied by the issue of how to attain peace in a political community.

Marsilius initiates his inquiry into how to attain peace by asking what the political association (*regnum*)[2] is. According to Aristotle in *Politics*, I. i,[3] the political association is "the perfect community having the full limit of self-sufficiency, which came into existence for the sake of living, but exists for the sake of living well."[4] Marsilius adopts Aristotle's view of the perfect final cause of the political association. Men are assembled for the sake of the sufficient life, being able to seek out for themselves the necessities of life and exchanging them with one another. So men have their partner, household, village and community.[5] Among many groups, the final assembly, which is perfect and fully self-sufficient, is called the political association (*civitas*).[6] However, for Marsilius, as the Aristotelians argued, the political association is not just a market in which people can exchange things necessary for mere subsistence. The political association exists to do more than give physical self-sufficiency to its own people who come together as a community. Beyond the meaning of political association as a physical gathering, the political association has a moral or rational character, that is the good as the expression of righteousness.[7] So Marsilius says that "men came together to the civil community in order to attain what was beneficial for sufficiency of life, and to avoid the opposite."[8] Thus, the purpose of the civil community is not only to get physical self-sufficiency but also to obtain a morally good life. But not every assemblage—couple, family, village and community—can automatically procure the good life as the highest good. Only when the assemblage is fully grown[9] does it exist for the sake of a good life, aiming at the greatest good, and then it is fully self-sufficient in the proper sense.[10] This assemblage is the political association.

As Wilks observes, for Marsilius it is goodness or right reason which distinguishes a *regnum* from a mere multitude.[11] In other words, it would be the will or the practical reason to live rightly which characterises the citizen as opposed to the loose individual man: Marsilius remarks, "Indeed, those who do not wish the polity to endure are classed among the slaves, not among the citizens, as are certain aliens."[12] That is for Marsilius, theoretically speaking, the citizens are those who can ensure the existence and prosperity of their polity, the purpose of which is to attain morally and physically the good life. Marsilius' definition of citizen does not necessarily entail the Aristotelian arguments about the correlation between being a man and being a citizen. What Marsilius was concerned with is the opposition of citizens against slaves in terms of their capacity to care for their political community. However, Marsilius would argue that being a man does not necessarily guarantee being a citizen, but citizens are good men in the sense that they know what is good or beneficial or not in order to make their polity endure, and that they can practise it. Without right reason or the will to live rightly, a man cannot be a citizen, and conversely a citizen cannot be a perfect man. It means that in order to be a citizen or a perfect man we need to join the political association which is established for the sake of living and living well.

However, Marsilius does not necessarily suppose that without the city individuals must fall into a state of nature in which there are men against men without any rule. Since for Marsilius 'natural' connotes being in accordance with the dictates of right reason,[13] human nature which includes reason does not allow man to be brought to the brink of such a disaster. Rather, as seen above, men by nature create a political association for their well-being. Even though Marsilius does not emphasise very much that the political association is a creation of nature and that man is by nature a political animal,[14] he, like Remigius, believes that without political association man cannot enjoy civil happiness, the best of the aims which we can reach in this world,[15] and cannot attain the greatest good of man, the physical and moral sufficiency of life which is necessary to make a man achieve perfection. For Marsilius, man cannot be complete without a perfect community, that is a *regnum* or a *civitas*.

According to Marsilius, being "well" means being with proper proportion. Since we do not receive entirely from nature the perfect means whereby these proportions are fulfilled, it is necessary for man to go beyond natural causes to form some means whereby to effect and preserve his actions and passions in body and soul. These imperfect means should be supplemented by reason, so that human beings can live well. Consequently, in order to proportion actions and passions, and to bring them to a fulfilment to which nature alone could not lead, there need to be discovered various kinds of arts and other virtues. And men of various offices are established for the purpose of supplying human needs.[16] These diverse orders or offices of men are none other than the many and distinct parts of the political association which supply such diverse things as men need for sufficiency of life both physically and morally.[17] In this respect too, the Marsilian *regnum* is very much Aristotelian. Aristotle supposed that for the sufficient life in a political association, there were to be various roles of human beings. However, Aristotle presumed a difference in terms of quality of the roles which human beings played. In contrast, as we shall see, Marsilius' view on the diverse offices of political association is not founded upon qualitative difference between men or offices which demonstrates which role is better or worse.

Concretely, relying on Aristotle's analysis of the structure of the state, Marsilius says that the parts or offices of the state are of six kinds: the agricultural, the artisan, the military, the financial, the priestly, and the judicial or deliberative:[18]

> The people, or the multitude composed of all the groups of the polity or city taken together, is composed of the common mass, "council" (*consilium*), such as the farmers, artisans, and others of that sort; or whether it be the "judiciary," ...... or whether it be the "honourable class."[19]

Three of these, the priestly, the warrior and the judicial, are in the strict sense parts of the state or the government ('*simpliciter sunt partes civitatis*'), and in civil communities they are usually called the honourable class (*honorabilitas*).[20]

The multitude belonging to other offices are usually called the common mass (*vulgaris*). However, Marsilius argues, unlike Aristotle, that the farmers and artisans are included in the category of the common mass. As we shall see further in the next chapter, in respect of its scope and its actual numbers, Marsilius' citizen-body is more comprehensive than Aristotle's. Aristotle confined the definition of citizens to participants in public services.[21] By contrast, for Marsilius citizens are defined to be those who make the polity endure for its self-sufficiency, from whatever social background they may be and whatever occupation they engage in. For Marsilius, it does not matter who has which job. What he is concerned with is that each person should be in his right position and can contribute to the maintenance of his polity.

Remigius and Ptolemy, whom we examined earlier, believed that the proportional constitution of parts led to peace, that is unity, in a civil community. This theme is consistently demonstrated in Marsilius' thought. For Marsilius too, the question of peace is the matter of how to put the various roles of the citizens in order. In Marsilius' view, when the parts of a *regnum* or the roles of citizens are properly ordered, there will be peace or tranquillity in the civil association. To live well physically and morally depends almost completely on the quiet or tranquillity of communities, because this leads to the perfectly sufficient life in the present world.[22] Marsilius interprets tranquillity as follows:

> Health is the best disposition of an animal in accordance with nature, and likewise that tranquillity is the best disposition of a state established in accordance with reason. Health, moreover, as the more experienced physicians describe it, is the good disposition of the animal whereby each of its parts can perfectly perform the operations belonging to its nature; according to which analogy tranquillity will be the good disposition of the city or state whereby each of its parts will be able perfectly to perform the operations belonging to it in accordance with reason and its establishment.[23]

As can be observed, this passage about health and peace is reminiscent of that of Remigius which followed Augustine's notion of health. Sharing his contemporary Aristotelians' analogy of health and peace, Marsilius says that an animal, when it is well disposed in accordance with nature, has certain proportioned parts ordered to one another and hence can attain health when these parts communicate their functions mutually and for the sake of unity. Likewise, by being well disposed and established in accordance with reason, the political association is properly constituted of certain such parts for the sake of unity.[24] The analogy of health as the best disposition of an animal corresponds to peace as the best disposition of a state.

The constitution of peace or tranquillity in a civil community reflects the extent to which it possesses a good disposition of its parts. Accordingly, the lack of tranquillity, like the illness of an animal, means the diseased disposition of the city or political association. In this disturbed situation, all or some of its parts are impeded from performing the roles belonging to them, either entirely or to the extent required for complete functioning in order for a state to endure. Marsilius takes the example of the Italian *regnum* to show what happens when discord, the opposite of tranquillity, befalls a civil regime or political association:

> From discord, the opposite of tranquillity, the worst fruits and troubles will befall any civil regime or state. This can readily be seen, and is obvious to almost all men, from the example of the Italian *regnum* ...... Misled through discord into the bypath of error, the Italian natives are deprived of the sufficient life, undergoing the gravest hardship instead of the quiet they seek, and the harsh yoke of tyrants instead of liberty.[25]

For Marsilius, tranquillity or peace is the prime requirement for having a perfect community of sufficient life, that is the political association. When the parts which constitute a political community deviate from their proper positions, there will be no peace and tranquillity, no self-sufficiency and therefore no *regnum*. Marsilius claims that when we do not obtain this 'civil peace' civil strife or revolutions emerge.[26] Thus, tranquillity is the basic principle of the order of civil association.[27]

Marsilius' literal definition of peace does not look different from Remigius' and Ptolemy's. All three theorists agreed that peace meant a good disposition of parts in a political community and that, for its members to achieve the sufficient life, peace was the most important and imminent matter to be achieved in the Italian context. However, although the three Italian Aristotelians shared the literal definition of peace and an understanding of its aim, Marsilius had a different point of view from his contemporaries about why and how to obtain peace in a political community. Remigius' and Ptolemy's notion of peace fundamentally depends upon a heavenly peace. For Remigius and Ptolemy, the earthly peace is of secondary importance after the heavenly one, the highest good. In addition, not only is the common good in this world the lesser good, but also its attainment is possible through the heavenly good, that is devotion to God. By contrast, the identity of Marsilius' peace lies entirely in civil peace. Marsilius' concern is with how to attain peace in this world. The matter of how to get heavenly peace was not totally disregarded by Marsilius, which would anyway have been impossible in the Italian context in the Middle Ages.

The framework set by Aquinas would continue to operate implicitly in Marsilius' thought too. However, what Marsilius intended most of all to investigate is how to get earthly peace, the real common good in this world.

As we shall see, this decisive difference between Marsilius and the contemporary Aristotelians about what peace is for and how to obtain it leads to differences about how politics, law and other related issues should be understood. For example, Aquinas and Remigius saw that politics and law had a firmly divine ontological foundation, and that the establishment of politics and law aimed fundamentally at divine enjoyment. By contrast, Marsilius' concern with politics, law and the common good of peace is clearly based on a human foundation and all of them aim for the common good of peace in order to achieve the morally and physically sufficient life in this world. Marsilius maintains that the attainment of peace, the highest good in this world, should be obtained through human devices, not through divine grace. One of the most effective devices would be law.

Civil Peace, the Common Good, and Law

Indeed, actually to live in peace is much more complicated to achieve, for men are inclined to be involved in various kinds of conflicts. Marsilius himself perceives that despite the 'right-willing' of the citizen, man is also born composed of contrary actions and passions. Moreover, man is born "bare and unprotected" from excesses of the surrounding air and other elements. So man is very fragile and is easily capable of suffering and of destruction.[28] This human weakness might lead to what is in effect a virtual state of men against men, although that is not what Marsilius supposed to be the state of nature before the formation of a civil society. In other words, if not regulated by a norm of justice, men might break into factions and fight which would eventually bring about the destruction of the political association. That is why Marsilius suggested that there had to be established in this association a standard of justice and a guardian or maker of that standard.

The argument for the necessity of making laws, a necessity which is due to human internal contradiction and inability to protect themselves from external circumstances, indicates that it is through law alone that judgements can be properly made and preserved from defect. Marsilius observes that the ruler should have "right emotion and true knowledge" of all cases to judge rightly, but not all rulers are possessors of these virtues. Law appears, in brief, as an antidote to the weakness of individual beings. In consequence, Marsilius argues that the law is superior emotionally and intellectually to individual human beings:[29]

> The primary necessity of the law, then, is as follows: it is necessary to establish in the polity that without which civil judgements cannot be made with complete rightness, and through which these judgements are properly made and preserved from defect so far as it is humanly possible.[30]

Without law, there would arise severe conflicts in which the strong brutally rules the weak and in which parts would be arranged for their convenience, not in a due proportion, and in which therefore there cannot be peace. However, as mentioned earlier, human beings are reasonable enough to create political association in order to live well together. Marsilius argues that right reason in a political association is actualised in law or what is commanded or permitted according to these laws.[31] Because the law, which is the concrete form of right reason, does not embody any subjective biases, judgements made in accordance with laws are just.

Political association has as its aim the good life—the sufficient life in its proper sense. This aim is implemented by making laws, the means by which parts of a state can be put in right position and the peace of the common good can be assured. Marsilius asserts that the principal end of law is civil justice and the common benefit in a civil community. Through law, the security of rulers and the long duration of governments is guaranteed,[32] which Marsilius says is the secondary end of law. Thus, Marsilius too, like Aquinas, Remigius and Ptolemy, believed that laws should be ordained for the common good, that is peace, the highest good. If men do not have the laws to say what is beneficial for sufficiency of life[33] and to avoid the opposite, the political association cannot endure. But, when Aquinas and Remigius stressed that law was ordained for the common good, this was ultimately only a means for obtaining the divine common good. However, Marsilius' assertion of the necessity of law came from his confidence in law as an instrument to keep civil peace, that is the common good in this world, not in the other world.

To clarify what Marsilius himself means by law and to elucidate what he intended to claim through the argument for the necessity of laws, it is helpful to examine his distinction between the four senses of law,[34] although he does not set out in detail what each means nor does he consider how they are related to one another. According to Marsilius, first, law means "a natural sensitive inclination toward some action or passion." This definition of law signifies a natural law in some sense. But Marsilius does not elaborate the notion of natural law. This makes it difficult to understand precisely what he means by natural law. Nevertheless, because Marsilius' notion of natural law is an important point of reference from which to interpret his political principles, it is necessary to ask what Marsilius might have meant by natural law (*ius naturale*).

Initially, we are given to understand that for Marsilius, natural law corresponds to the natural inclinations of a human being encompassing all the dispositions and tendencies to action or passion. But he does not seem to have a consistent conception of natural law or natural inclinations. Marsilius' conceptualisation of natural inclination is ambivalent. On the one hand, as mentioned above, he conceives natural law as the dictate of right reason. But it is important to see that his understanding of a natural law as the dictate of right reason is limited in character. It is not the absolute, universal ground which directs human life morally, like the reason of nature in the Ciceronian sense.[35] It is closer to Aquinas' conception of natural law, which says that natural justice is a basis of a human law. That is, Marsilius' understanding of natural law as reason is to be taken in the sense that it is reason which prompts men to create the political association and its laws, in order to live well.[36] On this understanding, Marsilius argues that all nations are in accordance with right reason, just insofar as they have laws in their polity: even though they may not agree about what is honourable or not.[37]

On the other hand, however, Marsilius generally seems to understand nature as something original and primitive; nature in this sense existed from the beginning of the world, and human beings were simply a part of this nature. But this does not presume that natural law is non-rational.[38] It merely implies notions of primitiveness and insufficiency. Since nature did not give to us the perfect means with which we could fulfil our life, it was necessary for man to have other means to overcome these imperfect natural conditions. Therefore, we need to establish human laws which can cover the incompleteness of natural law.[39] Through these supplementary means, appropriate proportion can be imposed on the actions and passions of human beings in respect of which nature itself may well fail to lead.[40] Thus, while the human will to complement the insufficiency is supported by nature as reason, the insufficiency which human beings have to fill out also results from nature. It is in this sense that I would conclude that Marsilius' understanding of nature is ambivalent.

Second, law means "a productive habit and in general every form, existing in the mind, of a producible thing, from which as from an exemplar or measure there emerge the forms of things made by art." When he wrote this passage, he seems to have had Aquinas' description of eternal law in mind. To recall, according to Aquinas, when the *ratio* of the things that exists already in the mind of an artist is produced by him it is called the art or exemplar of the things to be produced. Likewise, Aquinas sees that the *ratio* of divine wisdom pre-exists and controls the world. That is, God through his wisdom, creates all things and is related to them. The divine *ratio* is not subject to time but is eternal. Accordingly, for Aquinas, eternal law is nothing other than the *ratio* of divine wisdom to direct all actions and movements.[41] Marsilius does not directly mention Aquinas' notion of eternal law. However, this passage is close enough to Aquinas' to suggest that Marsilius intends this second meaning of law to cover eternal law.[42]

In the third sense, law is "the standard containing admonitions for voluntary human acts according as these are ordered toward glory or punishment in the future world." This third sense of law is divine law, meaning either the Mosaic law or the evangelical law of Christ.[43] The divine law deals with both transient and immanent acts according to how they affect the attainment of eternal life. It is a coercive standard in accordance with which a person is rewarded or punished in and for the status of the eternal life only.[44] Marsilius agrees that what is lawful and what is unlawful *in an absolute sense* must be viewed according to divine law rather than human law, when these disagree in their commands, prohibitions, or permissions.[45] Thus, for Marsilius too, divine law may constitute a higher standard than human law for human beings insofar as they hope to attain eternal life. However, insofar as they wish to live well here on earth, the human law is the only immediate and direct standard. In a differentiation of the function of divine law from that of human law, Marsilius does not see that the divine law is the higher law, which can impose upon human law a real power to constrain the actions of human beings in *this world*. Alternatively, what we can say at least is that it was not his concern at all, although he had this medieval framework in mind and he could not disregard it.

These, then, are the first three possible meanings of the term 'law'. Marsilius' immediate and main interest in law, however, is in human law. When Marsilius talks about law in general, he refers to law as a coercive command in this world. This is human law, the fourth sense of law: "the science or doctrine or universal judgement of matters of civil justice and benefit, and of their opposites."[46] This is a standard of transient human acts, what is beneficial or what is harmful, for sufficiency in this world. In comparison to Remigius and Ptolemy, who put higher priority on the heavenly good which men will eventually attain as the highest good, Marsilius, despite his belief in the eternal life, relies entirely on human law to lead to the common good of peace in this world. Marsilius claims that law is established for the common good in the civil community. This is also the law which bears on the issue of political representation. Let us make a close examination of this law in Marsilius.

According to Marsilius, for the law (the human law) to be ordained for the common good, there are two requirements—one is prudence and understanding about law, the other coercive force:

> Law, then, is a "discourse" or statement "emerging from prudence" and political "understanding," that is, it is an ordinance made by political prudence, concerning matters of justice and benefit and their opposites, having "coercive force," that is concerning whose observance there is given a command which one is compelled to observe, or which is made by way of such a command.[47]

Marsilius believes that coercive command with an appropriate punishment or recompense to be received in this world is a necessary part of the true understanding of law.[48] For Marsilius, human civil laws and customs are standards having coercive force. Law lacking such command, even though it is just and beneficial, does not have the nature of law. Again, Marsilius says:

> The true knowledge or discovery of the just and the beneficial, and of their opposites, is not law ...... whereby it is the measure of human civil acts, unless there is given a coercive command as to its observance, or it is made by way of such a command, by someone through whose authority its transgressors must and can be punished.[49]

Thus, the condition which makes the knowledge of the just and the beneficial into a law, to be enforced in a civil community, is coercive force. It implies that Marsilius supposes that the political association could scarcely achieve the common good as its aim without compulsory force imposed upon its members. As we shall see again later, Marsilius' differentiation between the judgement of priests and that of secular rulers, which constitutes a main point in his civil principles, depends upon the question of who has the coercive power with which to punish the transgressors of law. Marsilius insists that while secular rulers can regulate all matters (including matters relating to faith) in a civil community with a coercive force according to the laws, the priests, having no such force, only guide and only on matters relating to faith. This division ensures that for Marsilius secular rulers are in charge of securing the common good of peace in a civil community, but the priests are not—a subject with which we will deal in Ch. 9.

However, for Marsilius, laws merely having coercive command are not perfect. Marsilius takes an example of a barbarian law. Although barbarian laws have the proper form, that is a coercive command of observance, they lack a proper condition, that is the proper and true ordering of justice.[50] So Marsilius thinks that barbarian laws are not laws in the true sense. He suggests that a proper law be both just and coercive.[51] It is right to see the coerciveness of law as essential to law. But, at the same time, Marsilius envisions justice as an equally essential feature. Thus, Marsilius believes that when law meets the two requirements of justice and coerciveness which make law what it is, it would effect right reason in a political community and therefore would bring the common good of civil peace.

The Human Legislator, Citizenship, and Political Representation

For Aquinas, who believed that human laws depended on the divine laws, law is what the divine wisdom thinks, because anything except the divine wisdom cannot be absolutely just. We may ask *who* makes law in Marsilius, that is *who* is the legislator? Let me discuss this issue, which is the critical point in the construction of political representation in Marsilius. In Marsilius' thought, *ius* (law or right),[52] that is the standard of the just and the beneficial, is none other than what is willed by the active command, prohibition, or permission of the legislator.[53] In other words, there is no standard of right beyond the will of the legislator. Whatever the legislator wills is the law and whatever the legislator thinks is just and equal. In short, law is the legislator's craft. In this sense, the legislator is the sovereign without any superior (*superiore carens*), because the authority to make or establish laws belongs to him.

I intend to suggest that Marsilius' conception of legislator can be characterised by two aspects: one is that of a human legislator which is opposed to the divine one, the other is the populist aspect of the human legislator which is opposed to the elitist one. First, corresponding to his argument for the human foundation of the source of law, Marsilius claimed that the legislator should be a human agent, not a divine one or God. Indeed, in Marsilius' view, the legislator is the *person* who can make the law; to him belongs the authority or right reason to make such a command and to punish its transgressors with coercive force:[54]

> The power to cause the laws to be observed (*potestas observationis legum*) belongs only to those men to whom belongs coercive force over the transgressors (*potentia transgressorum coactiva*) of the law.[55]

Taking Marsilius' assertion of the human legislator, we may immediately pose the next problem—who is the human legislator, or who has the power to make laws and to create the coercive force? Concerning this question about the identity of the human legislator, Marsilius suggests a simple but convincing answer:

> *populum seu civium universitatem, aut eius valentiorem partem per suam electionem seu voluntatem in generali civium congregatione per sermonem expressam* (the people or the whole body of citizens, or the weightier part thereof, through its election or will expressed by words in the general assembly of the citizens).[56]

For Marsilius, the *legislator humanus* as the primary and proper efficient cause of the law is nothing other than the whole body of citizens (*universitas civium*) or its weightier part (*valentior pars*), which is the second distinction of Marsilius' legislator. That is, law means what the whole body of citizens or its weightier part, which must be taken for the same thing, think and wish. In consequence, the original and supreme authority and power to make laws lies in the whole body of the citizens or the people as a whole.

Marsilius' argument that the legislator is the whole body of citizens or its weightier part, and no one else, is based on his principle that "every whole is greater than its part," which is true with respect both to action and discernment.[57] That is, Marsilius' justification of the whole comes from the fact that the whole body of citizens knows best what is just and what is not in a political community. This shows that Marsilius follows Aristotle for the theoretical justification of the rule of many—"two persons are better able to act and to understand."[58] Aristotle himself admitted that the collective power of the multitude could be better than that of a few, but this did not lead him therefore to conclude that rule by the multitude was the best political rule.[59] Marsilius too, like Aristotle, realises that the laws can be better made by the wise and learned than by the less learned and uncultivated.[60] But he does not accept the view that it is therefore to be concluded that the laws are better made by the wise alone than by the entire multitude of citizens. For Marsilius did not believe that the few wise, despite their knowledge and practical competence, would discern or desire the common benefit as well as would the entire multitude of the citizens. Rather, in this respect, Marsilius is very much like Ptolemy, who maintained that the rule of the people was the political rule in its proper sense of looking after the common good. Marsilius contends that it is very unreasonable to presume that one man should perceive better, judging with only two eyes and two ears and acting with only two hands and feet, than many persons with many such organs.[61] Therefore, the whole body of the citizens or the weightier multitude thereof can better discern what must be taken and what rejected than any part of it taken separately.[62] Consequently, they have the authority to approve, interpret and suspend the laws.[63] Even though the wise and the learned know most about the laws, in particular about their technical aspects, their knowledge and judgement cannot be superior to the morality and knowledge of the whole body of citizens which considers the common good and hence make a political community endure for its complete aim:

> Most of the citizens are neither vicious nor undiscerning most of the time; all or most of them are of sound mind and reason and have a right desire for the polity and for the things necessary for it to endure, like laws and other statutes or customs.[64]

Marsilius' belief in the collective morality and intelligence of the people can be more clearly exposed in his understanding of history. For Marsilius, just as one man's judgement is inferior to that of the many, so what is observed by men of one era is quite imperfect by comparison with what is observed in many eras. Marsilius' understanding of the people as a collectivity is not confined to the legislator in a single political association and extends to the people beyond the era and the place:

> No single man, and perhaps not even all the men of one era, could investigate or remember all the civil acts determined in the law; indeed, what was said about them by the first investigators and also by all the men of the same era who observed such acts was meagre and imperfect, and attained its completion only subsequently through the additions made by later investigators. This can be sufficiently seen from experience, in the additions, subtractions, and complete changes sometimes made in the laws in different eras, or at different times within the same era.[65]

Thus, Marsilius argues for the superior capability of the collectivity of the people in theory and in history. In particular, he notices the cumulative power of the whole body of the citizens through various eras to know the common good. That is, history would teach us how to make the better judgement for the good of the whole or the laws which are of greatest importance for the common sufficiency of the people. This evolutionary historicity is a sign of Marsilius' consistent argument for the superiority of the collectivity of the people or of the whole to the part.

In this way, Marsilius makes sure that it is nonsense to say that an individual or a few would be better than the whole as a collectivity. However, what is noteworthy here is that Marsilius' argument for the whole body of citizens as the collective power does not necessarily put them in opposition to the few wise. When Marsilius talks about the citizens as a whole, it includes both the few wise and the less learned. The less learned citizens, being members of the whole, can perceive what must be corrected in a proposed law,[66] because they know what would be beneficial for their good life. Thus, by being legislators who make laws, they can make a contribution to maintaining a political association. So they are "weighty" enough to be citizens. Likewise, the few wise too are involved in making laws as members of the whole body of citizens, but in a different way from the multitude, for example, by proposing the contents of laws. Thus, in Marsilius' thought, by participating in making laws and hence being "weightier," both the less learned and the few wise constitute the whole body of citizenship.

Further, Marsilius' comprehensive scope of citizenship does not mean that all citizens have identical capabilities. Marsilius acknowledges that an individual could be more excellent than any other in respect of merit, knowledge, wisdom and education, but he argues that this difference does not necessarily lead to a difference of worth. As we saw, Marsilius suggested that the various roles be arranged in their right positions according to their natural characters in order to attain a unity of peace in a political community. But the various or different roles do not imply any qualitative discriminations in terms of worth or merit between the members of the citizen-body. Therefore, even though a few people are in a governmental position in a state—for example, the 'judicial' or 'ruling' and 'deliberative' part to be established 'to regulate justice and the common benefit' -[67] this does not signify at all that they are superior to any other members of a state. Whether they participate in the part of government or not, whether they are well-educated and qualified for politics or not, the true requirement of citizenship in Marsilius lies in the involvement in making a political community endure, that is of making laws for the common good in order to reach the sufficient life in which the whole of its members can enjoy their good life. To this end, Marsilius believes that theoretically and historically speaking, the whole people as a collective power is morally and politically superior to any individuals. That is, because the whole body of citizens know best what is good or not for the maintenance of a political community, they can discern and desire the common justice and benefit to a greater extent than can any separate part of that multitude. For Marsilius, what makes affairs of a state be decided in accordance with the common good for the whole people is not individual excellence, but the collective capability, power and perspective with which the whole people can look ahead to, and accomplish, the common good of peace. However, we must recognise that the question of how to attain the whole people's power which is distinguished from individual capability—the matter with which such utilitarians as Bentham are concerned and suggest a solution for—was outside Marsilius' interest.

On this basis, Marsilius argues that it would be hazardous to entrust the making of the law to the discretion of the few. When only a few people are given the authority to be in charge of making laws, they would be more likely to consider their own private benefit, as individuals or as a group, rather than the common good of the whole. Marsilius points out that this is quite apparent in those who make the decretals of the clergy, that is bishops or priests.[68] Thus, when one man makes a bad law, looking more to his own private benefit than to that of the community, the law will be tyrannical.[69] Accordingly, the law is not ordained for the common good any more and is no more law in the true sense:

> Every citizen must be free, and not undergo another's despotism, that is, slavish dominion. But this would not be the case if one or a few of the citizens by their own authority made the law over the whole body of citizens.[70]

Indeed, Marsilius maintains that the community itself or the people as a whole should be the political entity which has the authority to make laws. The will of the community as a legislator cannot be influenced by any superior—either by God or by their ruler—but should be their own. In these respects, Marsilius is remarkably in contrast to Aquinas, a medieval figure of overwhelming influence on ontology, who argued that human law absolutely referred to God and that the best rule was rule by a king because the king was the sole possessor of political prudence.

The relationship between the people as a collective power and the few wise—both of whom constitute the membership of the whole body of citizens—can be better understood by the following analogy. While many men are not able to produce a picture, a house, a ship, and other works of art, they appreciate them sufficiently to judge rightly about the quality of the final products.

In other words, the creator of things is not necessarily the only or the best judge of them. On that understanding, Marsilius argues that every citizen or even the majority of them are not the discoverers of the law but the "makers" of it in the sense that they can judge of what has been discovered and proposed.[71] In Marsilius' view, those who discover the laws are *prudentes*. But whatever the *prudentes* discover must be brought before the assembled body of citizens for its final and binding authorisation. This is because those matters which can affect the benefit and harm of all ought to be known and heard by the whole body of citizens, who know best about the benefit of the community and, moreover, observe the law better and more readily than any other.[72] Thus, the whole body of citizens approve or disapprove, add, subtract, revise or reject provisional laws which have been proposed. Marsilius says that after this process, the drafts in question would be recognised as laws.[73] The citizens, that is the people as a whole, are real and final judges who can judge about what others have discovered.

It is at this point that the idea of political representation in Marsilius takes a specific shape. Marsilius thinks that while the human legislator, that is the whole body of citizens, originally has the authority to make laws and to judge in this world with coercive power,[74] for some reasons they need to have some persons who can be the discoverers of the law or can execute the judgements and coerce their transgressors in accordance with laws on their behalf. This idea of appointing somebody to act on their behalf need not affect at all Marsilius' belief that the judgement or approval of the whole body of citizen is what establishes the law with the necessary coercive authority. However, the question still arises of how, after the power has been given to somebody, can the authority and power of the whole body of citizens still be consistently maintained in Marsilius' thought? This is the question which our modern thinkers have not seriously raised and therefore have not been keen to answer. We must consider this question in detail in the next chapter.

· 8 ·

THE HUMAN LEGISLATOR AND POLITICAL REPRESENTATION

As we saw in Ch. 1, the leading modern interpreters of political representation (Burke, Bentham and Mill) attempted to set up political representation as the authoritative scheme for public actions. To this end, they were concerned with how to establish the relationship between the represented and the representative. Their ideas about securing the common good or the public interest in a political community are still influential on our contemporary political understanding.

However, I suggest that for political representation to be seen as the legitimate as well as an effective scheme to secure public benefits in the state, the establishment of the relationship between two political actors alone, as these three thinkers suggested, is not enough. However various the political implications of the term representation are, the basic scheme of political representation involves some element of the alienation of the wills or judgement of the represented from themselves to those of the representatives. Whoever is represented or whoever is a representative, it is necessary that political representation be followed by an alienation of power or judgement. Even though we can explore the role of the represented and the representative, consider the relationship between them and hope that this will enable us to understand how the scheme of political representation works, any conception of political representation which fails to register the transfer of power as its fundamental aspect is seriously flawed.

Marsilius' treatment of political representation also encompasses the responsiveness between the represented and the representative, which must be a constitutive element in the idea of political representation. However, unlike the three later thinkers whom we examined in Ch. 1, he does not limit himself to a discussion of the relationship between two discrete political actors, but also considers how a community can realistically hope to combine a transfer of power with an effective scheme for securing the benefit of the whole people.

The issue of whether the power given to the ruler or the representative is permanent or not—the issue which we observed in Ch. 4 in the medieval debate over the *lex regia* and the concern to identify the source of jurisdiction in the Italian city-state—is crucial in identifying the nature of political representation. Even though the alienation of power is inevitable in the scheme of political representation and the representatives, after the transfer of power, certainly retain some of that power, it does not necessarily follow that the represented cede all their authority to their own representatives, in the sense that authority cannot be returned to the represented and as a consequence the represented must lose their political right. To see whether the alienation of power results either in a Rousseauian forfeiture of power[1] or in the people's continuous control over power, we need to examine how effectively the represented's—the people's—original legislative power actually persists within the scheme of political representation. Marsilius' conception of political representation suggests that the people's original power should be continuously activated in the representative system and that, as a result, its representation can work as an alternative scheme to act legitimately on behalf of the whole people. Marsilius' conception of political representation deals with the general issues considered central in any scheme of political representation: who is represented, who is the representative and how to structure the relationship between them. But, more importantly, the theoretical context within which he conceives the transfer of power can help us, beyond the establishment of the correct relationship between the two key political actors in representative government, to determine if a scheme of political representation can really function with any dependability for the people's well-being.

We are the Sovereign: The *Universitas Civium* or the *Valentior Pars*

To begin with, we must recall what law is and who the legislator is for Marsilius. For him, law means justice with coercive force and it is made according to the legislator's will. The supreme power to make laws and to judge belongs to the whole body of citizens (*universitas civium*) or the weightier part of it or the person who is authorised to do so by it:

> The authority to make or establish the laws, and to give a command with regard to their observance, belongs only to the whole body of the citizens or to the weightier part thereof as efficient cause, or else to the person or persons to whom the aforesaid whole body has granted this authority.[2]

In Marsilius, the concept of the sovereign is identified with that of the legislator because the legislator, who is the source of law, is the efficient cause of making a political association attain the sufficient life or of establishing the parts of the state.[3] According to Marsilius, the legislator is the person who can best discern what is good and beneficial and bring it into existence within the human community. Consequently the legislator itself is the sovereign over the affairs of state and therefore has an ultimate and final authority and power in deciding them. The sovereign legislator is nothing other than the whole body of citizens. The possessor of the legislative power, that is the best "maker" of law in Marsilius' terms, does not need to have any superior who would lord over it by reason of its lack of knowledge about the common good or how to preserve peace in a political association.

Who is the whole body of citizens which has the sovereign power? As seen in the previous chapter, Marsilius defines the citizens as those who are equipped with specific moral and political responsibilities to maintain a civil community. It is their participation in the collective entity that justifies and constitutes an individual's civic identity. More specifically, borrowing Aristotle's conception of a citizen in the *Politics*,[4] Marsilius defines a citizen as follows: the citizen is 'a participant in the governmental, deliberative or judicial functions of the civil community.'[5] Even though Marsilius himself says that his definition of a citizen is in accordance with Aristotle, Marsilius' citizenship is determined in broader terms than it is for Aristotle. For Marsilius, the citizen's participation demands, firstly, the knowledge that without law civil judgements cannot be made with complete rectitude and a political association cannot endure, and then, secondly, the activity of law-making in the political community. Moreover, Marsilius' citizenship, requiring both knowledge and activity, actually involves a more comprehensive scope of political agencies of the civil community than it does for Aristotle. That is, for Marsilius, the whole body of citizens consists of the many less learned and the few wise, including both the honourable classes of the priestly, the warrior and the judiciary and the common class of farmers and artisans.[6] But women, children, slaves and aliens are excluded from the category of citizens, because Marsilius does not think that they have the theoretical and practical abilities to be citizens or to cherish political association.[7]

Thus, when Marsilius argues for citizens' participation in the political process this does not mean, as in Aristotle's understanding of citizenship,[8] that they necessarily perform ruling or judicial functions in a limited sense. Marsilius did not deny that the rank or ability of an individual or the kinds of constitutions could determine the relative degree of political participation.[9] For example, Marsilius would agree that the honourable class, which is the group of the best men and those who are appropriately elected to the highest governmental offices,[10] could play a greater role in politics. However, without implying a difference of worth or merit, for Marsilius such conditions cannot be an absolute factor in determining whether an individual can be a member of the whole body of citizens or be able to participate in the civil community or not, as it did for Aristotle himself. For Marsilius, what counts for citizenship is not the offices or positions of government held by individuals but the moral and political ability to make their political community endure. To this end, in Marsilius' thought, as argued in Ch. 7, the citizens take part in the legislative process in a broad sense as a human legislator, and this constitutes the core of Marsilius' conception of citizenship. It is on this understanding that, for Marsilius, citizenship acquires an inherently participatory connotation.[11] In other words, citizens' political participation is embodied through their role of making laws, that is legislation. In this way, Marsilius' conception of the citizen, unlike Aristotle's, has more to do with the human legislator making the law than with individual political membership of a political association.

The whole body of citizens, who have the sovereign power of making laws, do not have any superior and therefore are entitled to decide the matters of a state. As discussed in Ch. 7, Marsilius finds the justification of the citizens' legislative power in their moral and political competence which is superior to that of any individual or group. In the previous chapter I have explained sufficiently not to require restatement on what grounds the whole body of citizens lacks a superior and forms the source of law. Instead, here I intend to examine who forms the weightier part (*valentior pars*), which Marsilius implies is the equivalent of the whole body of citizens by saying that the sovereign legislative power belongs to the whole body of citizens or its weightier part. In claiming that the sovereign power is held by the legislator, that is, the whole body of citizens who are involved in the legislative power, one of the difficulties which we meet is how to interpret the *valentior pars* in Marsilius' thought. Indeed, there has been extensive debate over what Marsilius intended to convey by *valentior pars*, in contrast to the whole body of citizens, which provokes the conflicting interpretations of Marsilius: does Marsilius add the *valentior pars* as an alternative to the whole body of citizens in order to give sovereign status to the ruling part of an individual or a group? Or does he maintain that the whole body of citizens actually means the same thing as the *pars valentior*? The examination of this question will make it clear whom Marsilius means by the sovereign legislator.

While some argue that the *valentior pars* designates virtually the entire citizen population of the community,[12] others view it as an instrument for limiting direct participation in the authorisation of law-making to a few men or to a single person.[13] For example, Quillet claims that there is only a small number of citizens who satisfy the criteria for membership of the *pars valentior*: the *valentior pars* is not a symbol of the people.[14] Rather, at the centre of Marsilius' doctrine of the *valentior pars* lies the idea of representation by delegation, which is embodied historically in the form of the imperial electors.[15] In a similar vein, according to Wilks, the *valentior pars* indicates a functionally qualified directorate of government, although it acts by virtue of the authority of the human legislator. That is, Wilks too asserts that the *valentior pars* in Marsilius is in effect the seven electoral princes and that his theory of government, thus, is aristocratic.[16]

In contrast to them, however, Marsilius himself says that the *valentior pars* should be understood to be the same thing as the whole body of citizens.[17] This implies that for Marsilius the *valentior pars*, whoever they are, signifies the *universitas civium* as a collectivity with moral and political competence, in the sense that the *valentior pars* can virtually do what the whole body of citizens would do. To speak in the light of history, what Marsilius had in mind with regard to the *valentior pars*, as Quillet and Wilks say, may well have been the seven electors.[18] However, even if this was in fact Marsilius' opinion, for which we have no clear and reliable evidence, for him the *valentior pars* is not opposed to the whole body of citizens. This is because Marsilius supposes that the source of the princes' right to elect originates from the authority of the whole body of people, the legislator,[19] which we will discuss in detail in Ch. 9.

Neither Quillet, nor still less Wilks, fully grasp this point in interpreting who the *valentior pars* must be. I suggest that on this basis, Marsilius' words that "the *valentior pars* represents the whole body of citizens" ("*civium universitas aut eius pars valentior, quae totam universitatem repraesentat*")[20]—the passage which produces some confusion in the interpretation of the *valentior pars*—can be clearly understood. This passage does not mean that the *valentior pars* is the representative as delegate who conveys the individual wishes and interests of the people.[21] When we pay attention to the context in which Marsilius says this, it signifies that the *valentior pars* is the agent who shows and connotes the will or intention of the *universitas civium* to make the political association endure by making laws. Rather, we find the representative who acts on behalf of the whole people, that is a qualified expert, to whom is delegated the legislative authority of the citizens, in Marsilius' terminology of *pars principans*, which we will be discussing in the next section.

Marsilius' position is that when a political association has important matters to be deliberated it relies on the whole body of citizens or the weightier part thereof. He considers the 'weightier part' (*valentior pars*),[22] the equivalent of the whole body of citizens, in its quantitative and qualitative characteristics:

> By "the weightier part" I mean to take into consideration the quantity and the quality of the persons in that community over which the law is made (*valentiorem inquam partem considerata quantitate personarum et qualitate in communitate illa super quam lex fertur*).[23]

By showing how the *valentior pars* is not different from the whole body of citizens in respect of quantity and quality, I intend to maintain that the *valentior pars* is assumed to be the same thing as the whole body of citizens. First, Marsilius indicates the whole body of citizens or its weightier part by the term "multitude," which includes the council, the judiciary and the honourable class.[24] Quantitatively Marsilius does not think that the *pars valentior* is distinct from the *universitas*; rather they are almost identical. To this extent, Gierke is right in insisting that the phrase *valentior pars* implies a recognition of the numerical majority.[25] But as Gewirth and d'Entrèves emphasise, *valentior pars* is more than a numerical majority.[26] The following sentence implies in a negative way what Marsilius means by *valentior pars*.

> The phrase "several taken together" (*simul plurium*) must be understood not in a comparative sense, as meaning "majority," but in a positive sense, according as it is

> derived from "plural number" in the sense of some multitude, but not the weightier part of the citizens.[27]

This passage shows that *simul plurium* is different from the majority but it does not mean the weightier part either. This implies that Marsilius distinguishes to some extent the weightier part from the simple numerical majority.

However, more significantly than this literal clue, the qualitative characteristic of the weightier part can be founded in the definition of the legislator or the citizens. When Marsilius excludes children, slaves, aliens and women from the category of the citizens for the reason of their lack of capability, he thinks that they are not qualified for making law. For this reason, they cannot become the members of the legislator who possesses the sovereign power in a state. However, the weightier part, which is differentiated from the excluded, is equipped with the moral and political capability to make laws and therefore can substitute for the whole body of citizens.

This quality of the weightier part takes concrete shape in the functional differentiation among the different parts of the state. Marsilius divides the parts into the honourable class, the *honorabilitas*, and the common class, the *vulgus*.[28] Marsilius' differentiation of these classes does not imply that qualitative considerations are invoked because, as seen in Ch. 7, he does not think of there being a difference between the classes in terms of quality in the sense of worth or merit. The quality of the weightier part is broadly understood in the light of Marsilius' view of the superiority of the multitude. That is, what Marsilius intends to express through the quality of the weightier part is not Aristotle's aristocratic position, but rather the qualitative collective character which reflects the moral and political excellence of the people as a whole. That is, the *valentior pars* too, like the whole body of citizens, is 'weightier' enough to understand that without the law a political association cannot exist and the best-ruled state cannot be imagined.[29] In this context, Marsilius insists that "the less learned, or those who do not have leisure for liberal functions," should nevertheless share in political power, for they "participate in the understanding and judgement of practical affairs, although not equally with those who have leisure."[30]

On this basis, as Gewirth points out,[31] what Marsilius intended to argue for the *valentior pars* is the combined participation of the *honorabilitas* and the *vulgus* in political power—which, again, is consistent with his comprehensive scope of citizenship, that is the multitude of less learned and the few wise. That is, by balancing the former's judgement and numbers with the latter's prudence and leisure, Marsilius makes the whole body of citizens more perfect. This balanced and more nuanced method of political participation gains plausibility by 'the qualitative change of quantity.' An increase in quantity could bring with it an increase in qualitative value. Marsilius says:

> Even if we assume what is indeed true, that some of the less learned do not judge about a proposed law or some other practical matter equally as well as do the same number of the learned, still the number of the less learned could be increased to such an extent that they would judge about these things equally as well as, or even better than, the few who are more learned.[32]

In this way, the quantitative character of *valentior pars* is linked with its qualitative one. It is exactly in this context that Marsilius repeatedly insists that the 'weightier multitude of men' wish the state to endure.[33] Just as for Marsilius "every whole is greater than its part," in respect both to magnitude or mass and to practical virtue and action,[34] so the *valentior pars* involves a complete agreement of the quantitative and qualitative aspects of the whole body of citizens. Thus, this *valentior pars* can comprise all persons, except for "some men who have a deformed nature" who disagree with the common decision.[35] The multitude of the whole people "is more ample, and consequently its judgement is more secure, than that of some part taken separately."[36] Therefore, the whole body of the citizens, or the weightier multitude of it, can better discern what must be done for the common benefit of a political association than any other part or any single individual. The *valentior pars*, which displays the superiority of the whole people, is the overwhelming majority of the citizens. To sum up, for Marsilius, the *valentior pars* is a quantitative majority of the citizens, precisely because the way in which he has theorised the citizen body ensures that the quantitative majority must also be the qualitative majority.

Marsilius' conception of the *valentior pars* with both a quantitative and qualitative character, which is almost identical with that of the whole body of citizens, reinforces his claim that the sovereign legislator is none other than the people as a whole with moral and political competence superior to any other. It is in consideration of the balance of quantity and quality that Marsilius leaves the judgement about what is best for the common utility to the whole body of citizens or its weightier part. In consequence, Marsilius claims that the sovereign power in a state should always reside with the people as a whole.

Making the Representative: The *Pars Principans*

As we saw earlier on, for Marsilius, without human standards of the just and the beneficial, fighting and separation happen and then the destruction of the state and the loss of a sufficient life result. Therefore, a political association establishes the law by which judgements can be made with complete rectitude. Marsilius asserts that the power to make the law, which is the sovereign power in a political association, belongs to the human legislator, that is the whole body of citizens or its weightier part, who know best what is beneficial and what is harmful in a civil community.

However, for some reasons, the sovereign legislator of the whole body of citizens needs to establish representatives, a number of persons to make civil judgements in accordance with the law on its behalf. Here is the point from which Marsilius' conception of political representation or the creation of the representative in relation to the law originates. To understand why Marsilius insists on the need for representation, a close look at the analogy concerning the relationship between the people as a whole and the few wise which is mentioned in the previous chapter is helpful. In Marsilius' view, the multitude of the whole people is the most proper entity to judge rightly about the quality of products of human work or art, even though they are unable to discover or produce such artifacts themselves.[37] Likewise, every citizen, although not himself a discoverer of the laws, is capable of judging the proposed laws which would be the science of civil justice and benefit,[38] because the whole body of citizens is the entity which discerns best the common good in a civil community. However, the citizen, albeit the legislator with the sovereign power, needs the ruling part (*pars principans*) in a governmental position which acts on behalf of the citizen. If we remember that Marsilius has confidence in the whole body of citizens as the agent which can make their political community endure better than any other, the following questions need to be raised. Why does the whole body of citizens need the representative, in Marsilius' terms the *pars principans*, to act on its behalf? Why does the whole body of citizens with the original legislative power give its representatives the authority to execute laws with coercive force?

Needless to say, in justifying the creation of the representative, for Marsilius there is no space in which the Burkean argument for the necessity of making the representative—the argument that the representative possesses greater capability and responsibility to look after the public interest than the represented—can find a place. Marsilius does not give to any other person except the whole body of citizens or its weightier part credit for the competence and moral responsibility to maintain a political association. If the justification in Burkean terms is not to be found in Marsilius, does he see the transfer as necessary, as Mill did, because of the representative's competence which, by promoting further the common good together with the people's participation, contributes to the overall scheme for public action? Or was it, as it was for Bentham, simply a matter of convenience which does not imply any qualitative difference of merit or worth?

We can surmise that for Marsilius, there are several reasons why the citizens as the legislator delegate their sovereign authority to be exercised on their behalf by a *pars principans*, the ruling part. First of all, Marsilius assumes that the *pars principans* is established as a matter of convenience. For the execution of legal provisions, as a technical method of exercising the legislative power in practical terms, is effected more conveniently by the ruling part than by the entire multitude of citizens. The entire community does not need to be occupied in the execution, so one or a few rulers are sufficient to ensure it. Being a few or only one in number, they can execute the legal provisions more easily. However, in arguing this, Marsilius does not assume that few necessarily implies better. Just as Mill thought that politics needed to be conducted by politicians or rulers because of the highly professional knowledge and skill which politics required, but that the morality and intelligence of the people were the real impetus behind making government work well, so for Marsilius the creation of rulers does not imply at all the moral and political dependence of the ruled on the rulers in terms of the latters' superiority. Marsilius recognises that among the citizens, the men who are able to have leisure, who are older and experienced in practical affairs, that is "prudent men" ("*prudentes*"), can carry out the inquiry into laws more competently than others.[39] In fact, the *prudentes* are best qualified to identify and frame legislative proposals.[40] In this respect, even though the *prudentes* in Marsilius' thought are not necessarily the rulers, they are more likely to be the rulers as the executives of the laws: not only because the *prudentes* actually have more leisure to engage in politics, but also because the judicial and the deliberative part of the state is the part which is naturally appropriate for prudent men.[41] But for Marsilius, this too is a sort of division of labour involving different functions, which originates from the diversity of the natural inclinations of men, for the attainment of sufficiency of life. Again, this does not imply a difference of quality in the sense of merit or worth between the various parts in a civil community.[42]

The other reasons for entrusting judgement to the discretion of rulers are because, it is difficult or impossible for all the people to agree upon one decision, owing to the malice or ignorance of some[43] or because it is impossible for laws to be framed so as to cover every eventuality. So, although the whole body of citizens has the power to make laws in order that the political association endures, the ruler's prudence helps in the judgement of such cases in which the laws do not speak with certainty or in detail.[44]

For these reasons, for Marsilius, the citizens need to depend on an instrument or external organ, that is the *pars principans*, as their representative whose function is to regulate the civil acts of men in accordance with the law. To this end, the whole body of citizens decides to give their power to the representative. The following passage aptly sums up the relationship between the legislator and the ruling part, the *pars principans*, or between the represented and the representative in Marsilius:

> The primary efficient cause we say is the legislator; the secondary, as it were the instrumental or executive cause, we say is the ruler (*principans*) through the authority granted to him for this purpose by the legislator, in accordance with the form which the legislator has given to him ...... Although the legislator, as the primary and proper cause, must determine which persons must exercise what offices in the state, the execution of such matters, as also of all other legal provisions, is commanded, or as the case may be, prohibited, by the ruling part (*pars principans*) of the state.[45]

As this passage indicates, as the consequence of the transfer of the authority, this representative or ruling part can command the just and the honourable and prohibit their contraries by rewarding or punishing the merits or demerits of those who observe or transgress legal commands.[46] Under the authorisation of the legislator, as Marsilius cites Aristotle in the *Ethics*, "the ruler is the guardian of justice."[47] Furthermore, by having the command and the common guardianship of things, this ruling part of the state conserves the other parts and assists them in the performance of their various functions. In this sense the ruling part (*pars principans*) is "the first of all the parts of the state, and the others are ordered to it."[48] However, I suggest that this passage should not lead us to interpret *pars principans* as the supreme part in a political association which is above the whole people.

For Marsilius, by the authority of the whole body of citizens or of its weightier part, the ruling part, which is analogous to the heart, is first formed in that whole body. In this part, the soul of the whole body of citizens creates a certain form with the active power or authority to establish the other parts of the political association. This is called the government (*principatus*): "its virtue is the law; and its active power is the authority to judge, command, and execute sentences concerning civil justice and benefit delegated from the legislator."[49] When the rulers do this, it means that the entire community acts through them, since the rulers do it in accordance with the legal determination of the community[50] and with the authority which the sovereign legislator has given to them. Thus, differentiating the legislator from the ruler, the *pars principans*, Marsilius supposes that the ruling part is one of the parts of the civic body, not the whole body of citizens themselves. This means that those who discharge the deliberative and judicial offices are not sovereign. In Marsilius' view, those who are entrusted with law-making "are not and cannot be the legislator in the absolute sense but only in a relative sense and for a particular time and in accordance with the authority of the primary legislator."[51] That is, while the sovereign legislator as the primary judge has the original authority and power to make laws which are the standard of justice in a political association, the ruler (the *pars principans*), who is the secondary judge, exercises civil judgements according to the laws made by the authority of the prime legislator. What allows the ruler or secondary judge to have the power of executing law—the power which makes him the first part of a state—is the sovereign legislator or the prime judge. By being authorised to do so, the ruler (the *pars principans*) as the representative can put laws into effect on behalf of the legislator. Insofar as there is the necessity to execute laws, the ruler or the representative is established by the sovereign legislator: although the ruling part appears to deal with important matters for government as the first part of a civil community, the true knowledge of the law which the rulers have to follow in their judgement is always given by the sovereign legislator or the whole body of citizens. Accordingly, for Marsilius, this lesser judge, that is the ruler as the executive of law, or *principans pars* in Marsilian terminology, should be under the control of the sovereign legislator, the judge at the primary level.

In this way, making laws and judging according to the laws, although they are separate matters in our legal practice today, are very closely interrelated in Marsilius' conception of political representation. To sum up, for Marsilius, the necessity of law requires a political association to create rulers who make judgements according to law. To this end, the legislator grants the authority which originally belongs to it to the ruler. This ruler, the *pars principans*, is the representative of the whole body of the citizens and acts on their behalf as the executor of legal provisions.[52]

Thus, for Marsilius, the conception of making the representatives is essentially instrumental in the sense that they can express and accomplish what all citizens want in a convenient and useful way. The rulers as the representatives do not have any discretion to authorise what has not been willed by the citizens. They are the persons who are selected by the whole body just to perform a specific function on behalf of the citizens.[53] Up to this point, Marsilius' understanding of making the representative hardly appears to differ from that of Bentham. However, the *pars principans* in Marsilius is more actively involved in acting for the whole people than the representative as a delegate is. Let me illustrate the active roles of the ruler (the *pars principans*) in the following two aspects.

First, the *pars principans* or the government, with the authority which the human legislator gives to him, establishes and distinguishes the other parts of the state.[54] The disposition of the parts by the *pars principans* is of great importance in making the political association ordered, that is in attaining peace. If everyone in the political association is free to choose whatever functional occupation he likes without the intervention of the governing part, then the immoderate excess of some parts of the state in relation to others would cause the state to be destroyed.[55] This implies that although Marsilius believes in the people's moral and political capability as a collective power, he, unlike Bentham, does not consider every single individual as the best judge of their own concerns. In order that the various parts of the state can be arranged in a good disposition in the political schema, the government or the *pars principans* distributes due places to its members in accordance with the establishment of law. In the respect that putting each part in its proper position is effectively caused by the due action of the ruler, the ruler (the *pars principans*) is "the efficient and conserving cause of peace and tranquillity."[56] Due to this decisive role of the ruler, the representative becomes the "first part" of the state and the principle of the "order" of all the other parts.[57] Whatever essentially promotes or impedes the action of this ruling part of the state, which aims to procure peace, brings either tranquillity or discord in a political association. As we will see in Ch. 9, the obstacles which hinder the task of the ruler, whatever they are, are considered to be the enemy of peace.

Insofar as the ruler, thus, is an active contributor to civil peace, the function of the *pars principans* as the representative is not simply that of a delegate. For Marsilius, to become the first part of a political association is a complicated job, requiring knowledge, prudence and experience. This job of the *pars principans* demands wider responsibilities than the mechanical implementation of what the citizens want and think. It is not just to be an executive governing with fixed rules. The ruler as the representative has to be equipped with moral and practical knowledge and competence in applying the law to various situations in a political association. When this qualified ruler governs, the effect will be a secure, long-lasting and tranquil reign.[58] Thus, for Marsilius, to rule in accordance with the law has a more active implication than may at first be apparent. When Marsilius remarked that the *pars principans* was the first part of a state, he stressed the importance of the task which it must undertake. Nevertheless, as far as the *pars principans* is concerned, however active it may be in bringing peace in a political association, it remains authorised by the people as a whole and, under its authorisation, executes the law which is made by the people. Accordingly, its authority and power can never surpass those of the whole body of citizens.

The Alienation and Reproduction of Power

Is there a continuing life of the whole body of citizens after setting up the representative? This question, however paradoxical it may sound, is of central importance in the assessment of any scheme of political representation for the public interests of the people. As mentioned earlier, Rousseau held that where the sovereign or the general will which was always right and always tended to the public advantage was mediated through the representative, this meant alienation without right.[59] That is, for Rousseau, representation is incompatible with the sovereignty of the general will.

However, I maintain that for Marsilius, unlike Rousseau, the sovereign can be represented and making a representative does not necessarily result in the cancellation of the people's power. In this section I intend to show that Marsilius is a consistent thinker arguing that the whole people, who have the real sovereign power, should continue to have final authority over a political community even after creating their representative. To this end, I will illustrate how, without losing their sovereign power, the whole body of citizens comes to terms with the creation of the representative in his thinking.

To begin with, let us go back to the question raised at the start of this section. Mill, who admits the competence of the representatives and therefore their influence in the representative system, leaves more space for the representatives' intervention in controlling a state than Bentham does. Bentham who observes the sinister interests of the representative argues that, even after setting up the representative, the sound operation of the representative system still depends on the people who remain the best equipped to judge matters of state. In this way, Bentham tries to ensure that the sovereign power genuinely resides in the people at all times. Bentham, Mill and most contemporary interpreters of political representation insist that in representative government the representative remains fundamentally under the control of the sovereign authority of the people. But, many of these thinkers have little, if any, interest in just how the sovereign power of the people continues to operate effectively once power has been transferred. What concerns them is not so much how to sustain the sovereign power of the people as how to operate the representative government well. That is, once the representative is established, their concern with how to operate the representative government for the benefit of the people focuses on those who in practice are in charge of the business of government. Their assessments of this issue, therefore, centre on their views of the respective capabilities of the represented and the representative.

The exploration of the idea of political representation in terms of the relationship between the represented and the representative is necessary to identify who the sovereign really is who has the supreme power, who is authorised to be its representative, and on what grounds the represented and the representative can and do play their respective roles. As with modern interpreters of political representation, the relationship between the two political actors is essential to Marsilius' conception of political representation. As we have seen, in maintaining that the whole body of citizens possesses the sovereign power, Marsilius relies on the superiority of the people as a whole in terms of their moral and political capability. Moreover, he finds a theoretical justification for the whole people's power in the human weakness of the ruler. According to Marsilius, since the ruler is a human being, he too, like all other people, may well have a false opinion or perverted desire in contrast to a civil community of the whole people. Accordingly, the ruler, despite his status as the first part of a state, is "not equal in virtue to the law,"[60] and this is an expression of the incompleteness of human beings in general.

However, I suggest that insofar as the idea of political representation is a process of the authorisation of legitimate public acts and presumes the supremacy of the people's part in providing such authorisation, then to justify the people's dependence upon the practical activity of their representative solely by insisting on the human nature of the represented and the representative will not itself prevent the scheme of political representation for public acts from degenerating into an instrument for a politics of the narrowest of interests. For example, when it is assumed that every human being is weak and vulnerable to exterior circumstances, no understanding of political representation which is restricted to these materials—whether it is on an individual basis or on a collective base—can work properly as a scheme for public action, because both of the key political actors are too incomplete to be entirely relied on. Hence, in order to fill in the vacuum of justification, the thinkers on political representation look for supplementary devices to fill up human incompleteness: as we saw in Ch. 1, whereas for Mill, these were the appointment of the representative, the technical device of plural voting and the opposition to the secret ballot, for Bentham they were the institutions of the 'temporary non-relocability system' of the legislature, the 'legislation penal judicatory' and the 'public opinion tribunal.' The failure of these devices will continue to provoke us to contrive other expedients. Therefore, to see how political representation can reasonably be expected to act for the public benefit after the representative has been appointed, we need to return to the fundamental point at issue in the debate over the *lex regia*: the transfer of power.

In order to judge whether political representation can function as a scheme of legitimate public acts genuinely authorised by the people, we need to examine how the scheme maintains the public interests of the people within the representative system. In this respect, Marsilius coherently argues that the whole body of citizens which has authorised the appointment of the representatives should continue to control them in a consistent way after the first part of a state is established. This is because the source of the ruling part as the first part of a state lies in the authorisation of the original possessor of the ultimate power. Marsilius does not see any reason why the entity which authorises the scheme for the performance of public action needs to lose this task after creating the representative. Indeed, given that the authority and power of the whole body of citizens is greater than that of the representatives, they simply cannot, by being given the power by the people, suddenly become superior to the people. Through the people's transfer of power, the representatives are authorised to make use of that power in order to act on behalf of the people, but they do not simply supplant the people and they never fully equal its power. So, Marsilius argues that when the ruling part acts contrary to the laws, the judgement, command and execution of any correction of the ruler must be done by the legislator itself.[61] Whenever the rulers do wrong and they cannot act properly on behalf of the legislator, their power may be taken from them and the people's original power will be resumed. To make the people as a whole consistently the sovereign, Marsilius argues that the whole body of citizens' control over the representative ought to remain consistently effective. In this way, in Marsilius' thought, even though the whole body of citizens grants their original power to the rulers and the representatives are thus empowered to execute the laws, the representative's power is purely temporary. This is an important point which any interpretation of the idea of political representation merely in terms of the human characteristics of its component elements misses and Marsilius fully grasps.

On this basis, and contrary to Nederman's view, although for Marsilius, due to the necessity to make laws and to create a ruler to execute them, the whole body of citizens must alienate their power, this alienation never leads to the permanent forfeiture of the people's power. Nederman argues that, if the citizen relies on the discretion or judgement of a representative as a delegate to perform the common good, this means that he surrenders his right of participation, the most crucial feature of citizenship, and then degenerates into subjection. On this understanding, Nederman asserts that Marsilius is a critic of political representation since he claims that the individual citizen can ultimately judge the common benefit and there therefore is no real necessity for political representation in the first place.[62] However, I maintain that Nederman's reading of Marsilius misinterprets his understanding of political representation. That is, in Marsilius, it is not true that the citizen does not need to be represented because he is perfectly capable of recognising the communal good. Nor is it true that the ordinary citizens do not require a representative to determine their interests because they naturally desire what is truly good for themselves, that which is conducive to the maintenance of a self-sufficient and tranquil life.[63]

As emphasised frequently, Marsilius contends that the whole body of citizens itself is the best judge of the common benefit, but this does not imply that Marsilius rejects political representation. Marsilius simply does not reject the idea of political representation. Rather, he sees that political representation is necessary for selecting those who execute the laws. As seen in the previous section, the main role of the representative is to determine the other parts of the state, that is to give due position to its members, and to rule in accordance with the law. Nevertheless, the representative authority of the legislative experts is severely limited, since their decisions must be ratified by the whole body of citizens (the *universitas civium*), the human legislator. In this sense, Marsilius' representative is an essentially instrumental conception. Again, for Marsilius, the representative is one of the various functions or parts of a civil community.

The role of the representative is the outcome of a division of labour rather than a direct expression of qualitative differences of worth between individuals.

More significantly, Marsilian citizens do not totally devolve their original legislative power to the representative, because Marsilius argues that, after the whole body of citizens grants authority to the representatives, the sanction of their judgement still directly concerns the people themselves and the final judgement of things in relation to the common good of the political association still belongs to the primary legislator. Thus, the alienation of the people's power is a limited and temporary form of transfer of power. For Marsilius, it is never a complete surrender of people's civil and political rights. The authority and power to make the law always remain in the whole body of citizens, *universitas civium*. The ultimate authority of the legislator (the represented's authority) stands above the practical business of implementing laws (the representative's business). The representative's power which itself results from the transfer of the people's power can be returned to the people. The abdication of the people's legislative power has no place in Marsilius' thought.

As we have seen in Ch. 4, in their argument over the source of jurisdiction in Italian city-states, at an earlier point, the Roman lawyers (Irnerius, Placentinus and Azo) discussed the issue of the transfer of power through the medieval debate over the *lex regia*. All of them largely shared the view that the basis of making laws originated from what the whole people had agreed. However, while Irnerius and Placentinus held that the people's power which was given to the emperor could not be revoked later, Azo claimed the perpetuity of the original power of the people. Concerning this issue Marsilius is no different from Azo: the whole body of citizens do not cancel their legislative power at all. The only point on which Marsilius appears to differ from Azo concerns the person to whom the people granted the power to legislate. While Azo argued that the people transferred it to the emperor (*princeps*), Marsilius maintained that in theory the authority was granted to the ruling part (*principans*) who are in charge of executing laws. But, it is both instructive and essential to examine who the Marsilian ruler actually was, in order to confirm Marsilius' position. Historically speaking, was there in Marsilius' view anybody who had higher authority than the whole body of citizens?

· 9 ·

POLITICAL REPRESENTATION IN HISTORY

In Discourse I of *DP*, Marsilius frequently remarks about the entity who has the authority to make laws as follows: "the whole body of citizens or its weightier part or the person to whom the whole body of citizens has granted the authority."[1] This passage implies that for Marsilius the legislative power virtually resides with the three agencies. We have examined what the whole body of citizens and the weightier part signified in Marsilius' thought. The question of who the person is who is authorised to hold the power by the whole body of citizens remains our concern.

The question about the locus of the legislative power in Marsilius' thought is a prime key to understanding Marsilius' overall theory. However, this issue is as controversial as it is important in Marsilius. Broadly speaking, there are two interpretations of Marsilius' legislator: the populist and the imperialist. These conflicting theories of the legislator in Marsilius' thought depend in particular upon how to interpret his imperial stance. In this chapter, contrary to the narrowly imperialist interpretation of Marsilius, I maintain that, although Marsilius appears to argue for the emperor as the legislator who makes laws in historical context, Marsilius' belief in the whole body of citizens as the sovereign legislator remains unchanged. To this end, I attempt to show that for Marsilius the emperor as the equivalent of the legislator does not stand opposed to the whole body of citizens or the whole body of the believers and they are in harmony. Rather, I suggest that Marsilius' imperial stance on the question of the legislator is to oppose the pope's power which is the real disturber of the common good of peace in a political community. The examination of this question aims to demonstrate that, for Marsilius, the holder of the sovereign power in the temporal and the ecclesiastical domains is the whole body of citizens (*universitas civium*) or the whole body of believers (*universitas fidelium*).

Whose Unity?: The Emperor's or City-states'?

Marsilius' assertion of the relationship between the whole body of citizens and the ruler does not always appear to be put forward in a consistent fashion. In particular, this is apparent when Marsilius moves to Discourse II of *DP*, to *De Translatione Imperii* (hereafter *TI*) and to *Defensor Minor* (hereafter *DM*).[2] As we saw earlier, according to Marsilius' theoretical argument in Discourse I of *DP*, while the whole body of citizens is the legislator who has the original power to make laws and the coercive force to punish transgressors, the rulers as the executors of laws can not have such powers unless they are authorised by the legislator. However, for Marsilius, despite this argument, sometimes the ruler with "*coactiva potestas instrumentalis*"[3] appears to be practically synonymous with the legislator. This impression is revealed in the following passage which we read very often in his texts: "the human legislator or the ruler by the authority of the legislator" ("*humanus legislator seu principans ipsius auctoritate*").[4] Our concern is with whom 'the ruler by the authority of the legislator' means. Even though Marsilius' political principles, in particular his concern with the whole body of citizens or their weightier part as the human legislator, are established in Discourse I of *DP*, yet in Discourse I Marsilius does not give a more clear and detailed account of whom 'the person who has the legislative authority given by the whole body of citizens' actually means. Moving to the Discourse II of *DP*, to *TI* and to *DM*, in which Marsilius develops the theory of the empire, he states that the legislative power belongs to the whole body of citizens or the emperor. In these texts, more specifically, Marsilius says much to support the opinion that 'the ruler by his own authority' is the emperor. On several occasions the Roman emperor is explicitly stated as the equivalent of the legislator. For example:

> *Est etiam similiter secundum legem humanam legislator, ut civium universitas aut eius pars valentior, vel Romanus princeps summus imperator vocatus. Est et iudex coactivus secundum legem eandem, ut universitas iam dicta, vel princeps, aut ille vel illi, cui vel quibus universitas*

aut princeps dederit auctoritatem et coactivam potestatem per poenam realem aut personalem in hoc saeculo legis humanae transgressores coercendi.[5]

This passage implies that for Marsilius, 'the person to whom the whole body has granted the authority to make the laws' indicates the Roman emperor. Here, to explore the emperor's position in Marsilius' thought, first, I wish to raise the question of whether the person authorised as the legislator's substitute, that is the emperor, means the *pars principans* who, as examined in the previous chapter, acts on their behalf to execute laws. Marsilius does not clearly elucidate the difference between the emperor (*princeps*) and the *pars principans*. In particular, when we recall that Marsilius says that the *pars principans* is the first part of the state or the efficient cause of peace, the identification, respectively, of who the emperor (*princeps*) is and who the ruler (*pars principans*) is does not seem to be easy.[6] But, as Marsilius' analogy of the *pars principans* as the heart of an animal[7] indicates, the emperor is obviously the *pars principans* in the respect that both of them, as the principal organ of the civil community or specifically the Roman empire, execute laws to regulate the civil acts of men. However, I suggest that the emperor is differentiated, analytically if not in practice, from the *pars principans* in two aspects.[8]

First, the legislator in Marsilius is to be differentiated from the ruler, the *pars principans*, on the grounds that while the whole body of citizens is the supreme judge, the *pars principans* is the executive of laws to act on its behalf, which means the secondary judge in respect of weight of judgement. That is, the *pars principans* at the second level of judge can not be of the same status as the primary judge which is the whole body of citizens or the weightier part or the person to whom they have given the authority. The authorised person —the emperor—, who is described as the equivalent of the legislator, is no more the *pars principans* as the secondary judge than the legislator is.

Another reason for the differentiation between the emperor (*princeps*) and the ruling part (*pars principans*), I suggest, is that even though both the emperor and the *pars principans* have the power of governing a state, the emperor has a higher status which unifies the first parts of the other, lesser states. When Marsilius mentions the emperor, he does so in the context in which the emperor exercises powers higher than that of the *pars principans*. In this respect, the emperor can be considered as the *pars principans*, but he means a single supreme ruler or government (*primus principans or principatus*) among many rulers (the *partes principantes*):[9] the emperor is outstanding in respect of capacity and function, which symbolically amounts to the qualitative distinction of the legislator.[10]

In these two aspects, I suggest making an analytical differentiation between the emperor and the *pars principans*, that is the difference between 'the ruler by the authority of the legislator,' who has the legislative power as the substitute of the legislator, and 'the ruling part,' which has the executive power. By doing so, I wish to make clear that Marsilius puts the whole body of citizens as the sovereign legislator and the Roman emperor as its equivalent in historical context. Failure to make a distinction between the holder of delegated legislative power and the *pars principans*, and lack of an understanding that the emperor, theoretically speaking, is authorised to have the power by the people as a whole, have lent support to a narrowly imperialist interpretation of Marsilius.

On the other hand, concerning Marsilius' statement of the Roman emperor being the equivalent of the legislator, which hardly occurs in Discourse I in *DP*, some Marsilian scholars point out that it shows the inconsistency of Marsilius' thought. And this inconsistency of Marsilius' view of the legislator has been explained by the question of the authorship of the *DP*[11] or by recourse to Marsilius' "careful ambiguity" which evades expressing his preference for a particular political unity.[12] However, I maintain that these explanations about the emergence of the emperor in Marsilius' thought are inappropriate rather than redundant in understanding his imperial outlook. Instead, by showing that Marsilius' mention of the emperor as the equivalent of the legislator is not at odds with his argument for the sovereign power of the people, I intend to explain his theory of the empire. To this end, I suggest looking at the relationship between the people and the emperor in two perspectives: one is in terms of the *lex regia*, the other is in terms of the context of the *Italicum regnum*.

First, as with such glossators as Irnerius and Placentinus whom we examined in Ch. 4, Marsilius' emperor can be understood as the political agency which, after the initial grant of power by the people, continues to hold power. Marsilius starts by stating how the people (*universitas*) or the Roman people is the source of political power as follows:

> We say that the supreme human legislator, especially from the time of Christ up to the present time, and perhaps for sometime beforehand, was and is and ought to be the community (*universitas*) of human beings who ought to be subject to the precepts of coercive laws, or their greater part (*eius pars valentior*), in each region and province. And since this power or authority was transferred by the communities of the provinces, or their greater part, to the Roman people, in accordance with their exceeding virtue, the Roman people have and had the authority to legislate over all of the world's provinces.[13]

That is, for Marsilius, regardless of the size of a political unit—whether it is a region, province or city—the source of the political authority comes from those who are components of the unit. Accordingly, the authority or power of the emperor or the Roman people too is given by the whole (*universitas*) of human beings from lesser to bigger communities, which are considered to be its components. Here, we have the understanding of the organic relation of the part to the whole in Marsilius, as in Remigius. Marsilius would have recognised well that the election of the emperor by the German princes was effectively the imperial creation.[14] But he would not have believed that the electoral rights of the princes explain the whole problem of the source of the imperial authority, since in his view, the basis of the imperial power originates from the authority of the whole people (*universitas*).[15] At this point, the historical matter of whether the German princes were the successors of the Roman people is not Marsilius' interest.[16]

Second, the conflicting views in Marsilius of the locus of the power to relax or dispense with laws are complicated further by the question of what constitutional arrangement Marsilius had in mind. That is, apart from the implicit or explicit mention of the legislator—the whole body of citizens or the emperor—Marsilius' remark about the supreme government and the plurality of governments may give rise to many conflicting interpretations of his overall theory about the legislator:

> There must be among them one in number which is supreme, to which all the other governments are reduced, by which they are regulated, and which corrects any errors arising in them.[17]

The argument is more explicitly stated as follows:

> If this plurality of government is assumed, one of the greatest effects of human reason and art will be useless and superfluous. For all the civil utility which would be had from many supreme governments can be perfectly had through one government or one supreme government without the harms resulting from a plurality of them.[18]

We saw earlier that in Marsilius, for peace and order, a political association should be in unity. The unity is possible through the government by which all the other parts of the state are ordered, that is one government within a single state. Marsilius remarks that if the state has two or more supreme governments this will lead to "fighting, separation, and finally the destruction of the state."[19] However, Marsilius' conception of unity does not necessarily mean numerical oneness as opposed to plurality because he understands that the city or state, its parts or offices are actually many in number. The unity of a state or city in Marsilius is not so much one in the numerical sense as one of a unified order. What Marsilius intends to argue is that for the state or city to be rightly regulated, that is for the unity of government, supreme government is necessary and, to this end, it is actually one in number.[20]

Concerning the reason why such a plurality is reduced to one, Marsilius says that, as every being is naturally inclined toward and depends upon the first being, plurality originates from the numerical unity of the first being. To speak in political terms, the unity of the first being is nothing other than supreme government:

> Hence the statement wherein all beings are said to be one world in number does not mean that some numerical unity is formally in all beings ...... rather it is a plurality of certain things, which plurality is called one because it is in relation to one thing and because of one thing. Similarly, the men of one city or province are called one city or state because they wish one government in number.[21]

In Marsilius' view, the oneness or unity toward which a plurality is inclined is not with respect to number of rulers but with respect to the office from which the numerical unity of every action, judgement and command come. Marsilius believes that if the numerical plurality of cities is spread out without the centripetal force of a government, the judgement, command, and execution of matters of benefit and justice in a city would fail. Therefore, the supreme government is necessary, so that the cities will not be broken up.[22] It is for this reason that a plurality of governments is to be integrated into one government. Marsilius supposed that the supreme government, historically speaking, was nothing other than the holy Roman empire.

Nonetheless, this understanding of the supreme government as the emperor provokes controversy as to what is the political unity which Marsilius actually refers to in developing his analysis of the state—the empire or the Italian city-states? As we examined in Ch. 5, the issue of the relative powers of the imperial law of the empire and the local law of the Italian city-states was being widely discussed in Marsilius' time. This controversy between the universal and the territorial might be expected in Marsilius too, who says from the start of *DP* that the originality of his book is to explicate the cause which has made the Italian city-states and the Roman emperor troubled.[23]

In a discussion of the institutional background in Marsilius, Rubinstein argues that, for Marsilius, to discuss the empire conceived as universal monarchy was to discover the causes of the loss of civic peace.[24] The Italian city-states in general, and Padua in particular, provided the institutional background for much of Marsilius' theory of the state.[25] More specifically, Marsilius' picture of a well-ordered state constituted an implicit condemnation of arbitrary rule as exercised by Italian *signori*, who had full legislative authority and were not bound by the statutes.[26] Rubinstein holds that Marsilius' conception of the *universitas* as the basis of political authority was to reply to the challenge of the *signoria* and, by doing so, suggested a solution for the endemic problems of the city-states and of Italy at large.[27]

On the issue of the background of the city-states, Gewirth maintains that Marsilius' preference for the political unit is opposed to the idea of a universal state and his whole doctrine is devoted to explaining his opposition to a world government. However, Gewirth, unlike Rubinstein, argues that this opposition to the empire as a universal idea was directed against the pretensions of the papacy's universal plenitude of power.[28] In Gewirth's view, what Marsilius intended to insist on is, in fact, that for men to live peacefully together it suffices to have "numerical unities of governments according to provinces,"[29] without going beyond these to a world government. By contrast, arguing that Marsilius' *DP* was written for Louis of Bavaria, Wilks argues that the political entity which Marsilius referred to was a single universal society with one political head—that is the holy Roman empire.[30]

At first glance, it seems to be contradictory to have the theories of empire and city-states - that is, locating the legislative power and coercive power in the citizens or the emperor respectively—put forward together in Marsilius. But I suggest that they are not antagonistic. To explain how the empire was a necessary reference for the Italian city-states without provoking conflict between the two, Bartolus is worth citing again. According to Bartolus, by acknowledging the emperor as *de jure* "*dominus omnium*," the *civitates* remained within the people. Otherwise they would be regarded as heretics, because the empire was the governing power of the *populus Romanus* which was equated with the community of the faithful.[31] Like Bartolus, Marsilius required the empire in order to preserve the civic peace. However, Marsilius' reference to the empire is not to accommodate a Christian empire, but is to attain civil peace against the priest and the pope. For Marsilius, the existence of the emperor was in practice necessary to prevent the popes from abusing their powers and hence to guarantee peace in the city-states. What Marsilius was opposed to was not the empire as a universal state but the universal power which the pope claimed to have, which we shall discuss in the next section.

Marsilius, like Bartolus, needed the empire, in which the Italian city-state was, *de jure*, subject to the imperial power, in order to secure civic peace. This can be clarified further by understanding the political status of the empire and the Italian city-states in fourteenth-century history.

The empire (*imperium*), geographically speaking, consisted of those lands which were subject to the rule of the Roman people and later of the emperor. This unity of the empire did not permit a plurality of *regna*. As the term changed, however, the emperor came to mean he who was pre-eminent in the whole world with the supremacy over the other kingdoms.[32] That is, as Folz points out, its head was 'the emperor in charge of the Roman empire' not 'the emperor of the Romans.'[33] In a similar vein, Marsilius himself indicates that 'Roman empire' means "a universal or general monarchy over the whole world or at any rate over the majority of the provinces" rather than "the monarchy or royal rule of the city of Rome."[34] Thus, Marsilius sees the Roman empire as a universal political entity rather than a particular one.[35] However, although Marsilius could not deny that in a sense the Roman empire is the political expression of Christian universality,[36] he never had in mind as the ideal empire the idea of a universal Christian body politic. Indeed, Marsilius' idea of the empire is distinguished from those such as Dante's 'universal Christian commonwealth'[37] in which the emperor or world ruler is dependent on God as a lofty ideal of mankind.[38] On this basis, what Dante dreamed of was the Roman empire with one single authority and legality. But for Marsilius the Christian idea of empire could not be identified with the historical empire in the West in which he was involved—that is with the holy Roman empire.[39] Marsilius' concern with the argument for truly universal empire was not such a construction of a kingdom of God on earth. Neither was it confined to the constitutional situation in Germany, that is the empire as a historical phenomenon. The idea of the empire in Marsilius' thought has a double character—the world domain as a universal idea and the Roman empire as a historical fact. In either case, as indicated in Ch. 7, what Marsilius believes as the ideal political entity is the secular state, in which the civil happiness is attained through human acts, and not the Christian commonwealth.

With this understanding of the empire in mind, we can observe the relation between the empire and the Italian city-states in Marsilius in the context of the *regnum Italicum*, that is the provinces of northern Italy which were, *de jure*, under the imperial jurisdiction.[40] In other words, the Italian city-states had political, social and judicial reference to the empire, but the relation of the empire to the city-states was *de jure*.[41] That is, the function of the empire essentially consisted in guaranteeing peace by regulating only the justice of relations between the city-states.[42] Thus, not at the level of the facts but at the level of right, in Marsilius' thought, the supreme government to which a plurality of government is reduced signifies the Roman empire, which is a comprehensive political unity composed of lesser kingdoms and city-states. But the authorisation of the emperor does not entail the suppression of city-states as lesser legislative bodies. In consequence, Marsilius' argument for the supreme government or the emperor does not imply an absolutist theory of the empire. Rather, for Marsilius, the people or its empire is the real *universitas*, without which the substantial and juridical unity of the *regnum Italicum* disappears.[43] In this way, the empire is in harmony with the city-states, which constitutes the political entity at the centre of the vision of Marsilius.

The Enemy of Peace: The Roman Bishop, the Pope

The understanding of the empire in terms of the *lex regia* and the context of *regnum Italicum* saves Marsilius' theory from the absolute interpretation of political rule.[44] In fact, if we read *DP* more carefully, we see that Marsilius' idea of the Roman emperor as the equivalent of the legislator is in particular pressed in a context where he is violently attacking the papal claim of 'plenitude of power' ('*plenitudo potestatis*').[45] In this respect, Marsilius' first priority is not that of explaining whether the empire is the supreme government or the best constitution. What Marsilius intends to maintain is that the evil of disrupting civil peace is not caused by the supreme government of the empire but by the so-called papal monarchy, founded on the claim of the plenitude of power. Indeed, Marsilius was well aware that the cooperative relationship between the empire and the city-states had another intention which was of great importance to both of them—that is their common defence against the pope's despotism. This is a matter to which neither Cynus nor Bartolus,[46] jurists contemporary with Marsilius, called attention, but which Marsilius insisted was the prime cause of lack of tranquillity in both the Italian city-states and the empire.

Marsilius' concern with the church-state problem which is shown, in particular in the whole Discourse II of the *DP*, is, in brief, to make clear that the power and authority which the popes claim to possess not only *outside* but also *within* the church is wrong and the main cause of civil disorder. In this section I attempt to explore Marsilius' arguments for opposition to the papal supremacy both *outside* and *within* the church. It will show that for Marsilius the papal authority is of human creation and that there is no necessary reason for maintaining the pope's or the priest's power over a temporal community. To this end, first, let me examine the arguments of Marsilius' opposition to the pope's jurisdiction *outside* the church.

As we saw in Ch. 7, Marsilius argues that peace consists in the right disposition of each part of a political association. When each part of the state performs its own functions in accordance with a right constitution, the state keeps its tranquillity. Nevertheless, in Marsilius' view, by deviating from their original position, and therefore by disturbing the good disposition of its parts, the pope or the priests in general affect badly the order of peace. Hence, the pope is the common enemy of the Italian city-states and the emperor. Indeed, for Marsilius the pope is 'the real disturber of the peace of Christendom' and 'the greatest impediment to the rightful functioning of the civil community.'[47]

According to Marsilius, the pope's despotism is founded on the claim of 'plenitude of power' in every domain—both the secular and the ecclesiastical—of a political association. To show that the papal claim is not valid, Marsilius differentiates the various senses of plenitude of power[48] and argues that the pope's or the priest's power never signifies the plenitude of power as the universal or sovereign power. Instead, what they can possess is confined only to the sacramental power for the cure of souls, so that men can attain eternal salvation. The pope or the priest could not have any power of interfering with the temporal community, not to mention coercive jurisdiction over it. Why is the extent of the priestly power so limited and how does Marsilius characterise the priest's power?

First, Marsilius maintains the pope's lack of coercive power. Corresponding to his differentiation of divine law from human law, Marsilius sees that eternal salvation and the sufficient life in this world are separate matters. Accordingly, only the legislator or the ruler by its authority has coercive power, an indication of legitimate jurisdiction in this world. By contrast, the priest as a teacher of divine law is not entitled to claim any coercive jurisdiction. We saw that the papalists argued for sacerdotal supremacy over the secular jurisdiction by the claim that the pope was the immediate vicar of Christ who ruled over the two domains.[49] For them, there could be no question about the exercise of the omnipotent papal power which is justified in the name of Christ, the lord of the universe. However, contrary to the papalists' argument, Marsilius has a remarkably different assumption: the priest or the pope is not the vicar of Christ. In Marsilius' view, the pope is not ordained by God and is neither the successor of Peter or any apostle.[50] Rather, as we shall see further on, historically speaking, the papal authority was granted by the secular ruler; Marsilius does not even imagine that the pope or the priests have jurisdictional power over the outside church. According to Marsilius, even Christ, who is the judge of divine law,[51] did not have the coercive jurisdiction in a secular domain. Rather, Christ himself as a man was subject to the secular ruler's jurisdiction[52] and taught such subjection to others.[53] Here, again, we see that for Marsilius the divine law is not the law of universal judgement of civil disputes.[54]

Marsilius' argument that the priest or the pope has no coercive power is a crucial point for defining the nature and extent of the priestly power in a political association. This is the second characteristic of priestly power: the priests, who lack coercive power, remain, like other parts, a part of the political association. This means that the judgement of civil disputes belongs to the whole body of citizens or to the secular rulers and no one else[55] and that the priests are bound by their jurisdiction. In consequence, peace and the sufficient life in a state can be preserved.[56] Marsilius maintains that this is the true role of Christian priesthood.

On this understanding, the temporal power and the spiritual power in Marsilius, in contrast to Gelasius, are no longer two separate swords from God. What is more, it does not presume the equality of the two powers. As Gewirth pertinently points out, Marsilius' discussion of the 'church-state' problem is not about the relation of 'church' and 'state' or of the spiritual and temporal 'powers' any more.[57] This is because insofar as the pope or priest is completely subject to the people's or the secular ruler's jurisdiction, the priesthood is not the spiritual power in juxtaposition to the temporal power. Instead it is simply one of the parts, the priestly part, of the political association. For Marsilius, the distinction between the two parts means the limitation of the priest's power, that is the dependence of *pars sacerdotalis* on the legislator or the secular ruler or the *pars principans* in a political association,[58] which is a complete reversal of the papalist theories of Innocent III and IV and Boniface VIII.

On this point, d'Entrèves' supposition, that "the priestly function is the purely spiritual function in which the secular ruler has not to interfere,"[59] needs to be reconsidered. In the discourse II of *DP* and *DM*, in which Marsilius adopts a stronger position in favour of the secular ruler, in particular the emperor, he actually suggests that, for the unity of the state the ruling part can intervene in the priestly part, but the reverse is not permitted. For it is the correct action of the ruler that is required to put each part in a proper position in order to attain peace. If the priests pretend to possess the coercive power, this brings about an unordered multiplicity of governments, which makes the polity fall into an improper arrangement of functions of the parts in a state.[60]

Marsilius' assertion of the secular ruler's jurisdiction over the ecclesiastical ruler in a political community constitutes an essential core from which to develop his general principles of the priesthood *within* the church—a marked contrast, as observed in Ch. 3, to the papalists' argument for the papal supremacy *outside* the church, which was developed as an extension of supremacy *within* the church. Of the power of order, of office and of jurisdiction which the papal hierocratic theory claimed to be the powers of the pope,[61] Marsilius insists that what the priest or the pope can exercise is solely the sacramental power (*potestas ordinis*). According to Marsilius, God bestowed upon the apostles and some others[62] the sacramental power and the administrative power (that is, the power to lay down rules for the services or to distribute temporal property).[63] However, the grant of the two powers by the immediate action of God was limited to the times of the apostles. Afterwards, due to the increases of the number of priests, while the sacramental power still pertains to the priests, the authority of *officium* does not. That is, the priesthood is only a dispenser of the sacraments and a teacher of the faith. In Marsilius' view, for the priest to perform the power of the keys, that is the power of loosing or binding men from or to sins, is confined to the priest's power of performing the sacraments for eternal salvation.[64] This does not indicate the power to punish with coercive force because eternal salvation is not a matter of coercion.[65] In addition, Marsilius argues that the second power, the *officium*, which used once to belong to the apostles or the persons whom they ordained, is not inherited by the priests or the pope. Instead, the *officium* is determined by the "will and mind of men," that is the whole people or the ruler by its authority.[66]

Moreover, contrary to papalist argument, which supposed that the sacramental power of the pope involved the power to administrate and judge within the church since justified by the papal vicariate of Christ, Marsilius argues that, as far as the sacramental power is concerned, it does not carry with it any administrative and coercive power of enforcement in the church,[67] because the priest is not the vicar nor divinely instituted. Simply, for Marsilius, the priest as a part of a state is like an expert in a political association—that is, the priest is the physician of souls whom the political community needs.[68] The priest can judge concerning heretics or other infidels but the judgement is effective only *within* the church.[69] For the judgement to have forms of compulsion in a temporal community, it requires the legislator with coercive power or the ruler by the authority of the legislator or the human law which deals with such matters.[70] In this respect, unlike John of Paris who approved the priest's jurisdictional power to the extent that it is limited to spiritual affairs,[71] Marsilius claims that the final judgement even over excommunication pertains entirely to the whole body of the faithful in a community or to a general council.[72]

Marsilius' assertion of the priest's lack of jurisdictional power even within the church extends to his denial of the hierarchical order in which the pope is the head of the church. Contrary to Innocent III, Innocent IV and Boniface, Marsilius advocates a theory in which all priests have equal rights. For Marsilius, insofar as the sacramental power is the sole power which all priests can perform irrespective of their place within the church, there is no need of the hierarchy with different powers.[73] Moreover, he argues that every member of the church is its head and that the pope is not in a special status which is approved by God's ordainment. The pope is in the same position as other priests in the church.[74] Marsilius argues that any greater authority of the pope over other priests and churches, if it existed, was based on custom and on their voluntary consent for the unity of the faithful.[75] However, more significantly, even the institution of the customary headship is through *human* appointment or election. That is, the source of the papal authority or the priestly power is a human creation.[76] *Who* is the person who established the papal authority? The answer to this question is clearly found in Marsilius' interpretations of historical events.

Marsilius' argument for the origin of the papal authority and the pope's lack of jurisdiction in this world is made more solid by his historical explanations about the 'Donation of Constantine' and '*Translatio* of empire'. We may begin with the historical argument of the 'Donation' in Marsilius. To recall what has already been said, the papalist interpretation was that the 'Donation' meant the restoration of the jurisdictional power to the pope who was the original holder of the power.[77] In contrast, Marsilius argues that Constantine's conversion was a historical event which demonstrated that the origin of papal authority *outside* and *within* the church came from the secular ruler. Historically speaking, the priests or bishops, till the time of Constantine, lived under the coercive jurisdiction of the secular rulers and no bishop exercised coercive jurisdiction over any of the others. It was Constantine who granted to the Roman church and its bishop its preeminence and authority over other churches which they had not possessed before.[78] Further, Marsilius insists that this grant simply signifies that the authority of the pope was not granted by God, but by the temporal power which had the coercive jurisdiction.[79]

Marsilius' argument for the secular ruler's jurisdiction over the priest is demonstrated in his interpretation of the 'Translation of empire' too. Marsilius' description of the historical facts about the imperial transfers[80] aims to claim the superiority of the secular ruler to the pope and the pope's lack of the coercive power. According to Marsilius, only the person who does not have any superior has the authority to establish a government and to transfer it from nation to nation. That person was no one other than the emperor because he transferred the empire from the Greeks to the Germans.[81] Contrary to the papal argument for the initiative of the spiritual power in the '*Translatio*,' Marsilius says that the imperial transfers did not have any connection with the popes but resulted from the legitimate processes for transfers of power—in particular since the time of Gregory V, the election by seven princes.[82] Marsilius admits the pope's involvement in the imperial election. However, for the pope to confirm the elected person to be emperor and to crown him is just a formal ceremony and purely honorific and incidental.[83] Marsilius, unlike Innocent III, does not see that the coronation of the emperor by the pope is the final process which establishes the imperial authority.[84] Moreover, Marsilius remarks that if the princes' election of the emperor depends solely upon the will of the pope, the duty of the electors would be an empty one, that is nothing other than a nomination.[85] So, for Marsilius, the pope's confirmation of a man elected as a king is a customary process without any political implications.

To conclude, for Marsilius, the papal claim of plenitude of power is the prime cause of a plurality of supreme governments in a state,[86] which interferes with the secular government which is the entity which has the responsibility to implement civil peace. Marsilius maintains that Christ did not give any superior office or dignity to the pope[87] and that all priests are called to be teachers of divine law. In fact, the papal authority in this world was given by Constantine, the secular ruler who was outside the church. Even this authority which the emperor granted to the pope is so limited that it solely connotes the power to govern the churches for administrative convenience, which does not include coercive jurisdiction.[88]

Coercion, Jurisdiction, and the *Universitas*

Marsilius' argument for the emperor as the source of the papal authority brings us back to the issue of the imperial interpretation of Marsilius' theory. We face the question of whom Marsilius in practice thought to be the sovereign without any superior who has the supreme power. My answer to this question is consistent with what has been argued earlier: that is, that the whole body of citizens has the sovereign power. Despite Marsilius' acceptance of imperial power in the ecclesiastical domain, imperial authority does not involve for him an absolute theory of the empire. Earlier, we saw how in Marsilius the emperor comes to terms with the people as a whole in terms of *lex regia* and the context of *regnum Italicum*. In this concluding section, I intend to demonstrate that the imperial power in the ecclesiastical domain is not in conflict with the ecclesiastical equivalent of the whole body of citizens, that is the whole body of the believers (*universitas fidelium*) or the faithful legislator (*legislator fidelis*).[89] By doing so, I suggest that in Marsilius' thought the position of the whole people (*universitas civium*) as sovereign is coherently maintained in the ecclesiastical, as in the temporal domain. The whole body of citizens being the sovereign in the two domains makes Marsilius' theory of the *universitas* more convincing.

To maintain that Marsilius does not suggest absolute claims for the sovereignty of the emperor, it may help to go back to our understanding of the *lex regia* in which the original grant of authority by the Roman people to the emperor is treated. That is, our understanding that the emperor's position is the result of the transfer of the whole people's original authority and that in historical context the emperor is the equivalent of the whole people as the legislator, but does not have the temporal lordship as a whole, is also important for understanding Marsilius' imperial argument in the question of ecclesiology. Marsilius argues that Constantine is the source of the papal authority. However, this argument does not lead to the absolute theory of the emperor because for Marsilius the exercise of the imperial authority in the ecclesiastical domain too presupposes the prior authorisation of the whole people. Unless the whole body of citizens authorises the emperor to grant the power to the priest or the pope, the emperor cannot grant it and the priests cannot be given it. This *lex regia* principle explains not only the source of imperial authority but also that of papal authority in Marsilius. On this basis, Marsilius maintains that while, historically speaking, it was Constantine who granted the Roman bishop power, analytically speaking, the whole body of faithful citizens, which has the supreme authority to establish other parts of the state, is the immediate efficient cause of the papal authority.[90] Constantine is the equivalent of the faithful legislator in the respect that the emperor is nothing other than 'the ruler by the authority of the legislator,'[91] but is never its superior. It is on this foundation that Marsilius' argument for the priest's subjection to the coercive judgement of secular rulers is based.[92] The relationship between the whole body of citizens or between the faithful citizens and the emperor, which presumes their superiority to the emperor, extends to Marsilius' theory of ecclesiology, in which the sovereign power of the church is held by the whole body of the believers.

The papalists argued that the pope, the vicar of Christ, personified the church and so embodied in himself the whole of its authority.[93] Against this papalist argument, Marsilius defines the church, that is the whole mystical body of Christ,[94] as the whole body of the faithful Christians in which both priests and non-priests equally are included:

> The "church" means the whole body of the faithful (*univesitas fidelium*) who believe in and invoke the name of Christ, and all the parts of this whole body in any community, even the household.[95]

For Marsilius, church specifies 'the universal church' or the congregation of the believers, whatever their dignity or condition.[96] Christ granted all members equal entitlement to be a member of the church since Christ purchased and redeemed everyone with his blood.[97] Accordingly, the priest or the pope is not in status superior to other members of the church. Marsilius' definition of the church as the congregation of the faithful provides a crucial implication about who has coercive jurisdiction in the church. That is, for Marsilius, it is upon the whole body of the faithful which constitutes his mystical body—the church—that Christ bestowed coercive authority or jurisdiction.[98] The ultimate ecclesiastical authority rests with the congregation of all Christian believers (*universitas fidelium*) which lacks a superior, and not with any special person or group. The coercive jurisdiction *within* the church, like that *outside* the church, pertains to the whole body of the believers or the faithful in the church, which means the whole body of citizens in a political community.[99] By the coercive jurisdiction, the whole body of the believers or its weightier part have the authority to make decisions over important ecclesiastical matters: for example, they can convoke a general council[100] and enforce its decisions.[101] Moreover the election or approval of the ecclesiastical orders,[102] the appointment or the removal of the priestly office,[103] including that of the head of all bishops and churches,[104] pertain to the whole body of the faithful or to the ruler by the authority of the legislator.[105]

Here, what is noteworthy again is Marsilius' argument for imperial power in these crucial matters of the church. Marsilius argues that coercive authority in the church belongs to the emperor too.[106] However, as emphasized often, despite the imperial power in the church, the emperor is never superior to the whole body of believers. I intend to show this in terms of the difference of the scope of the power in the church, which can be exercised by the whole body of believers and by the emperor respectively. That is, for Marsilius, there is one power which the whole body of the believers can give to the priests but the emperor cannot. This is the coercive force which the priests are allowed to have. At this point, Marsilius seems to be ambivalent about the coercive power of the priest. As mentioned earlier, when differentiating eternal salvation from the sufficient life in this world, Marsilius maintains that since the former is not a matter of coerciveness,[107] the calling of the priest is the teaching of faith and that in this world, the priests cannot possess any coercive power. But, on the other hand, Marsilius implies that there is the possibility for the priest to have a coercive power, if he is authorised by the whole body of believers. The following passage indicates it:

> Nor does any bishop or pope have coercive jurisdiction over any priest or non priest in this world, unless it shall have been granted to him by the human legislator, who always has the power to revoke this jurisdiction...... especially in communities of the faithful.[108]

Earlier, Marsilius argued that coercive judgement in the church (i.e. excommunication), insofar as it is concerned with the present life, must be made by the whole body of the faithful or its weightier part or by the ruler by the authority of the legislator.[109] However, as the above passage says, Marsilius implies that the priests could have coercive jurisdiction which the whole people or the ruler by the authority of the legislator implements. At the same time, however, Marsilius' ambivalence about the priests' coercive power reinforces his belief in the whole body of the faithful as the sovereign entity in the church. Initially, he argues that the punishment of priests or the grant of authority can be exercised by Christ alone, the absolute head of the church.[110] By allowing the whole body of the faithful to give the jurisdictional power to the priest, Marsilius makes the power of the whole body of the believers the power which amounts to Christ's in the other world.

Marsilius' argument for the ecclesiastical sovereignty of the whole body of believers is further manifested in his idea of the general council. According to Marsilius, the general council is composed of all Christians and inherits the power of the whole body of believers.[111] The general council elected to act on behalf of the faithful people has the principal authority and makes decisions with regard to faith and the coercive authority for their observance. The observance of the ordinances which the general council enacts is binding on all men including the pope. Its authority is not confined to specific matters but extends to every concern of the church.[112] An individual pope could err, but the general council could never fail, because the authority of the general council is given by the Holy Spirit or the whole body of believers.[113] The general council truly acts for the faithful Christians, that is the church in its truest sense. In this respect, the council is a faithful delegate conveying the will of the whole body of the believers or of the faithful legislator.[114] Marsilius' discussion of the general council promotes nothing other than confirmation of the sovereignty of the whole body of the faithful in the ecclesiastical domain.

In Marsilius' thought, 'the whole body of faithful citizens' ('*universitas civium fidelium*') is the entity which is the final judge in dealing with matters in both the secular and the ecclesiastical domain. His philosophical principle 'the whole is greater than any of its parts taken separately' is valid in the church,[115] as well as in the temporal domain. For Marsilius, the power and jurisdiction, spiritual and temporal, is concentrated in the sovereign human legislator (*legislator humanus*), that is the faithful people (*fidelis*). In either domain, there was no question for Marsilius of an abdication of the people's sovereignty to the emperor. Both historically and theoretically speaking, the locus of the legislative power remains in the whole body of citizens: as he remarks, "the whole body of the believers or their weightier part cannot be misled either in civil affairs or in spiritual affairs."[116]

CONCLUSION: LAW, CITIZENSHIP, AND DEMOCRACY

The following contrast between two classic treatments is a good example of how evaluations of Marsilius' thought move in two directions. On the one hand, McIlwain writes:

> Most of the mistakes made in interpreting this interesting political treatise are the result of reading into it a meaning which was never there. There is nothing in it of democracy, nothing of majority rule, no "separation of powers."[1]

On the other hand, Poole says:

> The two books of the *Defensor Pacis* thus comprise...... the whole essence of the political and religious theory which separates modern times from the Middle Ages...... Marsiglio belongs to that rarest class of doctrinaires whom further ages may rightly look back upon as prophets.[2]

These interpretations offer guides which suggest to us different ways of reading a text. But in reading Marsilius, the absence of modern terms does not mean that it is not interesting from a modern point of view; conversely, the presence of modern ideas does not necessarily make a political thinker worthwhile reading. Either way we are forced to go back again to the questions with which we started this work: why and how can we attempt to understand Marsilius' thought in terms of political representation? Or simply why do we read Marsilius today; what does Marsilius' thought mean today and give to us?

Our attempt to answer this question requires first, that if we intend to understand Marsilius' thought, it is our duty to grasp what Marsilius argued and tackled through his texts. Through the preceding chapters we have explored Marsilius' conception of political representation together with the context in which contemporary issues associated with it were articulated. Further, in this conclusion I attempt to consider what my historical study on Marsilius' thought can suggest for our contemporary claims about political representation, which we practice today as our intellectual and political commitment. Many scholars on Marsilius find in him a relevance or contribution to modern democratic theory,[3] in particular for the purpose of explicating the origin of the theory or its influence or continuity.[4] In contrast, I intend to make some suggestions about why Marsilius' case for political representation has its own distinctive attractions and merits, and why it may still be possible to develop it coherently today.

To begin with, I need to point out Marsilius' notion of democracy. Marsilius, following Aristotle, explicitly distinguished republicanism from democracy: that is, whereas in republicanism every citizen participates, democracy is government by the *vulgus* alone, i. e. the multitude of the poor.[5] In this sense, for Marsilius republicanism is more inclusive than democracy.[6] In fact, as seen earlier, while like Aristotle, Marsilius defines polity as a temperate government in which "every citizen participates in some way in the government or in the deliberative function in turn according to his rank and ability or condition, for the common benefit and with the will or consent of the citizens," democracy, the opposite of polity, is "a government in which the masses or the multitude of the needy establish the government and rule alone, apart from the will or consent of the other citizens and not entirely for the common benefit according to proper proportion."[7]

Thus, despite sharing the same name for the form of rule, Marsilian democracy is to be distinguished from democracy today—the people's rule. In Marsilius' definition of democracy, we cannot see any current democratic element of political rule. What we call democracy today is similar to what Marsilius defines as the polity, that is a temperate government of republican form. Marsilius' argument for the people's rule starts from his definition of polity, not from a definition of democracy. Otherwise, these definitions might cause some confusion in understanding Marsilius' thought.

Today democracy is a form of state in which the people's rule is the standard for legitimate political authority. This indicates that the people is the sovereign entity which rules a state. This right of the people justifies its direct participation in the process of politics. Taking this characterisation of democracy for granted, we believe that although, for various reasons, the people's participation in politics is not always actualised in a modern representative democratic state, the locus of sovereignty in a state is still in the people. It signifies that the will of the people constitutes the basis of the special legitimacy and moral authority of representative government. Thus, at least at the level of its theorisation, political representation today incorporates the doctrine of popular sovereignty as an essential component of its theory.

On this basis, the scheme of political representation involves some elements of substitution of the wills or judgements of the representatives for those of the represented. Most modern interpreters of political representation see the validity of political representation in terms of the responsiveness between the represented and the representatives: this responsiveness is efficient when the representatives listen to the voters and do something on their behalf. Their common view, then, supposes that the aggregation of the interests of many particular constituencies, through the relationship between the two political actors, can yield the interests of the whole people in a state. On this more or less utilitarian understanding of public interests, political representation focuses on how to operate the representative government or how to work the representative's business once the people transfer their power to the representative.

However, I claim that for political representation to work as a legitimate scheme for public action, there should be more than this utilitarian calculation of the whole, which downplays the notion of the common good as the universal value. When the focus is on interest understood in this mechanical way as a basic theme which underlies political representation to the exclusion of an understanding of a good government for all, interests eventually degenerate into factional or particular interests. Indeed, political representation today is mostly concerned with technical issues concerning the use of election for political power, in the determinants of electoral victory, and in the conditions for the effective pursuit of interests. Such technical discussions hardly help to improve the well-being of the whole people. Contrary to the expectation of the modern interpreters of political representation (in particular Burke and Mill), the representative becomes in practice no more than a functional politician acting for his or her particular constituency, not for the whole people in a state. Moreover, as any political actors have in practice the weakness of human beings in general, the analysis of political representation in terms of human nature based on the capabilities of the representative or the represented,[8] is flawed. Seen in these narrow terms, political representation cannot reasonably be expected to function as a dependable scheme for good government.

At this point, Marsilius' conception of political representation is worth close attention. It too includes the relationship between the represented and the representative, but understands political representation as more than a matter of responsiveness between the political actors. Marsilius offers a broader perspective in identifying the fundamental aspects of political representation. These aspects are, first, the alienation of judgement; second, the location of the power to judge what is necessary and what is best for the common good;[9] third, the political implications of the transfer of power to the representative; fourth, the assessment of how the civil and political rights of a given people can be effectively secured through political representation. Let me sum up.

First, Marsilius' viewpoint of the necessity of the alienation of power as the scheme of political representation comes from the requirement of laws. According to Marsilius, law is right reason with which to control a civil community with proper proportion and therefore to maintain the common good of peace in a political association. The source of law, the standard of judgement of civil justice and benefit, is the whole body of citizens (*universitas civium*). This is because the people as the whole is superior to any individuals or groups, not only in respect of its numerical superiority but also of its moral competence and judgement. When particular views prevail over a civil community, there would not be law and the common good of peace, but instead a tyranny ruled by private interests.

However, as in modern theories of political representation, Marsilius recognises that for the reason of convenience or the political division of labour[10] the people can transfer the power to somebody, the *pars principans* in Marsilius' terminology. The *pars principans* mandated as a representative is to order civil acts on behalf of the people. But, for Marsilius, since the representative's power is given by the whole body of citizens, the representative is simply a part which the sovereign legislator establishes for peace in a political association. The representatives do not have any discretion in authorising what is willed by the people. The representatives know about the technical aspects of the affairs of state, but it is the people that has final authority over them. Accordingly, when the ruler as the representative transgresses laws or acts against justice, the people can check and depose him and then can resume its full power because the representatives' power is authorised by the people. Thus, the people's power is activated in the representative system, that is *after* appointing the representative. In this sense, for Marsilius, even though the alienation of the represented's power is necessary in the scheme of political representation, it does not necessarily follow that the people, after the transfer of power, cede their authority permanently to the representative. Since the people's grant of power to the representative is intended for the good working of government through its substitute and for nothing else, if the scheme of political representation does not work well, it need no longer be accepted. In that case authority can be returned to the represented and hence the sovereign power of the people continue to operate effectively. By doing so, Marsilius makes political representation work as a scheme for good government, which is beneficial to its citizen-body or the people as a whole.

This is a way in which Marsilius' conception of political representation is differentiated from those of the modern interpreters of political representation. That is, for the latter, the relationship between the represented and the representative by itself is efficient enough for the working of representative government. However, for Marsilius, such analysis of political representation in terms of the relationship is simply a constitutive element of the theory of political representation. What is more crucial to Marsilius is that for political representation to be a genuine scheme for public action the people must not lose their power and authority after the creation of the representative. To this end, the understanding of political representation in terms of the transfer of power is essential because, when the representatives cannot do their roles properly, the delegated power can be withdrawn by the people. Thus, by leaving the authority with which to control a state to the people even after the grant of the power to the representatives, Marsilius makes the people always remain the holder of the sovereign power in the exercise of political authority. In consequence, even though the act of instituting a ruler involves the citizens in alienating or in delegating the original sovereign authority, the alienation does not result in the forfeit of the people's power. The alienation of power is merely a way of temporarily transferring the people's power.

The interpretation of political representation in terms of the transfer of power is valid in understanding Marsilius' historical argument for the emperor. Sometimes, the emperor in Marsilius is regarded as the sole legislator. However, as we have shown, for Marsilius, on the bases of *lex regia* and *Italicum regnum*, the emperor in historical context is the equivalent of the legislator of the whole body of citizens. Moreover, in Marsilius' ecclesiology too, the whole body of believers is the key factor which has the sovereign power in the church. Thus, in Marsilius' view, the people as a whole is theoretically and historically proven to be right and therefore more powerful than any individual persons.

The substitution of individuals' judgement for authoritative collective decision-making as the nature of political representation has survived today. But, few any longer take note of the normative and fundamental issues of political representation as the authoritative and binding public action on behalf of the whole people, which has always been at the centre of the history of the idea of political representation. Insofar as democracy is the name for the good intentions of states which we want to persist and representative democracy aims to function as a desirable alternative to direct democracy, we should not give up asking whether political representation—modern constitutional representative democracy—really works for the public benefit of the people.

In fact, we observe today that it is never the people who decide the affairs of state and people are seldom the first element to be consulted when governmental decisions are going to be made. Some people or groups are excluded and isolated from political considerations. The people is not a political agent and their formal authority becomes notional. There is a sufficient justification for it: less because of the representative system itself, than because of the practical requirements for their own survival and the complicated considerations and quick judgement which political situations require, the people usually have great difficulties in participating in politics. Or, more effectively, because of the lack of ordinary people's professional knowledge, direct and active participation in politics is assigned to the professional politicians and political parties. But, with this justification, the opinion and decision of a few leading persons are imposed on the people, whose own will and judgement are disregarded. The existence of the people today is a political ideology intended to function for interest representation within the capitalist democratic state.[11] That is, in contemporary politics, in which the task of politics seems to be concentrated on articulating and resolving the particular interests of a constituency or a group without respect for the whole people, even a referendum as a political practice, which is based on the theory of popular sovereignty, very easily degenerates into a political performance which looks far from being a contribution to a political condition which is for the benefit of the people, including the whole range of groups or classes, or to good government in general.

Here, I suggest that Marsilius' case for political representation may in principle offer a coherent alternative approach to making political representation an effective scheme for authoritative and binding public action on behalf of the whole people. In particular, in our modern political community in which the professionalisation of career politics and the intensification of interests lobbying are dominating and there is little of a more genuinely democratic public space, Marsilius' conception of political representation, in which the power of the people, despite its internal variety, is the most trustworthy political entity on which a state should depend in moral and political judgements, needs to be considered. In maintaining this, however, it is important to grasp that Marsilius' conception of the people has different assumptions from those of the modern theory. That is, the Marsilian citizen-body, unlike the people today, is not inclusive of the whole range of the people because some people are excluded due to their lack of abilities to judge. Further, the people in the modern theory of political representation is considered on an individual basis in which the individual is the basic unit of the sovereignty of the people. In contrast, Marsilius' conception of the people has a very emphatic collective character. It does not completely develop its modern shape, but shows a great step forward beyond a medieval idea of sovereignty, in which the king was a sole agent to exercise public power. However, my emphasis is that Marsilius provides a justification for denying the elitist understanding of politics, i.e. that a few excellent people are better able than the whole body of citizens in morality and political judgement to maintain the good life in a civil community. What Marsilius asserts is that the task of politics is within the initiative of most ordinary people and this is the way in which to maintain the good management of a state for the whole people. For Marsilius, it would be a passive political idea that the people's right as citizens can be achieved through their participation in elections on a regular basis—by reelecting or not reelecting their representatives. Indeed, the good government for the representation of all can be possible in polities in which the people continue to have the power and authority of deciding affairs of state. That is, Marsilius' intention is not confined to the people's view being made known and expressed through their intermediaries in the process of deciding and implementing public affairs, but lies in the people's control over them—the permanent power which would not be withdrawn from it in his scheme of political representation.

To conclude, Marsilius rejects the depoliticisation and deauthorisation of ordinary citizens which are so central to modern interest-based visions of political process. By doing so, Marsilius provides a conception of political representation as a coherent system for public action, in which the people's role occupies the prime part - just the element which is conspicuously missing from the routine political science analysis of the representative politics of contemporary capitalist democracies. Hence, his conception of political representation provides us with a critical instrument for evaluating the ideological pretensions of modern representative democracy. I believe that this is what historical research on Marsilius' thought may offer to our contemporary theory of representative democracy.

NOTES

Introduction

1. R. Tuck, "The Contribution of History," in *Companion to Contemporary Political Philosophy*, ed. by Robert E. Goodin and Philip Pettit (Oxford: Blackwell, 1993), pp. 72–89. See also Tuck, "History of Political Thought," in *New Perspectives on Historical Writings*, ed. by Peter Burke (Cambridge: Polity Press, 1991), pp. 193–205.
2. For example, Peter H. Merkl, *Political Continuity and Change* (New York: Harper and Row, 1967); Mulford Q. Sibley, "The Place of Classical Theory in the Study of Politics," in *Approaches to the Study of Politics*, ed. by Roland Young (Chicago: University of Chicago Press, 1958), pp. 125–48; F. M. Watkins, "Political Theory as a Datum of Political Science," *ibid.*, pp. 148–55; Leonard Nelson, "What is the History of Philosophy?" *Ratio*, 4 (1962), pp. 22–35; A. Bloom, "Leo Strauss," *Political Theory*, 2 (1974), pp. 372–92.
3. For the important turning points for a new approach of history of political thought appearing in the late 1960s, see John Dunn, "The Identity of the History of Ideas," *Philosophy*, 43 (1968), pp. 85–116; Quentin Skinner, "Meaning and Understanding in the History of Ideas," *History and Theory*, 8 (1969), pp. 3–53. Before these articles of the late 1960s, a number of scholars had acknowledged the merits of a historical approach of this kind. The foremost example was R. G. Collingwood—see his *Autobiography* (Oxford: Oxford University Press, 1939). Another prominent recent example was John Pocock—see his "The History of Political Thought: A Methodological Enquiry," in *Philosophy, Politics and Society*, ed. by P. Laslett and W. G. Runciman, 2nd ser. (Oxford: Basil Blackwell, 1962), pp. 183–202.

4. Skinner, "Meaning and Understanding," repr. in *Meaning and Context: Quentin Skinner and His Critics*, ed. by James Tully (Cambridge: Polity Press, 1988), p. 30. Here and after I cite Skinner's article from Tully's book (pp. 29–67).
5. Concerning this so-called retrospective mind reading, see Donald R. Kelley, *Foundations of Modern Historical Scholarship* (New York: Columbia University Press, 1970), pp. x–xi.
6. Skinner, "Meaning and Understanding," pp. 63–4.
7. *Ibid.*, pp. 60–1.
8. *Ibid.*, p 64.
9. *Ibid.*, p. 58 and p. 64.
10. For example, C. B. Macpherson, *The Political Theory of Possessive Individualism* (Oxford: Clarendon Press, 1962).
11. Skinner, "Meaning and Understanding," p. 32.
12. Tuck's argument ("The Contribution of History," p. 86) that we still lack a fully developed and coherent account of why historical enquiry should matter is stimulating enough to make us think about these issues.
13. Skinner, "Meaning and Understanding," p. 67. Cf. For Skinner's recent change of his position about the particularism of the context approach, see Skinner, *Liberty before Liberalism* (Cambridge: Cambridge University Press, 1998).
14. See Tuck, "The Contribution of History," p. 85; Pocock, "The History of Political Thought," pp. 198–201.
15. Pocock, *ibid.*, p. 183.
16. See Dunn, "The History of Political Theory," in *The History of Political Theory and Other Essays* (Cambridge: Cambridge University Press, 1996), p. 26.
17. H. J. Laski, "Political Theory in the Later Middle Ages," in *CMH*, VIII (Cambridge: Cambridge University Press, 1936), p. 629; R. L. Poole, *Illustrations of the History of Medieval Thought and Learning* (London: S. P. C. K., 1932), p. 240; C. W. Previté-Orton, "Marsiglio of Padua, Doctrines," in *EHR*, XXXVIII (1923), p. 2; "Marsilius of Padua," in *the Proceedings of the British Academy*, 21 (1935), p. 137; J. B. Morrall, *Political Thought in Medieval Times*, 3rd edn (London: Hutchinson, 1971), pp. 112–3.
18. R. W. and A. J. Carlyle, *A History of Medieval Political Theory in the West* (London: William Blackwood & Sons Ltd., 1903–36), Vol. VI, p. 9. Also see C. H. McIlwain, *The Growth of Political Thought in the West* (New York: Macmillan, 1932), p 304 and p. 307; Michael J. Wilks, *The Problem of Sovereignty in the Late Middle Ages The Papal Monarchy with Augustinus Triumphus and the Publicists* (Cambridge: Cambridge University University Press, 1963), p. 196; Leo Strauss, "Marsilius of Padua," in *The History of Political Philosophy*, ed. by Strauss and J. Cropsey (Chicago: Chicago University Press, 1964), pp. 235–38.
19. G. de Lagarde, *La Naissance de l'Esprit Laïque au Déclin du Moyen Age, Vol. I: Bilan de XIII Siècle*, 3rd edn (Louvain: Éditions E. Nauwelaerts, 1956), p. 157.
20. *Ibid.*, p. 188; Lagarde, *ibid.*, *Vol. III: Le Defensor Pacis* (Louvain: Éditions Nauwelaerts, 1970), pp. 178–89.
21. Alan Gewirth, *Marsilius of Padua, Vol. I. Marsilius of Padua and Medieval Political Philosophy*, (New York: Columbia University Press, 1951).

22. For example, Gewirth's interpretation that Marsilius did not consider the universal state to be related to a *civitas*, is caused by his lack of historical understanding of the period. See Gewirth, *Marsilius of Padua*, pp. 127–8.
23. J. Quillet, *La Philosophie Politique de Marsilie de Padoue* (Paris; Librairie Philosophique J. Vrin, 1970), p. 48.
24. *Ibid.*, p. 75.
25. *Ibid.*, p. 44.
26. See Gewirth, *Marsilius of Padua*, Vol. I, Ch. 5.
27. Quillet, *La Philosophie Politique de Marsile de Padoue*, p. 85.
28. Cary J. Nederman, *Community and Consent: the Secular Political Theory of Marsiglio of Padua's Defensor Pacis* (Lanham, Md.: Rowman & Littlefield, 1995), p. 3.

Chapter 1

1. John S. Mill, 'Considerations on Representative Government,' in *Collected Works of J. S. Mill*, ed. by J. M. Robson (Toronto: University of Toronto Press, 1977), Vol. XIX, p. 422 (hereafter referred to as *Considerations*).
2. The term political representation connotes a more general category than representative democracy. I regard representative democracy as the dominant version of contemporary political representation, because representative democracy as a state form is now the most influential form of political representation. On representative democracy in this sense, see Paul Hirst, *Representative Democracy and Its Limits* (Cambridge: Polity Press, 1990), Ch. II. In this book I more often use 'political representation' as a general term, in particular when talking of the context of the Middle Ages when Marsilius was writing, because 'representative democracy' or 'republican democracy' in that period is clearly anachronistic.
3. *The Compact Edition of the Oxford English Dictionary* (Oxford: Oxford University Press, 1971), Vol. II, p. 2498.
4. Pitkin, *The Concept of Representation* (Berkeley: University of California Press, 1967).
5. Griffths and Wollheim, "How Can One Person Represent Another?" *Aristotelian Society, Supplementary*, Vol. XXXIV (1960), pp. 187–224.
6. For example, in the fourteenth century, the pope, the cardinals and priests were said to represent Christ, because they bore his image and took his place by succession. See Lagarde (1937), "L'idèe de Représentation dans les Œuvres de Guillaume d'Ockham," *International Committee of the Historical Sciences, Bulletin*, XI (December, 1937), pp. 429–30.
7. Griffths, "How Can One Person Represent Another?" pp. 188–90.
8. Ernest Barker, *Essays on Government* (Oxford: Clarendon Press, 1951), pp. 199–200 and pp. 229–30.
9. Burke, 'Speech on Fox's East India Bill (1783),' in *The Works of the Right Honourable Edmund Burke*, new edn, ed. by W. King and F. Laurence (London: Rivington, 1826–7), Vol. IV, p. 11.
10. Burke, 'Speech on Moving his Resolutions for Conciliation with the Colonies (1775),' in *The Works of Burke*, Vol. III, p. 110–1; 'Reflections on the Revolution in France (1790),' in *The Works of Burke*, Vol. V, pp. 122–3.

11. Burke, 'Reflections,' p. 124.
12. Burke, 'Speech to the Electors of Bristol at the Conclusion of the Poll (1774),' in *The Works of Burke*, Vol. III, pp. 18–9.
13 *Ibid.*, p. 18.
14. Burke, 'A Letter to the Sheriff of Bristol on the Affairs of America (1777),' in *The Works of Burke*, Vol. III, p. 180.
15. *Ibid.*, p. 183.
16. Burke, 'Speech on the Reform of the Representation in the House of the Commons (1782),' in *The Works of Burke*, Vol. X, p. 97.
17. Burke, 'An Appeal from the New to the Old Whigs (1791),' in *The Works of Burke*, Vol. VI, p. 216.
18. *Ibid.*, p. 216.
19. *Ibid.*, pp. 210–1.
20. *Ibid.*
21. However, the division between "men" and "the public" in Burke is not necessarily the dichotomy between natural state and civil society, because in a civil society there still exist "men."
22. Burke, 'Reflections,' pp. 120–23.
23. Burke, 'First Letter on the Proposals for Peace (1796),' in *The Works of Burke*, Vo . VIII, pp. 140–1.
24. Burke, 'Reflections,' pp. 121–2.
25. Burke, 'An Appeal from the New to the Old Whigs,' p. 218.
26. Actually, this criticism of Burke would be reinforced, if we consider his case for natural aristocracy and virtual representation which take the conventional order of society for granted and assume the coordination between various elements of the people. For these ideas, see *ibid.*; 'A Letter to Sir H. Langrishe, Bart. M.P. (1792),' in *The Works of Burke*, Vol. VI, p. 360.
27. Burke, 'Speech on the Reform of the Representation,' p. 97.
28. Burke, 'Speech to the Electors of Bristol,' p. 20.
29. Burke, 'Reflections,' p. 122.
30. In this respect, as we shall see later, Burke's conception of public utility differs from those of Bentham and Mill which presume that the aggregation of individuals' utility leads to the utility of the whole. For Burke's understanding of public utility, see his 'Reflections' and 'The Thoughts and Details on Scarcity (1795),' in *The Works of Burke*, Vol. VII, pp. 373–419.
31. Burke, 'Speech to the Electors of Bristol,' p. 20; 'Speech on the Reform of the Representation,' p. 97.
32. On the greatest happiness principle, see R. Harrison, *Bentham* (London: Routledge & Kegan Paul, 1983), Ch. 7.
33. Bentham, 'Constitutional Code,' in *The Collected Works of Jeremy Bentham*, ed. by F. Rosen and J. H. Burns (Oxford: Clarendon Press, 1983), Vol. I. p. 2. Rosen and L. J. Hume say that the *Code* is "the classic utilitarian text on representative democracy" and "a culminating product of his many years' work on jurisprudence and codification." See Rosen, *Jeremy Bentham and Representative Democracy* (Oxford: Clarendon Press,

1983), p. 2; Hume, *Bentham and Bureaucracy* (Cambridge: Cambridge University Press, 1981), p. 1.

34. Bentham, *An Introduction to the Principles of Morals and Legislation*, ed. by J. Burns and H. L. A. Hart (Oxford: Clarendon Press, 1996), p. 12.
35. Bentham, *Code*, Ch. III, Art. 1, p. 25.
36. *Ibid.*, Ch. V, Section I, Art. 1–3, p. 29.
37. Bentham avoided the use of the word 'representative' and, instead, used the word 'deputy,' because the word 'representative' was less apposite and not exclusively characteristic. In the concerns of individuals, for example, in the field of private right, many are the cases in which it is necessary that one person should act on behalf of another, without having been appointed by him for that purpose: witness guardians of orphans, administrators of property interests, and the like (*ibid.*, Ch. V, Section 2, Art. 2, p. 30). However, for the sake of terminological consistency, hereafter I continue to use the word 'representative.'
38. See Rosen, *Bentham*, p. 187.
39. Cf. Hume, *Bentham and Bureaucracy*, pp. 244–5. Hume's interpretation is that Bentham's government is a trust for the benefit of the people.
40. Cf. Rosen, *Bentham*, pp. 232–6.
41. Bentham, *First Principles Preparatory to Constitutional Code*, ed. by P. Schofield (Oxford: Clarendon Press, 1989), p. 270; *Code*, Ch. VI, Section 24, Art. 12, p. 70.
42. Bentham, *Code*, Ch. V, Section 4, Art. 4, p. 36.
43. *Ibid.*, Ch. IX, Section 15, Art. 34, p. 304.
44. On the public opinion tribunal, see *ibid.*, Ch. V, Sections 4–5.
45. *Ibid.*, Ch. VI, Section I, Art. 10, pp. 43–4.
46. *Ibid.*, Ch. VI, Section I, Art. 9 and 11–2, pp. 43–4.
47. Bentham supposes that the voters can be manipulated in many ways. However, he thinks that with secret voting, the voters can secure their right to choose the representative because, despite the voters' selling of their vote, they can vote as they will in secrecy. In addition, secret voting can be a security for good government because it allows the best men to be elected. See Bentham, *Radical Reform Bill*, cited from Rosen, *Bentham*, p. 186.
48. Bentham, *Code*, Ch. VI, Section 25, Art. 2, pp. 72–91. Because Bentham is in doubt that representatives elected for a limited term can act always for the interests of the people, he presents a system according to which the members of the legislature cannot be reelected for a certain time.
49. *Ibid.*, Ch. V, Section 3, Art. 4–10, pp. 33–5; Ch. VI, Section 28, pp. 111–14. 'Legislation penal judicatory' is a security for checking members of the legislative, in particular the prime minister, the justice minister. This system for removal from office and eventual punishment applies to all governmental officials.
50. Bentham, *An Introduction to the Principles of Morals and Legislation*, p. 13; *First Principles Preparatory to Code*, p. 3.
51. Mill, *Considerations*, p. 383 and p. 390.
52. *Ibid.*, p. 390.
53. It is on this understanding that Mill regards the operation of government as an agency of national education. *Ibid.*, p. 393.

54. *Ibid.*, p. 405.
55. *Ibid.*, p. 403.
56. *Ibid.*, p. 392.
57. *Ibid.*, pp. 404–5 and p. 412.
58. *Ibid.*, pp. 383–4 and p. 490.
59. For Mill's distinction between various kinds of interests, see *ibid.*, pp. 444–5; Dennis F. Thompson, *John Stuart Mill and Representative Government* (Princeton: Princeton University Press, 1976), p. 15, n. 5.
60. Mill, *Considerations*, pp. 381–2.
61. *Ibid.*, p. 380.
62. *Ibid.*, p. 379.
63. *Ibid.*, p. 381.
64. *Ibid.*, p. 412. According to Mill, direct democracy is in practice not feasible except in a tiny town.
65. Mill, *Considerations*, Ch. III, in particular p. 399 and p. 412.
66. *Ibid.*, p. 470.
67. *Ibid.*, pp. 470–2. Mill argues that because the persons have not demonstrated even the most minimal interest in taking care of themselves, let alone an interest in the general good, they are excluded.
68. To redress this evil, Mill suggests the system of proportional representation. For it, *ibid.*, pp. 448–50 and p. 515.
69. See *ibid.*, p. 447 and p. 467. For example, Mill notes that a numerical majority of poorer citizens may well enact laws weakening the security of property and reduce economic incentives to produce, so violating the rights of a wealthy minority. Likewise, the interests of a ruling class is to assume themselves an endless variety of unjust privileges at the expense of the people (see *ibid.*, pp. 441–2). In either case, Mill says that this is not in the real interest of the whole society.
70. *Ibid.*, pp. 446–8. On Mill's view of true democracy and false democracy, see *ibid*, Ch. VII.
71. Mill, *Considerations*, p. 527.
72. *Ibid.*, p. 457 and p. 473. Mill was worried that in the circumstance in which the great majority of voters in most countries were in practice manual labourers, universal suffrage would produce those dangers.
73. *Ibid.*, p. 455 and p. 506.
74. *Ibid.*, pp. 475–9 and p. 506. To find a criterion for determining who are entitled to extra votes, Mill suggests some sorts of examination or a sufficient standard of education (see *ibid.*, p. 475 and p. 508).
75. *Ibid.*, pp. 508–10.
76. *Ibid.*, p. 390.
77. Mill, *Considerations*, pp. 441–6.
78. For example, there are the idea of the main checks to popular power exercised in the democratic assembly (see *ibid.*, pp. 501–3), the rejection of the doctrine of parliaments of short duration (*ibid.*, p. 191) and the opposition to the secret ballot (*ibid.*, pp. 489–90).
79. On a politics of trust, see Dunn, "Trust and Political Agency," in *Interpreting Political Responsibility* (Cambridge: Polity Press, 1990), pp. 26–44.

80. Cf. Mill's preference for the role of the representative in 'Rationale of Representation (1835),' *Collected Works of Mill*, Vol. XVIII, pp. 23–4 and pp. 39–41; 'De Tocqueville on Democracy in America (1835),' *ibid.*, pp. 72–3.
81. On the mandate-independence controversy, see Pitkin, *The Concept of Representation*, Ch. 7. See also S. E. Finer, *The History of Government from the Earliest Times*, Vol. II (Oxford: Oxford University Press, 1997), p. 1033.
82. Thompson, *John Stuart Mill and Representative Government*, p. 112.
83. For example, Suzanne Berger points out that in political representation today, those classical issues of representation remain as major themes: the relations between leader and members, and the assessment of who among the various rival interpreters of the group's interests knows best. *Organising Interests in Western Europe: Pluralism, Corporatism, and the Transformation of Politics*, ed. by S. Berger (Cambridge: Cambridge University Press, 1981), p. 10.
84. For these issues, see Bernard Manin, *The Principles of Representative Government* (Cambridge: Cambridge University Press, 1997); Pizzorno, A. "Interests and Parties in Pluralism," in *Organising Interests in Western Europe*, pp. 247–84.

Chapter 2

1. For this view, see R. and A. Carlyle, *A History of Medieval Political Theory*, Vol. V, pp. 464–74; Antony Black, *Political Thought in Europe 1250–1450* (Cambridge: Cambridge University Press, 1992); Brian Tierney, *Religion, Law and the Growth of Constitutional Thought 1150–1650* (Cambridge: Cambridge University Press, 1982); C. H. McIwain, "Medieval Estates," in *CMH*, VII, p. 679. On the other hand, for the view that the modern conception of political representation has no relation to that of the medieval period, see Pitkin, "Appendix on Etymology," in *The Concept of Representation*, pp. 241–52; Harvey C. Mansfield, Jr, "Modern and Medieval Representation," in *Nomos X: Representation*, ed. by J. R. Pennock and J. W. Chapman (New York: Atherton, 1968), pp. 55–82. In contrast to these two views, Arthur P. Monahan and Gaines Post find relevance for the medieval and the modern conceptions of political representation through featuring their different aspects. See Monahan, *Consent, Coercion and Limit: The Medieval Origins of Parliamentary Democracy* (Kingston: McGill-Queens University Press, 1987); Post, *Studies in Medieval Legal Thought: Public Law and State 1100–1322* (Princeton: Princeton University Press, 1964).
2. Historically speaking, medieval assemblies had a variety of forms, characters or functions and structures, differing from country to country. Here, what it indicates is the widespread phenomenon of gatherings of the community as a whole held in the twelfth and thirteenth century to discuss public affairs, whether in the form of a council or parliament or court of justice. For various kinds of medieval assemblies in European context, see Antonio Marongiu, *Medieval Parliaments, A Comparative Study*, trans. by S. J. Woolf (London: Eyre & Spottiswoode, 1968), pp. 19–33 and Parts II–III.
3. Ullmann, *Principles of Government and Politics in the Middle Ages*, 4th edn (London: Methuen, 1978), pp. 19–21. Corresponding to Ullmann's descending theme, Fritz Kern maintains that in the early Middle Ages the monarchical form of government, that is kingship, was believed to derive from God, not from the people. Kern, *Kingship*

and Law in the Middle Ages, trans. by S. B. Chrimes (Oxford: Basil Blackwell, 1939), p. 5. On the other hand, taking Ullmann's ascending thesis, Kenneth Pennington sees its emergence in the twelfth century. The mainstream of legal thought in this period says that laws are established through promulgation and validated by the approval of the people. Pennington, "Law, Legislative Authority and Theories of Government, 1150–1300," in *CHMPT*, ed. by Burns (Cambridge: Cambridge University Press, 1988), p. 424–25. In addition, Skinner argues that in the late twelfth and the early thirteenth centuries the emperor is said to have the authority to make laws, but by the end of twelfth century many glossators, with the *de facto* independence of the Italian cities, supported the ascending thesis for the autonomy of the cities and their republican way of life. Skinner, "Political Philosophy," in *CHRP*, ed. by C. B. Schmmit, Q. Skinrer and E. Kessler (Cambridge: Cambridge University Press, 1988), pp. 390–1.

4. Ullmann, *Principles of Government*, p. 21.
5. See E. H. Kantorowicz, *The King's Two Bodies* (Princeton: Princeton University Press, 1957).
6. Gierke, *Political Theories of the Middle Ages*, trans. by F. W. Maitland (Cambridge: Cambridge University Press, 1987), p. 62.
7. Lord names this medieval representation parliamentary monarchy or quasi-constitutionalism, which continued from the thirteenth to the seventeenth century. He states that the development of the representative system and parliaments was one of the greatest achievements of the Middle Ages. Lord, "The Parliaments of the Middle Ages and the Early Modern Period," *Catholic Historical Review*, XVI (1930), p. 125. Similarly, R. and A. Carlyle argued that the development of the representative of the community in the Spanish *Cortes* or English parliaments or French États-Généraux signified that the principle was assured that the king was bound by law, the embodiment of the life and will of the community (see their *A History of Medieval Political Theory*, Vol. V, pp. 464–74). See also Maude V. Clarke, *Medieval Representation and Consent* (London: Longman, Green & Co., 1936), p. 5.
8. Pitkin makes the etymological point that it was not until 1595 that we find an example of 'represent' meaning specifically 'to act for someone as his authorized agent or deputy.' Pitkin, *The Concept of Representation*, p. 243.
9. McIlwain, "Medieval Estates," p. 689; Helen M. Cam, *Liberties and Communities* (Cambridge: Cambridge University Press, 1944), Ch. 15; A. F. Pollard, *The Evolution of Parliament* (London: Longman, Green & Co., 1926), p. 109 and pp. 158–9. These scholars say that in the early period of medieval assembly the crucial role of the representatives was to bind their communities to pay taxes which were decided by the king. Later on, they gradually began to demand from the king what the communities wanted before consenting to taxes.
10. For detailed functions of the representative assemblies, see Lord, "The Parliaments," p. 128 and pp. 141–2; Finer, *The History of Government*, pp. 1037–8.
11. Lord, "The Parliaments," p. 141. Also, on the actual power relationship between these two political entities, see Finer, *The History of Government*, p. 1036–9. Finer argues that, generally speaking, the weaker the monarch the stronger the power of the assembly
12. Gierke, *Political Theories*, p. 67. Cf. Monahan, *Consent, Coercion and Limit*, p. 114.

13. See Lord, "Parliaments," p. 143; Finer, *The History of Government*, pp. 1039–49; Marongiu, *Medieval Parliaments*, p. 226–7.
14. Even by the fifteenth century, the knights, burgesses and the members of the Commons were named as attorneys or procurators of their communities, not as their representatives. See Cam, *Liberties and Communities*, Ch. 15–16; S. Chrimes, *English Constitutional Ideas in the Fifteenth Century* (Cambridge: Cambridge University Press, 1936), pp. 131–3.
15. On consent as a source of political legitimacy in modern theory of democratic polity, see Patrick Riley, "How Coherent is the Social Contract Tradition?" *Journal of the History of Ideas*, 34 (1975), pp. 543–62, in particular p. 543 and p. 551.
16. Tierney, *Religion, Law and the Growth of Constitutional Thought*, pp. 40–2; Clarke, *Medieval Representation and Consent*, p. 267.
17. The *Decretum* of Gratian written about 1140 is said to be the first successful effort at a synthesis of church law. See Monahan, *Consent, Coercion, and Limit*, p. 81: Robert L. Benson, *The Bishop-Elect, A Study in Medieval Ecclesiastical Office* (Princeton: Princeton University Press, 1968), p. 23. For an excellent study on Gratian's work, see Stanley Chodorow, *Christian Political Theory and Church Politics in the Mid-Twelfth Century: The Ecclesiology of Gratian's Decretum* (Berkeley: University of California Press, 1972).
18. Monahan, *Consent, Coercion and Limit*, p. 98.
19. Benson, *The Bishop-Elect*, p. 27.
20. For the debate about Gratian's view of the laity's participation in episcopal election, see Chodorow, *Christian Political Theory and Church Politics*, pp. 200–3, in particular p. 201, n. 26.
21. See Gratian, *Decretum*, Dist. lxiii. c. 25.
22. Post, *Studies in Medieval Legal Thought*, p. 112.
23. See Marongiu, *Medieval Parliaments*, p. 32.
24. Post, *Studies in Medieval Legal Thought*, p. 111.
25. Monahan, *Consent, Coercion and Limit*, p. 131. For example, even consent with full power arose from an extraordinary demand by the king for a subsidy (see Post, *Studies in Medieval Legal Thought*, p. 111).
26. For this argument, Post, *ibid.*, pp. 310–414; Kern, *Kingship and Law in the Middle Ages*, Part I; Kantorowicz, *The King's Two Bodies*, pp. 336–83.
27. A law of Justinian, *Code* 5.59.52, cited in Post, *ibid.*, p. 164. Fundamental research on this principle can be found in Post, *ibid.*, Part I, Ch. IV; Yves M. J. Congar, "*Quod Omnes Tangit, ab Omnibus Tractari et Approbari Debet*," in *Revue Historique de Droit Français et Étranger*, 4th ser., 36 (1958), pp. 210–59.
28. Monahan, *Consent, Coercion and Limit*, p. 98.
29. *Ibid.*, p. 100.
30. Finer, *The History of Government*, p. 1030.
31. Post, *Studies in Medieval Legal Thought*, p. 175.
32. Tierney argues that q.o.t. was adapted by the canonists to express a doctrine of consent in the ecclesiastical sphere. Tierney, *Religion, Law and the Growth of Constitutional Thought*, p. 24.
33. Monahan, *Consent, Coercion and Limit*, p. 102.
34. Post, *Studies in Medieval Legal Thought*, pp. 109–10.
35. For examples of its use, see *ibid.*, pp. 89–90.

36. *Ibid.*, p. 169.
37. Monahan, *Consent, Coercion and Limit*, p. 102.
38. Monahan, *ibid.*; Post, *Studies in Medieval Legal Thought*, p. 178. Cf. Pitkin, *The Concept of Representation*, p. 245. Presuming that parliament was a court rather than a legislative agency, Pitkin says that "parliament is essentially a legal fiction that parties who have legal rights at stake in a judicial action are entitled to be present or at least consulted in its decision." By contrast, Marongiu argues that the assembly or parliament was more than merely a legal fiction, that is it was the political representative body of the entire community to exercise constitutional powers. Marongiu, *Medieval Parliaments*, pp. 225–6.
39. Post, *Studies in Medieval Legal Thought*, pp. 175–6.
40. Monahan, *Consent, Coercion and Limit*, p. 87.
41. Cf. For the interpretation that this maxim appears to be evidence of the constitutional principle which sees the popular consent as the source of political legitimacy, see Marongiu, "The Theory of Democracy and Consent in the Fourteenth Century," in *Lordship and Community in Medieval Europe*, ed. by F. L. Cheyette (New York: Holt, Rinehart and Winston, 1968), pp. 404–14.
42. Monahan, *Consent, Coercion and Limit*, p. 110 and p. 127.
43. *Ibid.*, pp. 124–6. For an appreciation of *plena potestas* by legists and canonists, see Post, *Studies in Medieval Legal Thought*, pp. 95–102.
44. Post, *ibid.*, p. 93; Tierney, *Religion, Law and the Growth of Constitutional Thought*, pp. 23–4.
45. According to Post, by 1300, it was common for representatives with full powers to be sent to assemblies, whether ecclesiastical councils or high courts and councils of princes—for example, to the English parliament by 1268, to the Cortes of Aragon by 1307, and to the French États-Généraux in 1302. See Post, *ibid.*, pp. 109–10.
46. For the former view, see J. G. Edwards, "The *Plena Potestas* of English Parliament Representatives," in *Oxford Essays in Medieval History Presented to H. E. Salter*, ed. by J. Jolliffe (Oxford: Clarendon Press, 1934); McIlwain, "Medieval Estates," pp. 679–80; Clarke, *Medieval Representation and Consent*, p. 291. For the examples of the latter, see McIlwain, "Medieval Estates," p. 686; Post, *Studies in Medieval Legal Thought*, p. 111 and p. 119.
47. Lord, "The Parliaments," p. 128 and p. 141; Edwards, "The *Plena Potestas*," pp. 146–7; McIwain, "Medieval Estates," p. 678.
48. T. F. T. Plucknett, "Parliament," in *The English Government at Work, 1327–1336*, Vol. I, ed. by J. F. Willard and W. A. Morris (Cambridge, Mass.: The Medieval Academy of America, 1940), p. 101; Monahan, *Consent, Coercion and Limit*, pp. 125–6. For illustrations to show that the full powers are not the same as the absolute power of the representatives from the entire community in Italy or Spain, see Marongiu, *Medieval Parliaments*, p. 231.
49. See Lords, "The Parliaments," pp. 127–8; Post, *Studies in Medieval Legal Thought*, p. 115 and p. 119; Marongiu, *Medieval Parliaments*, pp. 223–4.
50. However, Post argues that in contrast to other European countries, in north Italy, due to the independence of the cities from the imperial authority, the *plena potestas* was not conceived with reference to consent for the emperor. Post, *ibid.*, p. 124. Cf. Marongiu who argues that from the time of the diet by Frederick Barbarossa in 1158 the representatives continued to attend imperial curias. This implies the close connection between the representatives of the cities and the emperors (see his *Medieval Parliaments*, pp. 27–8). More specifically,

on the Italian assemblies in the twelfth and thirteenth centuries, see Marongiu, *ibid*., pp. 109–27. We shall deal with this issue of the relationship between the city and the emperor in northern Italy in Chapter 5 below.

Chapter 3

1. Marsilius of Padua, *Defensor Pacis*, ed. by C. W. Previté-Orton (Cambridge: Cambridge University Press, 1928); *Defensor Pacis* (hereafter referred as *DP*), trans. by A. Gewirth (New York: Columbia University Press, 1956), II. xxiii. 11. Throughout my dissertation, I use the English translation of *DP*, but when necessary for more accurate understanding of Marsilius I cite the Latin text as well.
2. *DP*, II. xxiii. 11.
3. A. P. Monahan, "Introduction," in John of Paris, *On Royal and Papal Power*, trans. by Monahan (New York: Columbia University Press, 1974), p. xvi.
4. For further details of the conflict, see W. T. Waugh, "Germany: Lewis the Bavarian," in *CMH*, VII, pp. 118–28; Black, *Political Thought in Europe*, pp. 54–6.
5. For example, the first papal process which John XXII issued against Louis on 8 October 1323 provides us with a clue about the issues of the conflict concerning the relation between the two authorities. Louis was threatened with excommunication under the following headings: 'i) though his election as king of the Romans had been made *in discordia*, he had dared to assume the royal title without papal approval; ii) he had performed acts of administration in the realm and the empire, although the empire was vacant and its administration consequently pertained to the pope; iii) he had shown favour to the Visconti of Milan, who had been condemned for heresy, and to various other rebels against the church.' See '*Iohannis XXII, Papae Primus Processus Contra Ludewicum Regem*,' in *MGH*, *Constitutiones et Acta Publica Imperatorum et Regum*, V (Hanover, 1909), p. 617. Translation is from H. S. Offler, "Empire and Papacy: the Last Struggle," *TRHS*, 5th ser., 6 (1956), pp. 23–4. On the development of the controversy, see Wilks, *The Problem of Sovereignty*, pp. 233–53; R. and A. Carlyle, A *History of Medieval Political Theory*, Vol. IV and Vol. V, Part II.
6. Wilks, *The Problem of Sovereignty*, p. 237. Cf. McIlwain, *The Growth of Political Thought*, p. 313.
7. As Monahan argues, study of the history of church-state relations, like that of other subjects, exhibits two distinct but related facets. First, its factual side, the historical data concerning the actual relationships between ecclesiastical and political circumstances. Second, a theoretical, ideological side which let both exist as concrete entities. See Monahan, "Introduction," p. xi. That is, theories as to what should be the proper relationship between church and state too are in a real sense historical facts to be considered by the scholar who studies the problem of church-state relations, which reminds us of Skinner's contextual approach again. It is with this set of historical facts that I am concerned in this chapter as well as in other chapters of Part II.
8. I owe the distinction of the powers in the papal-hierocractic theory to Wilks. See his "*Papa est Nomen Jurisdictionis*: Augustinus Triumphus and the Papal Vicariate of Christ, Part I," in *Journal of Theological Studies*, N.S. 8 (1957), pp. 71–91, in particular pp. 75–9.

9. Cf. Gratian who saw the *officium* as the possession of the sacramental power itself, namely of 'order.' Chodorow, *Christian Political Theory and Church Politics*, pp. 155–8.
10. Wilks, "*Papa est Nomen Jurisdictionis*," pp. 72–3. According to Wilks, the idea of the pope as the vicar of Christ to justify the absolute power of the pope in the church was not common until about 1150. See *ibid*, p. 74.
11. Watt, *The Theory of Papal Monarchy in the Thirteenth Century: The Contribution of the Canonists* (London: Burns & Oates, 1965), p. 4.
12. *Decretum*, Dist. xcvi. c. 10, *Corpus Iuris Canonici* I, ed. by A. Friedberg (Graz, repr. 1959), col. 340: '*Duo sunt quippe, inperator auguste, quibus principaliter hic mundus regitur: auctoritas sacra Pontificum, et regalis potestas. In quibus tanto grauius est pondus sacerdotum, quanto etiam pro ipsis regibus hominum in diuino sunt reddituri examine rationem.*'
13. Wilks, *The Problem Of Sovereignty*, p. 233. Cf. Cecil N. S. Woolf, *Bartolus of Sassoferrato: His Position in the History of Medieval Political Thought* (Cambridge: Cambridge University Press, 1913), pp. 53–7. However, how actually persuasive the 'Gelasian doctrine' is as a medieval category, is a controversial issue. On this, see Watt, *The Theory of Papal Monarchy*, p. 11.
14. '*Solitae* (Decretals i.33.6),' *Corpus Iuris Canonici* II, col. 196-8: '*Ad firmamentum igitur coeli, hoc est universalis ecclesiae, fecit Deus duo magna luminaria, id est, duas magnas instituit dignitates, quae sunt pontificalis auctoritas, et regalis potestas. Sed illa, quae praeest diebus id est, spiritualibus, major est; quae vero carnalibus, minor, ut, quanta est inter solem et lunam, tanta inter pontifices et reges differentia cognoscatur.*'
15. For more, see *Per Venerabilem* (Decretals iv.17.13) and *Novit* (Decretals ii.1.13). Cf Watt, *The Theory of Papal Monarchy*, p. 56.
16. Matthew 18:15.
17. '*Novit*,' *Corpus Iuris Canonici* II, col. 243: '*Non ergo putet aliquis, quod iurisdictionem aut potestatem illustris regis Francorum perturbare aut minuere intendamus, quum ipse iurisdictionem et potestatem nostram nec velit nec debeat etiam impedire, quumque iurisdictionem propriam non sufficiamus explere, cur alienam usurpare vellemus? Sed quum Dominus dicat in evangelio: si peccaverit in te frater tuus, vade et corripe eum inter te et ipsum solum. Si te audierit, lucratus eris fratrem tuum...... Quod si non audierit eos, dic ecclesiae.*' The translation is Tierney's. *The Crisis of Church and State 1050–1300* (Englewood Cliffs, N.J.: Prentice-Hall, 1980), p. 134.
18. *Ibid.*, col. 243: '*Non enim intendimus judicare de feudo, cuius ad ipsum spectat iudicium, nisi forte iuri communi per speciale privilegium vel contrariam consuetudinem aliquid sit detractum, sed decernere de peccato, cuius ad nos pertinet sine dubitatione censura, quam in quemlibet exercere possumus et debemus.*'
19. Generally, the decretal *Per Venerabilem* is regarded as Innocent's most comprehensive statement on the relationship between *sacerdotium* and *regnum*. Pennington, "Pope Innocent III's Views on Church and State: A Gloss to *Per Venerabilem*," in *Law, Church and Society: Essays in Honor of Stephen Kuttner*, ed. by Pennington and C. Somerville (Philadelphia: Pennsylvania University Press, 1977), p. 50.
20. '*Per Venerabilem*,' *Corpus Iuris Canonici* II, col. 715–6: '*Eius vicarius, qui est sacerdos in aeternum secundum ordinem Melchisedech, constitutus a Deo iudex vivorum et mortuorum. Tria quippe distinguit iudicia: primum inter sanguinem et sanguinem, per quod criminale intelligitur et civile; ultimum inter lepram et lepram, per quod ecclesiasticum et criminale notatur; medium inter*

causam et causam, quod ad utrumque refertur, tam ecclesiasticum quam civile, in quibus quum aliquid fuerit difficile, vel ambiguum, ad iudicium est sedis apostolicae recurrendum.'

21. *Novit*, col. 242–4: '*Quum enim non humanae constitutioni, sed divinae legi potius innitamur, quia potestas nostra non est ex homine, sed ex Deo: nullus qui sit sanae mentis ignorat, quin ad officium nostrum spectet de quocunque mortali peccato corripere quemlibet* Christianum, *et, si correctionem contempserit, ipsum per districtionem ecclesiasticam coercere.*'
22. R. Folz, *The Concept of Empire in Western Europe from the Fifth to the Fourteenth Century* (London: Edward Arnold, 1969), p. 87.
23. On Frederick's position in this struggle, see Ullmann, "Some Reflections on the Opposition of Frederick II to the Papacy," *Archivio Storico Pugliese* 13(1960), pp. 3–26.
24. R. and A. Carlyle, A *History of Medieval Political Theory*, Vol. V, p. 324; J. Rivière, *Le Problème de l'Église et de l'État au Temps de Philippe le Bel* (Paris, 1926), p. 39 and p. 46.
25. Tierney, *The Crisis of Church and State*, p. 150; Watt, *The Theory of Papal Monarchy*, p. 59.
26. 'On *Quod Super* (Decretals iii.34.8),' *Commentaria Super Libros Quinque Decretalium* (Frankfurt, 1570), fol. 429–30, cited in Tierney, *The Crisis of Church and State*, pp. 155–6.
27. 'On *Licet* (Decretals ii.2.10),' *Commentaria*, fol. 197–8, cited in Tierney, *ibid.*, p. 154.
28. '*Licet* (Decretals ii.2.10),' *Corpus Iuris Canonici* II, col. 251: '*Mandamus, quatenus, si quando a laicis Vercellensibus tales literas super rebus, praecipue quae forum saeculare contingunt, a sede apostolica contigerit impetrari, eas sublato appellationis obstaculo, decernas auctoritas nostra irritas et inanes, dummodo dicit consules et commune de se conquerentibus in iudicio saeculari exhibeant iustitiae complementum. Licet tamen ipsis, qui sub eisdem consulibus taliter duxerint contendendum, si se in aliquo senserint praegravari, ad tuam, sicut hactenus servatum est, vel ad nostram, si maluerint, audientiam appellare, hoc praesertim tempore, quo vacante imperio ad iudicem saecularem recurrere nequent, qui a superioribus in sua iustitia opprimuntur.*'
29. For example, the pope can intervene in secular jurisdiction for the protection of widows and church property. For more cases, see *On Licet*, fol. 197–8.
30. See Innocent IV, *Apparatus super Quinque Libris Decretalium* (Augustae Taurinorum, 1581), ii.2.17, f. 84. For earlier uses of this doctrine, see also Watt, *The Theory of Papal Monarchy*, pp. 92–7.
31. According to Watt, it was the culmination of the papal ideology. Watt, "Introduction," in John of Paris, *On Royal and Papal Power*, trans. by Watt (Toronto: Pontifical Institute of Medieval Studies, 1971), p. 28.
32. M. Pacaut, "L'Autorité Pontificale selon Innocent IV," *Le Moyen Age*, 66 (1960), p. 88. Cf. Watt, *The Theory of Papal Monarchy*, p. 60.
33. '*Unam Sanctam*,' *Corpus Iuris Canonici* II, col. 1245–6.
34. *Ibid.*, col. 1246: '*Ergo, si deviat terrena potestas, iudicabitur a potestate spirituali; sed, si deviat spiritualis minor, a suo superiori; si vero suprema, a solo Deo, non ab homine poterit iudicari...... Porro subesse Romano Pontifici omni humanae creaturae declaramus, dicimus, diffinimus et pronunciamus omnino esse de necessitate salutis.*'
35. Cf. Janet Coleman's argument that John's intention in writing *De Potestate Regia et Papali* was to demonstrate Dominican positions against Franciscan ones in the debate over the relationships between the pope and the church, between the pope and temporal rulers, between the church and its collective property and between temporal rulers and the private property of their subjects. Coleman doubts the traditional view that John's *De Potestate* was

written to refute Boniface's bulls against Philip. Rather, she argues that the *De Potestate* aimed to oppose Boniface's assertion of the papal supremacy against the cardinals' power within the church. See Coleman, "The Dominican Political Theory of John of Paris in its Context," in *The Church and Sovereignty c. 590–1918*, ed. by Diana Wood (Oxford: Basil Blackwell, 1991), pp. 187–223, in particular p. 190 and pp. 219–20. I agree that John's *De Potestate* is a presentation of Dominican theory on those issues. However, even though John did not mention the name of Boniface, it would be difficult to say that he did not know or consider the conflict between Philip and Boniface during the end of the thirteenth and the beginning of the fourteenth when John was writing. Moreover, the discussion of the relationship between the *sacerdotium* and the *regnum* is of great importance in *De Potestate*.

36. McIlwain, *The Growth of Political Thought*, p. 263. Cf. Tierney who interprets the *De Potestate* as a work of canonistic thought. Tierney, *Foundations of the Conciliar Theory: The Contribution of the Medieval Canonists from Gratian to the Great Schism* (Cambridge: Cambridge University Press, 1956), pp. 157–78.
37. John, *On Royal and Papal Power*, trans. by Watt, Ch. XII, p. 142; Ch. II, p. 82.
38. *Ibid.*, Ch. VI, pp. 97–100.
39. *Ibid.*, Ch. XII, pp. 147–8.
40. *Ibid.*, Ch. XII, p. 146.
41. At this point, it is worthwhile mentioning Tierney's analysis of John's argument for church government in terms of corporation. According to Tierney, John's understanding of the pope as the head of church, like that in corporation theory, is not greater than that of all the members in the church. In this aspect, Tierney sees in John the conciliar doctrine, which argued the limitation of papal power and instead the supreme authority of the general council. See Tierney, *Foundations*, p. 47 and p. 165.
42. John, *On Royal and Papal Power*, Ch. VIII, pp. 109–10.
43. *Ibid.*, Ch. XII, p. 144.
44. *Ibid.*, Ch. XIII, p. 156.
45. *Ibid.*, Ch. XIII, pp. 156–9.
46. Cf. *ibid.*, p. 159. By saying that "the emperor, as a member of the church, at the request of the cardinals, should proceed against him to accomplish his deposition," John is not consistent about the principle of the distinction between the two powers. We shall observe the inconsistency later in this chapter.
47. *Ibid.*, Ch. VI, pp. 99–102.
48. See *ibid.*, Ch. XIII, pp. 156–7.
49. *Ibid.*, p. 157. To repeat, in this respect John is regarded as the exponent of conciliarism that affirms the people or the general council to be the supreme judge of the church. For such hints of conciliarism in John, see also *ibid.*, Ch. X, p. 124; Ch. XXIV, pp. 242–3.
50. *Ibid.*, Ch. XIII, p. 160.
51. *Ibid.*, p. 158. It is in the context of John's support for Emperor Henry's deposition of candidates for the papacy that he argued so. However, John's appraisal of Henry's deposition is in contradiction to his theoretical proposition about the distinction of the two authorities and jurisdictions and hence undermines his arguments. Cf. Coleman, "The Dominican Theory of John of Paris," p. 221.
52. John, *On Royal and Papal Power*, Ch. XXV, p. 252.

53. *Ibid.*
54. Throughout this book, the 'Donation of Constantine' and the 'Translation of empire' indicate both the documents which record the historical events and the historical facts. I do not imply any difference in employing the terms as documents or historical facts in the sense that both of them are our subject of attention in our examination of how the papalists and the imperialists interpret the relationship between the spiritual and temporal powers.
55. The theoretical significance which the 'Donation of Constantine' occupies in medieval political thought does not necessarily correspond to the actual use which the popes themselves made of it. One view holds that the papacy—Gregory VII, Innocent III, Innocent IV, or Boniface VIII—very rarely used the 'Donation' to enhance its power, even at the very serious crises of their struggle with emperors and other secular rulers (see Woolf, *Bartolus*, pp. 315–6). Others consider it the foundation of the temporal power of the papacy. According to Zinkeisen, although the 'Donation' was embodied in the collections of canon law from that of Anselm of Lucca (1086) onwards, the popes for some centuries rarely availed themselves of it. Innocent III, Gregory VII, Innocent IV and Boniface VIII did not, despite their extreme claims, rely on the authority of the 'Donation.' Only Urban II and some of the popes from Nicholas V to Leo X (1447–1521), derived a practical benefit from the forged grant. The use of the 'Donation' by popes was less common than has been generally supposed. See F. Zinkeisen, "The Donation of Constantine as Applied by the Roman Church," *EHR*, IX (1894), p. 626 and pp. 630–2. Cf. C. B. Coleman who argues that those popes referred to the validity of 'Donation' and used it in support of their arguments. Coleman, *Constantine the Great and Christianity* (New York: Columbia University Press, 1914), pp. 178–83.
56. Folz, *The Concept of Empire*, p. 11; Woolf, *Bartolus*, p. 321. It is generally agreed that the document is a papal forgery, which was exposed in the fifteenth century by Nicholas of Cusa (in his *De Concordantia Catholica*, Book III, Ch. 2) and Lorenzo Valla (in his *De Falso Credita et Ementita Constantini Donatione*). For the critical exposure of the forgery, Coleman, *ibid.*, pp. 184–99; R. W. Dyson, "Introduction," in James of Viterbo, *De Regimine Christiano*, trans. by Dyson (Woodbridge: The Boydell Press, 1995), p. xxiv; E. Lewis, *Medieval Ideas* (New York: Cooper Square Publisher INC., 1974), p. 620, n. 10; J. B. Morrall and S. Ehler (ed.), *Church and State Through the Centuries* (London: Burns & Oates, 1954), p. 15.
57. *Select Historical Documents of the Middle Ages*, ed. and trans. by Ernest F. Henderson (London: Bell, 1903), pp. 324–5.
58. *Ibid.*, p. 326.
59. *Ibid.*
60. *Ibid.*, p. 328.
61. Innocent IV was the first to see the donation as the restitution of that which *de jure* belonged to the vicar of Christ. See Poole, *Illustrations of the History of Medieval Thought*, p. 250.
62. See D. Maffei, *La Donazione di Costantino nei Giuristi Medievali* (Milan: Dott. A. Giuffrè Editore, 1964), pp. 78–82.
63. R. and A. Carlyle, *A History of Medieval Political Theory*, V, p. 306. Cf. The text of 'Donation' which says that '*unde coram Deo vivo, qui nos regnare precepit et coram terribili eius iudicio obtestamus per hoc nostrum imperialem constitutum omnes nostros successores imperatores vel*

cunctos optimates, satrapes etiam, amplissimum senatum et universum populum in toto orbe terrarum, nunc et in posterum cunctis retro temporibus imperio nostro subiacenti, nulli eorum quoquo modo licere, hec, que a nobis imperiali sanctione sacrosanctae Romanae ecclesiae vel eius omnibus pontificibus concessa sunt, refragare aut confringere vel in quoquam convelli.' For the Latin text of 'Donation,' see Coleman, *Constantine the Great and Christianity*, pp. 228–37.

64. James of Viterbo, *On Christian Government*, trans. by R. W. Dyson (Woodbridge: The Boydell Press, 1995), Ch. X, p. 119.
65. *Ibid.*, Ch. X, p. 153.
66. John, *On Royal and Papal Power*, Ch. X, p. 124.
67. *Ibid.*, Ch. XIII, p. 106.
68. *Ibid.*, Ch. X, pp. 121–2.
69. *Ibid.*, p. 122.
70. *Ibid.*, Ch. XV, p. 173.
71. *Ibid.*, *Proemium*, p. 70.
72. For the reasons why the donation does not apply to France, see *ibid.*, Ch. XXI, pp. 221–6. In fact, John's historical explanation about why the 'Donation' does not demonstrate the papal sovereignty over the empire is more concerned with explaining the exclusion of the French kingdom from the authority of the pope.
73. Folz, *The Concept of Empire*, p. 85.
74. On the conflict between two candidates for the imperial throne, Otto and Philip, see Poole, "Philip of Swabia and Otto IV," in *CMH*, VI, pp. 44–79.
75. '*Venerabilem* (Decretals i.6.34),' *Corpus Iuris Canonici*, II, col. 80: '*Verum illis principibus ius et potestatem eligendi regem, in imperatorem postmodum promovendum, recognoscimus, ut debemus, ad quos de iure ac antiqua consuetudine noscitur pertinere; praesertim, quum ad eos ius et potestas huiusmodi ab apostolica sede pervenerit, quae Romanum imperium in personam magnifici Caroli a Graecis transtulit in Germanos. Sed et principes recognoscere debent, et utique recognoscunt, sicut iidem in nostra recognovere praesentia, quod ius et auctoritas examinandi personam electam in regem et promovendam ad imperium ad nos spectat, qui eum inungimus, consecramus et coronamus:*' 'Indeed we acknowledge, as we should, that the right and power to elect a king, who is afterwards to be promoted emperor; belong to those princes by right and ancient custom; it is especially so since this right and power came to them from the apostolic see, which transferred the Roman empire from the Greeks to the Germans in the person of the great Charles. But the princes should acknowledge, and certainly they do, as they themselves have recognised in our presence, that right and authority to examine the person who is elected as king and is to be promoted to the imperial status belong to us who anoint, consecrate and crown him.'
76. John, *On Royal and Papal Power*, Ch. XV, p. 173.

Chapter 4

1. Accursius, *Gl. notitia ad* D. 1.1.10, cited in Stein, "Bartolus, the Conflict of Laws and the Roman Law," in *The Character and Influence of the Roman Civil Law: Historical Essays* (London: Hambledon Press, 1988), p. 84.

2. For the development of Roman law in Italy, see Paul Vinogradoff, *Roman Law in the Medieval Europe*, 3rd edn (Oxford: Clarendon Press, 1961), Ch. II.
3. For the compilation of Roman law under the Emperor Justinian (c. 482–565), known as the *Corpus Iuris Civilis—Institutiones, Digesta, Codex* and *Novellae* —, see A. Arthur Schiller, *Roman Law: Mechanism of Development* (The Hague: Mouton, 1978), pp. 29–40.
4. D. Kelley, *The Human Measure: Social Thought in the Western Legal Tradition* (London: Harvard University Press, 1990), p. 56.
5. Stein, "Bartolus, the Conflict of Laws and the Roman Law," p. 84; J. M. Kelly, *A History of Western Legal Theory* (Oxford: Clarendon Press, 1992), p. 128.
6. Stein, "Judge and Jurist in the Civil Law," in *The Character and Influence of the Roman Law*, p. 134. See also M. H. Keen, "The Political Thought of the Fourteenth Century Civilians," in *Trends in Medieval Political Thought*, ed. by Beryl Smalley (Oxford: Blackwell, 1965), p. 106.
7. J. Canning, *The Political Thought of Baldus de Ubaldis* (Cambridge: Cambridge University Press, 1987), pp. 58–9 and p. 62. Cf. Wilks, *The Problem of Sovereignty*, pp. 184–8; Ullmann, *Law and Politics in the Middle Ages* (London: The Sources of History Limited, 1975), pp. 109–10; Skinner, *The Foundations of Modern Political Thought* II (Cambridge: Cambridge University Press, 1978), pp. 130–1.
8. Wilks argues that Marsilius' theory of government was basically only an elaboration of the *lex regia* idea. Wilks, *The Problem of Sovereignty*, p. 186.
9. For example, D. 1.3.32.1 says that, at the more concrete and real level, the people's opinion, that is custom, should be taken as a law because *leges* themselves have been accepted by decision of the people. Cf. C. 8.52.2 which says that custom is only authoritative when not contrary to *lex* or to reason. For the theoretical discussion of the conflict and the harmony between the Imperial law and custom, see André Gouron, "Coutume contra Loi chez les Premiers Glossateurs," in *Renaissance du Pouvoir Législatif et Genèse de L'État* (Montpellier: Société d'Histoire du Droit et des Institutions des Anciens Pays de Droit Écrit, 1988), pp. 117–30.
10. Stein, "Roman Law," in *CHMPT*, p. 47.
11. Canning, *The Political Thought of Baldus*, p. 62.
12. D. 1.4.1.1. For the same justification of the imperial power, see *Institutes* 1.2.6 which says that '*principi placuit legis habet vigorem, cum lege regia, quae de imperio eius lata est, populus ei et in eum omne suum imperium et potestatem concessit;*' C. 1.17.1.7 ('*omne ius omnisque potestas populi Romani in imperatoriam translata sunt potestatem*').
13. See H. Kantorowicz, *Studies in the Glossators of the Roman Laws* (Cambridge: Cambridge University Press, 1938), Ch. II; Stein, "The *Digest* Title, *De Diversis Regulis Iuris Antiqui*, and the General Principles of Law," in *The Character and Influence of the Roman Civil Law*, p. 60.
14. Irnerius, *Gloss on the Digest*, 1.6.2, cited in F. K. von Savigny, *Geschichte des Römischen Rechts in Mittelalter* (Heidelberg, 1826), Vol. IV, Ch. XXVII, p. 37, n. 49. Cf. W. E. Brynteson, "Roman Law and Legislation in the Middle Ages," *Speculum*, 41 (1966), p. 432.
15. Irnerius, *Gloss on Digest*, 1.3.32, cited in R. and A. Carlyle, *A History of Medieval Political Theory*, Vol. II, p. 60: '*Loquitur haec lex secumdum sua tempora, quibus populus habebat potestatem condendi leges, ideo tacito consensu omnium per consuetudinem abrogabantur. Sed quia hodie potestas translata est in imperatorem, nihil faceret desuetudo populi:*' 'This law is speaking in accordance with its own times, in which the people had the power of making

laws. Therefore they could be abrogated through custom by the tacit consent of all. But because today that power is transferred to the emperor, the people's abandonment (of the law) would be of no moment.' For more on Irnerius' views of law and legislative power, see also Savigny, *Geschichte des Römischen Rechts in Mittelalter*, Vol. IV, Ch. XXVII, pp. 9–62; Gouron, "Coutume contra Loi chez les Premiers Glossateurs," p. 119.

16. It was H. Fitting who attributed the *Summa Trecensis* to Irnerius. But the *Summa Trecensis* is not accepted any more to be Irnerius' work. Kantorowicz maintains that the *Summa Trecensis* is Rogerius' work written in the middle of the twelfth century. For the debate about the authorship of the *Summa Trecensis*, see Kantorowicz, *Studies in the Glossators of the Roman Laws*, pp. 146–80. Here, I use the formerly titled *Summa Codicis des Irnerius*, edited by Fitting, which remains the standard edition of the *Summa Trecensis*.
17. *Summa Codicis des Irnerius*, ed. by H. Fitting (Berlin: J. Guttentag Verlagsbuchhandlung, 1894), "*De Legibus et Constitutionibus*" (C. 1.14), p. 16.
18. *Ibid.*, "*Quæ Sit Longa Consuetudo?*" (C. 8.52), p. 306: '*nichil enim interest, populus suffragio voluntatem suam declaret, an ipsis negotiis cotidie ex usu et consuetudine hoc ostendit.*'
19. According to the *Summa Trecensis*, long-standing customs which are approved by the agreement of the users, are preserved as law. But the difference between the two laws is that while written law is not admitted unless it is law of the city of Rome, customary law has to be received not only by the city of Rome but also by any town, as long as it is not contrary to written law. See *ibid.*: '*diuturni enim mores consensu utencium comprobati pro lege seruantur. set in hoc differunt, quod ius scriptum nisi ciuitatis Romane non admittitur, ius autem consuetudinarium non solum urbis Rome sed etiam cuiusuis oppidi recipiendum est, dum tamen iuri scripto non obuiet.*'
20. *Ibid.*, p. 305: '*Quem ad modum ius scriptum auctoritate populi Romani nititur, imo eius cui a populo hoc permissum est, ita ius non scriptum rebus ipsis et factis eodem iudicio declaratur.*'
21. *Ibid.*, p. 16: '*is quidem auctoritatem legis condende habet qui potestatem precipiendi habet. ergo Populus Romanus, ille immo cui a populo hoc permissum est: principes enim hanc facultatem habent. nam populo seu principi hoc officium imminet, ut singulis hominibus prouideant ut filiis propriis seu membris.*'
22. *Ibid.*: '*hodie leges confici non debent nisi secundum tenorem eius constitutionis. iubet enim leges non aliter promulgandas esse, nisi causa necessaria hoc exposcat et antiquis sanctionibus non inserta. et hoc faciendum est causa in auditorio a proceribus discussa, maxime a senatoribus, et cum eorum consilio ordinata.*'
23. *Ibid.*
24. *Ibid.*, p. 306: '*consuetudo etiam optima legum interpres est, nec non per consuetudinem quoque leges ipse abrogantur.*'
25. Placentinus, *Summa Codicis* (Mainz, 1536; repr. Torino, 1962), p. 16: '*lex dicitur stricto modo proprie censura, lex vocatur largissimo modo quaecumque lectio, ut lex Iuliana: dicitur largo modo quicquid sancitur de Iusticia, secundumque hanc exceptionem lectio est santio sancta, iubens honesta, prohibens contraria, vel lex est commune praeceptum & c.*'
26. *Ibid.*: '*quia populi censura lex specialiter appellatur, populus primo habuit potestatem condendi legem.*'
27. *Ibid.*
28. *Ibid.*

29. *Ibid.*: '*De condendis exponitur a quo debeant condi, & dicitur ab Imperatore, vel ab eo tantum cui Imperator permiserit.*'
30. *Ibid.*, p. 17: '*De legibus conditis tripliciter agitur de legibus intelligendis, interpretandis, obseruandis: Ab omnibus inquam intelligi debent etiam a rusticis, etiam a fœminis, a clericis, a militibus, licet quandoque pareatur praedictis: hoc ita si leges possunt intelligi. Siquid ergo in legibus obscure dictum inueniatur, ad principem referatur ut dilucidet.*'
31. *Ibid.*
32. *Ibid.*
33. *Ibid.*: '*Porro hodie solus Imperator, uel is cui Imperator permisit, potestatem habet condendi iura, & interpretandi. Ergo hodie nec populus Romanus, nec Senatus.*'
34. *Ibid.*, p. 416.
35. *Ibid.*: '*Quod ergo dicitur ff. de legi. ibi consuetudinem abrogare legem, sic debet intelligi, id est consuetudinem non aliam ...... in principem per regiam legem populus Romanus omne ius transtulit. ergo ius condendi iura & abragandi: sicque ius tale sibi non reseruauerit.*'
36. *Ibid.*, p. 17. The full text of *Digna Vox* (C. 1.14.4) is as follows: '*Digna vox maiestate regnantis legibus alligatum se principem profiteri: adeo de autoritate iuris nostra pendet autoritas. et re vera maius imperio est submittere legibus principatum*': 'It is a statement worthy of the majesty of the ruler that the prince proclaims himself to be bound by the law: indeed our authority depends on the authority of law. And in truth the submission of the principate to the laws is greater than *imperium*.' In the sense that the emperor should declare himself bound by the laws, Pennington says that *Digna vox* is one of the medieval jurists' most important constitutional texts. Pennington, *The Prince and the Law, 1200–1600: Sovereignty and Rights in the Western Legal Tradition* (Berkeley: University of California Press, 1993), p. 78.
37. Placentinus, *Summa Codicis*, p. 17: '*Inquit Imperator, leges obseruari debere a subiectis ex necessitate, a principibus ex uoluntate.*'
38. Azo, "*De Legibus* & *Constitutionibus Principum & Edictis*" (C. 1.14), *Summa super Codicem* (Pavia, 1506; repr. Augustae Taurinorum, 1966), pp. 8–9: '*Lex autem ponitur quandoque stricte quandoque large. Stricte ut cum ponitur pro statuto populi romani. et hoc est quod dicitur. lex est quod populus romanus senatorio magistratu interrogante, veluti consule constituebat. i.e aliquo qui erat de senatorio magistratu ...... Quandoque ponitur large pro omni rationabili statuto. unde et dicitur lex et santio sancta, iubens honesta, prohibens contraria. Et ita est regula iustorum et iniustorum ..... Constitutio vero principis et edictum legis patres sunt, ut lex largo modo intelligatur. et ita large positum esse in rubrica dici potest.*'
39. For the pretor as judicial magistrate, see Schiller, *Roman Law*, pp. 404–9; Adolf Berger, *Encyclopedic Dictionary of Roman Law* (Philadelphia: American Philosophical Society, 1953), p. 647.
40. Azo, "*De Legibus* & *Constitutionibus Principum & Edictis*," p. 9: '*Si tandem consentiant omnes recitabitur in sacro palatio vel consistorio, ut confirmetur per principem et per populos iussu principis diuulgetur ...... Item potest condi a prefecto pretorio si non fit contraria legibus principis ... ... Item ab his quibus mandat imperator.*'
41. *Ibid.*: '*A populo autem romano forte et hodie potest condi lex, ut ex-predicta diffinitione legis ponitur, licet dicatur potestas translata in principem ...... Dicitur enim translata, i.e. concessa, non quod populus omnino a se abdicauerit eam ...... Nam et olim transtulerat sed tamen postea*

reuocauit.' See also Azo, *Lectura Super Codicem* (Paris, 1577; repr. Augustae Taurinorum, 1966), p. 44 (C. 1.14.11).

42. Azo, *Lectura super Codiciem*, p. 44: '*ergo si populus ante habebat, & adhuc habebit. Dic ergo quod hic non excluditur populus, sed singuli de populo, & est simile in illo exemplo, Solus Scipio ciuitatem vel uniuersitatem Romanam liberauit. Non enim excluditur hic populus, quia falsum esset: sed singuli de populo: quia plus fecit ipse quam aliquis aliorum, ideo singuli excluduntur, non vniversitas siue populus.*'
43. *Ibid*, p. 671 (C. 8.52): '*unde non est maioris potestatis Imperator quam totus populus, sed quam quilibet de populo.*'
44. Cf. Pennington, *The Prince and the Law*, p. 80.
45. Azo, *Summa super Codicem*, p. 9 (C. 1.14): '*Omnis anima sit subdita principi tanquam praecelenti & ducibus a deo missis....Imperator tamen unus successori suo imparare non potest. sed suadere ut leges seruet. et suasionis causam proponere. ut quia de lege, i.e. regia pendet auctoritas principalis. quia per eam populus trastulit omne imperium in principem. merito et ipse hoc retribuat legi ut seruet eam.*'
46. Azo, *Lectura super Codicem*, p. 40 (C. 1.14.4): '*Pone casum quia bene scis quod imperator non est alligatus legibus, sicut dicunt multe leges, sed tamen adeo de auctoritate iuris pendet auctoritas imperialis, ut Digna vox...... et re uera quia maius est si aliquis leges obseruet quam si esset imperator.*'
47. Ullmann, *The Medieval Idea of Law* (London: Methuen, 1946), p. 48. For a broad-ranging survey of the thirteenth- and fourteenth century materials concerning this issue, see L. Waelkens, *La Théorie de la Coutume chez Jacques de Révigny* (Leiden: E. J. Brill: Universitaire Pers Leiden, 1984).
48. Ullmann, *Law and Politics*, p. 106–7; Canning, A *History of Medieval Political Thought 300–1450* (London: Routledge, 1996), p. 161.
49. Cynus, *Commentarium in Codicem et Digestum Vetus* (Francofurti, 1578), fo. 8, no. 1, cited in Ullmann, "A Medieval Document on Papal Theories of Government," *EHR*, LXI (1946), p. 185, n. 5.
50. Cynus maintains that while unwritten customary law comes from the tacit consent of the people, written law proceeds from the people's express consent. Cynus, *ibid.*, C. 8.53.2, no. 23 ('*consuetudo sicut statutum introducitur ex consensu populi*'); *ibid*, no. 5 ('*differunt ergo statutum et consuetudo inter se sicut expressum et tacitum*'). Cited in Ullmann, *Medieval Idea of Law*, p. 63.
51. See *ibid.*, p. 174.
52. Cynus, *Lecture on C. 1.1.1*: '*temporaliter sub imperio omnes populi omnesque reges sunt, sicut sunt sub papa spiritualiter.*' See also *ibid.*, C. 5.16.26, no. 1: '*talis dominus, qui non recognoscit superiorem, est princeps in terra sua de facto,*' cited from Ullmann, "The Development of the Medieval Idea of Sovereignty," *EHR*, CCL (1949), p. 5.
53. See Innocent III's *Per Venerabilem*.

Chapter 5

1. On this, see Stein, "Judge and Jurists in the Civil Law: A Historical Interpretation," in *The Character and Influence of the Roman Civil Law*, p. 135.

2. Lockwood, "Marsilius of Padua and the Case for the Royal Ecclesiastical Supremacy," *TRHS*, 6th ser., I (1991), p. 95. See also Ullmann, "Personality and Territoriality in the *Defensor Pacis*: the Problem of Political Humanism," *Medioevo: Rivista di Storia della Filosofia Mediovale*, VI (1980), pp. 397–410.
3. Skinner, *The Foundations of Modern Political Thought* I, pp. 61–5.
4. Woolf, *Bartolus*, pp. 382–3. Cf. J. W. Allen who argues that in the fourteenth century the empire was dead. He maintains that it is unrealistic to suppose that the empire had practical power in the period. Allen, "Marsiglio of Padua and Medieval Secularism," in *The Social and Political Ideas of Some Great Medieval Thinkers*, ed. by F. J. C. Hearnshaw (London: Harrap, 1923), pp. 169–70.
5. For the use of '*princeps*' by jurists in the thirteenth century, see Pennington, *The Prince and the Law*, pp. 90–1. Pennington himself explains that the jurists created the 'prince' as a generic term to define a ruler who had no superior (*ibid.*, p. 91).
6. For example, four of the leading Bolognese Doctors of Law—Bulgarius, Martinus, Jacobus, and Ugo—declared at the Rongalia Diet of 1158 in favour of Frederick I's right to tax the cities of Lombardy. Vinogradoff, *Roman Law in Medieval Europe*, pp. 61–2; Canning, "Ideas of the State in Thirteenth and Fourteenth-Century Commentators on the Roman Law," *TRHS*, 5th ser., 33 (1983), p. 7.
7. On the outline of development of the idea of territorial sovereignty before Bartolus, see Canning, *ibid.*, pp. 6–8.
8. For the full content of the 'Peace of Constance,' see MGH, *Constitutiones et Acta Publica Imperatorum et Regum*, I (Hanover, 1893), pp. 411–8.
9. Skinner notes as one of its characteristics that "the city-states placed their highest executive and judicial functions in the hands of a salaried official elected for a strictly limited period of time." Skinner, "Political Philosophy," p. 390; *Foundations of Modern Political Thought* I, pp. 3–4. For the *podestà* as a republican office, see also Pennington, *The Prince and the Law*, pp. 40–1. On the change from the rule of consuls to that of *podestà*, see J. K. Hyde, *Society and Politics in Medieval Italy: the Evolution of the Civil Life, 1000–1350* (London: Macmillan, 1973), pp. 94–104. For the origin and development of the *podestà*, see Daniel Waley, *The Italian City Republics*, 3rd edn (London: Longman, 1988), p. 35 and pp. 41–5.
10. According to Waley, Frederick I set up the *podestà* by appointing or recognising the officials in towns of Lombardy and Emilia after 1160. Then in 1162 Milan agreed to 'receive the *podestà* whom the emperor wishes, whether he be a German or a Lombard' (*ibid.*, p. 41). However, this office was not successful in taking root in Rome and Venice (Hyde, *ibid.*, p. 101). Contrary to the emperor's intention in establishing the post, ironically the *podestà* contributed to the development of the cities.
11. Skinner, "Political Philosophy," p. 390.
12. Skinner, *Foundations of Modern Political Thought* I, pp. 8–9; Black, *Political Thought in Europe*, p. 115. Before Bartolus such commentators as Jacobus and Oldradus, even though less explicitly, had acknowledged that some Italian cities did not recognise a superior. See Canning, "Law, Sovereignty and Corporation Theory, 1300–1450," in *CHMPT*, p. 470.
13. Keen, "The Political Thought of the Fourteenth Century Civilians," in *Trends in Medieval Political Thought*, ed. by B. Smalley (Oxford: Basil Blackwell, 1965), p. 118.

14. Bartolus, *Commentaria on Digestum Vetus* (Basileæ, 1562), 6.1.2, p. 419: '*Ergo dico quod Imperator est dominus totius mundi vere. Nec obstat quod alii sunt domini particulariter, quia mundus est universitas quaedam; unde potest quis habere dictam universitatem, licet singulae res non sint suae.*'
15. Canning, "Ideas of the State," p. 4.
16. Bartolus, like other commentators, distinguishes the *terrae imperii* and the *terrae ecclesiae*, but he does so in support of a pro-papal and hierocratic interpretation of the relationship between papal and imperial authority. That is, Bartolus argues that through the 'Donation of Constantine' imperial authority was ceded by the pope and the *terrae ecclesiae* were attached to the Roman empire. Through the '*Translatio imperii*' the emperor received temporal government from the papacy. Nevertheless, the pope as Christ's vicar retained the universal jurisdiction in both the *terrae ecclesiae* and the empire. See Bartolus, *Commentaria on Digestum Novum* (Basileæ, 1562), 49.15.24. § 4, p. 983; Woolf, *Bartolus*, pp. 99–100. Further, for Bartolus' favouring the pope in the respect that the pope could rule in the *terrae imperii* but the emperor could not in the *terrae ecclesiae*, see *Comment. on Dig. Nov.* 50.16.2, p. 1027: '*Et nos possemus intrare in istam quaestionem quando possent ex se homines constituere civitates, an possint sua authoritate, an requiratur authoritas superioris. Et dicit Innocentius quod homines sua sponte possunt sine authoritate superioris......Et ibi dicit ipse, non intelligas de ea quae habet episcopum, sed in aliis quae non habent episcopum, quia istud est in Italia, quando habent episcopum, est civitas*:' 'We can go into this question whether the people could from themselves make cities, whether they can with their own authority, or the authority of a superior is required. Innocent says that the people of their own will can do it without the authority of a superior...... There he himself says that you should not understand it in the city which has a bishop, but in other cities which do not have a bishop. Because that is the situation in Italy—when they have a bishop, they are a city.'
17. On the basis that Christ confirmed the empire, Bartolus depicts as heretical those who deny that the emperor is *dominus mundi*. See *ibid.*, 49.15.24. § 7, pp. 983–4.
18. Bartolus, *Commentaria on Infortiatum* (Basileæ, 1562), 36.1.26, p. 860: '*Civitatibus, quae non sunt hostes Imperii, potest fideicommissum relinqui, et agere poterunt per suos syndicos. Innuit quod quaedam civitates non sunt sub imperio......Solutio: Intelligo, sub imperio omnes sunt de jure, de facto non. Sunt tamen quaedam, quae etiam sub imperio de jure non sunt, ut civitates donatae ecclesiae.*'
19. Bartolus, *Comment. on Dig. Vet.* 2.1.1, § 16, p. 109: '*Et ista aequiparatio de jurisdictione ad dominum probatur sic, Princeps habet omnem jurisdictionem...... et ex hoc dicitur dominus totius mundi...... Sicut quilibet judex dicitur princeps civitatis, vel territorii, cui praeest...... Et recte potest dici dominus totius illius territorii universaliter considerati*:' 'The equation of jurisdiction and *dominus* is proved thus: the emperor has the whole jurisdiction...... and from this is said to be the lord of the world...... Just as every judge is said to be the emperor of a city, or a territory, of which he is a leader...... And rightly the emperor can be said to be the lord of a territory taken universally.'
20. Cf. the thirteenth- and fourteenth-century French publicists, who denied imperial sovereignty over their kingdom, whether it was *de jure* or *de facto*, and elaborated a theory of the *de jure* sovereignty of their king in a particular territory. They did not reject the distinction between the *de jure* dependence and the *de facto* independence in general. But they held

that the French king had both *de jure* and *de facto* independence from the emperor. Whereas this theory for the *de jure* sovereignty of the king of France was the majority opinion amongst the French writers and jurists, the minority opinion (e.g. Johannes Blancus and Petrus de Bellapertica) upheld the universal overlordship of the emperor. See Ullmann, "The Development of the Medieval Idea of Sovereignty," pp. 7–8. For the majority view, see Canning, "Law, Sovereignty and Corporation Theory," p. 466; Canning, "Ideas of the States," p. 4 and pp. 7–8.

21. D. 2.1.3: '*Imperium aut merum aut mixtum est. Merum est imperium habere gladii potestatem ad animadvertendum facinorosos homines, quod etiam potestas appellratur. Mixtum est imperium, cui etiam jurisdictio inest, quod in danda bonorum possessione consistit. Iurisdictio est etiam iudicis dandi licentia.*' This passage is cited from *The Digest of Justinian*, Latin text ed. by Theodor Mommsen; English translation ed. by Alan Watson (Philadelphia: University of Pennsylvania Press), 1985.
22. For the differentiation of various kinds of jurisdiction, see Bartolus, *Comment. on Dig. Vet.* 2.1.1, p. 105.
23. Bartolus, *Consilium*, I. 189. § 1, p. 119: '*Nos habemus triplicem universitatem habitationum et praediorum: unam largam quae facit provinciam, et haec universitas habet jurisdictionem et mer. et mixt. imperium de jure communi...... Secunda universitas minus larga quae constituit civitatem, et huic universitati cohaeret jurisdictio tantum usque ad certam quantitatem in levioribus criminibus, sed merum et mixtum imp. non habet.....Fallit in quibusdam civitatibus in quibus est hic specialiter concessum a jure, ut Romae...... et in aliis civitatibus quae hoc habent ex consuetudine vel privilegio...... Ex his causis jurisdictio dicitur cohaerere loco seu territorio. Tertia universitas est minima ut castrum, villa, vicus...... et huic universitati nulla cohaeret jurisdictio, sed alterius civitatis jurisdictioni subesse dicitur, etc.*:' 'We have three sorts of *universitas* of habitations and lands: one is the large one which makes up a province, and this *universitas* has jurisdiction and simple and mixed *imperium* by common law (*de jure communi*)...... The second *universitas* which constitutes a city is less large, and to this *universitas* belongs only jurisdiction up to a certain quantity in less important crimes, but it does not have simple and mixed *imperium*. It is not the case in some cities in which this is specially conceded by a law, like Rome...... and in other cities which have this from custom or privilege...... For these reasons jurisdiction is said to belong to a place or territory. The third *universitas* is very small like a little town, an estate, a village...... and no jurisdiction belongs to this *universitas*, but it is said to be under the jurisdiction of another city.' I owe the Latin reference to Woolf. See Woolf, *Bartolus*, p. 123, n 2. See also Bartolus, *Comment. on Dig. Nov.* 39.2.1. § 3, p. 58; *Commentaria on Codex* (Basileæ, 1562), 11.21.1, pp. 910–1.
24. Bartolus, *Comment. on Cod.* 11.21.5. § 6, p. 910.
25. Bartolus, *Comment. on Dig. Nov.* 43.6.2, p. 346: '*Istae duae leges sunt contra homines hujus civitatis, qui habent domos suos supra muros civitatis, quod non licet sine permissione Principis, ut hic videtis. Tamen ipsi habent permissionem a populo et communi hujus civitatis, et dicunt quod est populus nemine subditus: ideo hic populus est princeps in hac civitate, ideo potest permittere*:' 'These two laws are against the people of the city, who have their own houses on the wall of the city, which is not allowed without the permission of the emperor, as you see here. But they have the permission from the people and community of the city, and say that the people is not subject to anybody: therefore this people is *princeps* in this city, and can permit it.'

By contrast, concerning the limits within which the legislation of the *civitas* was valid, Bartolus says that '*civitas non potest facere statuta de his qui suae jurisdictionis non sunt.*' See *Comment.* on *Cod.* 3.13.2, p. 290.

26. Bartolus gives a number of examples to show this. See *Comment. on Dig, Vet* 2.1.1, pp. 107-9; *ibid.*, 3.1.1, pp. 234–5; *ibid.*, 4.4.3, p. 323; *Comment. on Cod.* 10.46.1, p. 383.
27. In his *Tractatus de Regimine Civitatis*, Bartolus accounts for the reason why the discussion of small cities is excluded as follows: '*De populis autem parvis non dico, quia illi vel alteri civitati subsistunt...... vel alteri civitati seu regi confederantur aliquo federe, ita quod alterius maiestatem venerentur......Et videmus in civitatibus et castris, que sunt sub protectione huius civitatis Perusine. Sicut enim corpus humanum debile et parvum non potest per se regi sine auxilio tutoris et curatoris, ita isti populi parvi per se nullo modo regi possunt, nisi alteri submittantur vel alteri adhereant*': 'I do not talk about small peoples, because these people are under another city...... or are allied to another city or king by some treaty, in such a way that they respect the authority of someone else ...... as we see in the cities and towns which are under the protection of this city of Perusia. Just as the weak and small human body cannot be governed by itself without a guardian's and a curator's help, so these small people cannot be governed by themselves, unless they are submitted to others or are allied to another.' Bartolus, '*Tractatus de Regimine Civitatis*,' in *Politica e Diritto nel Trecento Italiano: il 'De Tyranno' di Bartolo da Sassoferrato (1314–1357): con l'Edizione Critica dei Trattati 'De Guelphis et Gebellinis,' 'De Regimine Civitatis' e 'De Tyranno'*, ed. by D. Quaglioni, *Il Pensiero Politico Bibliotheca* 11 (Firenze: Olschki, 1983), p. 168.
28. For the exercise of the power by *populus liber*, see for example, Bartolus, *Comment. on Cod.* 11.31.3, p. 915.
29. Bartolus, *Comment. on Dig. Vet.* 5.3.20. § 2, p. 408: '*Nota glossam quae dicit quod bona vacantia non applicantur alteri civitati sed fisco. Et verum dicit in civitatibus quae recognoscunt superiorem; sed in his quae non recognoscunt superiorem de jure vel de facto ut civitates Tusciae est ipsamet civitas fiscus. Vocatur enim populus liber*:' 'Note the gloss which says that *bona vacantia* (property without a legal owner) should not be given to another city but the imperial treasury (*fisc*). This is true of the cities which recognise a superior; but in the cities which do not recognise a superior *de jure* or *de facto* like the cities of Tuscany, the city itself is *fisc*. For it is called as a *populus liber*.'
30. Bartolus, *Comment. on Dig. Nov.* 48.1.7. § 14, p. 792: '*Quaelibet civitas Italiae hodie, praecipue in Tuscia, dominum non recognoscit, in se ipsa habet liberum populum et habet merum imperium in se ipsa, et tantam potestatem habet in populo quantam imperator in universo*.' See also *Comment. on Cod.* 10.63.5, p. 892.
31. Bartolus, *Comment. on Dig. Vet.* 4.4.3. § 2, p. 323 ('*ipsamet civitas sibi princeps est*'); *Comment. on Dig. Nov.* 43.6.2, p. 346 ('*populus liber nemini subditus, ideo hic populus est princeps in hac civitate, ideo potest permittere*'); *Comment. on Cod.* 11.31.3. § 2, p. 915 ('*dico, quod in civitatibus, quae in temporalibus non recognoscunt superiorem, ut est civitas Perusina, et sic populus liber est, ut natatur in l. Hostes, ff. de cap., quod venditio rerum immobilium possit fieri auctoritate eius concilii, apud quod est omnis potestas, illud enim vicem Imperatoris gerit in civitate illa*').
32. Bartolus, *Comment. on Dig. Vet.* 1.1.9. § 4, p. 17: '*Quando populus habet omnem iurisdictionem potest facere statutum non expectata superioris auctoritate ...... Et quod isto casu non expectetur*

superioris auctoritas patet exemplo consuetudinis, quae inducitur ex tacito consensu populi et aequiparatur statuto in quo constat quod non requiritur superioris auctoritas.'

33. *Ibid.*, 1.3.32. § 4, p. 37: '*tacitus et expressus consensus aequiparantur et sunt paris potentiae:*' 'tacit and express consent are equal and are of equal power.'
34. For the definition of custom and its binding force, see *ibid.*, 1.3.32, p. 46. About statute, see *Comment. on Infort.* 28.1.3. § 4, p. 240. Ullmann points out that it is at this point that Bartolus' conception of the *civitas sibi princeps* assumes it full significance. Ullmann, "*De Bartoli Sententia: Concilium Repraesentat Mentem Populi*," in *Bartolo Da Sassoferrato; Studi e Documenti per ILVI Centenario II* (Milan, 1962), p. 712. See also Woolf, *Bartolus*, p. 159.
35. Bartolus, *Comment. on Dig. Vet.* 1.1.9. § 4, p. 17. However, just as there was not always harmony between universal sovereignty and territorial sovereignty, conflicts between the imperial law and the statutes or custom occurred. For this, see *ibid.*, 1.1.9, pp. 16–24; *Comment. on Cod.* 8.53.2. § 45, p. 815.
36. Bartolus, *Comment. on Dig. Vet.* 12.1.27, p. 530: '*concilium quod totam civitatem repraesentat.*' For more, see *Comment. on Cod.* 4.32.5. § 2, p. 430 ('*totus populus quia eius vicem concilium repraesentat*'); *Comment. on Dig. Vet.* 1.4.1, p. 47 ('*concilium repraesentat mentem populi*'); *ibid.*, 12.1.27, § 2, p. 530 ('*ipsa civitas seu concilium, quod tantum civitatem repraesentat*').
37. Bartolus, *Comment. on Cod.* 10.31.2. § 10, p. 868: '*Nota quod de jure communi ad concilium civitatis spectat facere electiones officialium et syndicorum...... et sic non erit opus arenga vel adunantia generali. tamen parliamentum ubi non est aliquis superior, habet ab initio concilium eligere...... Istud concilium sic electum postea repraesentat totum populum.*'
38. Bartolus, *Tractatus de Regimine Civitatis*, p. 150.
39. *Ibid.*, p. 164: '*Et saepe visum est per consilium hominum communium deliberari quaedam, quae a sapientibus et prudentibus malefacta visa sunt: eventus vero manifestavit esse prudentissima facta.*'

Chapter 6

1. Ullmann, *Medieval Political Thought* (Harmondsworth: Penguin Books Ltd., 1975),p. 159.
2. Kristeller, *Renaissance Thought and Its Sources*, ed. by M. Mooney (New York: Columbia University Press, 1979), p. 128. See also Wilks, *The Problems of Sovereignty*, p. 84; Tierney, *Religion, Law and the Growth of Constitutional Thought*, p. 29; Canning, "Introduction: Politics, Institutions and Ideas," in *CHMPT*, p. 360.
3. For alternative sources of Aristotelianism, see Georg Wieland, "The Reception and Interpretation of Aristotle's *Ethics*," in *CHLMP*, ed. by N. Kretzmann, A. Kenny and J. Pinborg (Cambridge: Cambridge University Press, 1982), pp. 657–72; Nederman, "Aristotelianism and the Origins of 'Political Science' in the Twelfth Century," *Journal of the History of Ideas*, 52 (1991), pp. 180–1.
4. Nederman, "Nature, Justice, and Duty in the *Defensor Pacis*: Marsiglio of Padua's Ciceronian Impulse," *Political Theory*, 18 (1990), p. 616 and p. 633; Nederman, *Medieval Aristotelianism and Its Limits* (Aldershot: Variorum, 1997), Ch. XI and XII; Maurizio Viroli, *From Politics*

to Reason of State: The Acquisition and Transformation of the Language of Politics 1250–1600 (Cambridge: Cambridge University Press, 1992), p. 6.

5. For example, Aristotle's treatises on natural philosophy and the whole *Nicomachean Ethics* were translated respectively in the twelfth century and in 1246–7. See Nederman, "Aristotelian Ethics before the *Nicomachean Ethics*: Alternative Sources of Aristotle's Concept of Virtue in the Twelfth Century," in *Medieval Aristotelianism*, Ch. I, pp. 55–8.
6. See Aristotle, *Politics*, I. ii, 1252b28–1253a20. As well known, for Aristotle, the *polis* was the natural product of human beings and constituted the highest form of human association to express the moral and physical characteristics of human nature.
7. See Albertus Magnus, *Commentary on Politics* (*Opera Omnia*, Vol. IV) (Lyon, 1651), I. i, pp. 4–10.
8. For an outline of Albert's commentary on Aristotle's *Politics*, see also Jean Dunbabin (1982), "The Reception and Interpretation of Aristotle's *Politics*," in *CHLMP*, pp. 724–5.
9. For the process of the recovery of Aristotelianism as scholastic political thought in the thirteenth century, see Skinner, *Foundations of Modern Political Thought* I, pp. 49–50.
10. Augustine, *The City of God against the Pagans*, ed. and trans. by R. W. Dyson (Cambridge: Cambridge University Press, 1998), XIX. xv.
11. See Thomas Aquinas, '*De Regimine Principum Ad Regem Cypri*' (hereafter *De Regimine*), in *Thomae Aquinatis Opuscula Omnia*, ed. by J. Perrier, Vol. I (Paris: P. Lethielleux, 1949), I. ii, p. 223; Aquinas, '*Summa Theologiae*' (hereafter *ST*), in *Opera Omnia Iussu Impensaque Leonis XIII Edita*, Vol. V (Rome, 1882), 1a q. 103 a. 3; Vol. VII, 1a2ae q. 91 a. 2.
12. Aquinas, *De Regimine*, I. ix, pp. 243–4.
13. *Ibid.*, I. xvi, p. 262.
14. *ST*, 1a2ae q. 96 a. 3.
15. *ST*, 1a2ae q. 92 a. 1; *De Regimine*, I. xv.
16. *ST*, 1a2ae q. 90 a. 2.
17. *ST*, 1a2ae q. 92 a. 1.
18. *ST*, 1a2ae q. 90 a. 2; *De Regimine*, I. ii, p. 224; XVI, p. 261.
19. *ST*, 1a2ae q. 91 a. 1–2.
20. *ST*, 1a2ae q. 91 a. 2.
21. *ST*, 1a2ae q. 91 a. 3.
21. *ST*, 1a2ae q. 91 a. 4.
23. *ST*, 1a2ae q. 92 a. 1
24. *De Regimine*, I. i and xiv.
25. *Ibid.*, I. ii. Cf. *ST*, 1a2ae q. 105, in which Aquinas argues for a mixed constitution.
26. *ST*, in *Omnia Opera*, Vol. VIII, 2a2ae q. 47 a. 12
27. *ST*, 1a q. 103 a. 3; *De Regimine*, I. ii.
28. *ST*, 1a2ae q. 105 a. 1.
29. For example, in contrast to the nature of the *polis* in Aristotle' thought, medieval thinkers applied the category *polis* (*civitas*) to whatever political units existed—that is to empires and kingdoms, which are geographically larger political arrangements than a *polis*. This often ignored the crucial aspect of Aristotelian teaching. See Mario Grignaschi, "La Definition du 'Civis' dans la Scolastique," in *Anciens Pays et Assemblées d'État*, 35 (1966); Nederman, *Medieval Aristotelianism*, Ch. II, p. 185.

30. For example, Albert, like other commentators, agrees that the end of political science is the human good. But he says that the good is in the civil governor who is exalted. Albert, therefore, is more dependent upon the ruler in order to achieve the good in a society. See Albert, *Commentary on the Nicomachean Ethics* (*Opera Omnia*, Vol. IV) (Lyon, 1651), I. iii. 14, p. 28.
31. Nederman, *Medieval Aristotelianism*, Ch. I, p. 55.
32. Dunbabin, "The Reception and Interpretation of Aristotle's *Politics*," p. 723. Black says that medieval authors used Aristotle to support papal authority, the supremacy of church over state, imperial overlordship, monarchical sovereignty, as well as government in accordance with the laws and rule by the few or the many (see his *Political Thought in Europe*, pp. 10–2). To some extent, different interpretations were caused by William of Moerbeke's translation of the *Politics* which led to misinterpretation of some passages.
33. Black, *ibid*., p. 10.
34. Skinner, *Foundations of Modern Political Thought* I, p. 52; Charles T. Davis, "Remigio de' Girolami and Dante: A Comparison of their Conceptions of Peace," *Studi Danteschi*, 36 (1959), p. 105.
35. Remigius, '*De Bono Communi*,' in *La Teologia Politica Communale di Remigio de' Girolami*, ed. by Maria C. De Matteis (Bologna: Pàtron Editore, 1977), p. 43: '*Caritas proprie habetur non nisi ad res rationales sed ipsum commune in se non est quid rationale, ergo etc. Et dicendum quod commune non accipitur hic secundum totalitatem totius universalis, sed secundum totalitatem totius integralis, non quidem ex partibus corporalibus directe et principaliter, sed ex partibus rationalibus. Unde ex ista ratione directe amatur, praeamatur autem post Deum propter similitudinem quam habet ad Deum, qui certe summe rationalis est*:' 'Love is not properly had except to rational things, but the *commune* in itself is not something rational. And it has to be said that the commune is here understood not according to the totality of the universal whole but according to the totality of the integral whole, not indeed composed from corporeal parts directly and principally, but from rational parts. Whence, from this reason it is loved directly, and is loved first after God because of the similarity which it has to God, who is certainly perfectly rational.' See also Richard Egenter, "Die Soziale Leitidee im '*Tractatus de Bono Communi*' des Fr. Remigius von Florenz," *Scholastik* 9 (1934), p. 84.
36. Remigius, '*De Bono Communi*,' pp. 21–2: '*coniuntio quam habet pars ad se ipsam causatur a coniuntione quam habet pars ad totum et conservatur ab ipso, quia pars extra totum existens non est pars ut patet ex dictis. Quod autem non est nulli potest coniungi nec sibi nec alteri, quia coniunctio praesupponit esse ...... Ergo totius ad partem maior extat coniunctio quam partis ad se ipsam*': 'union which the part has toward itself is caused by union, which the part has toward the whole and is conserved by it, because the part existing outside the whole is not a part, as is clear from what it is said. But that which does not exist cannot be joined to anything, either to itself or to another, because union presupposes existence ...... Therefore the union of the whole toward the part is greater than that of the part toward itself.'
37. *Ibid*., p. 17: '*Primo quidem quia totum plus habet de entitate quam pars tota. Enim ut totum est existens actu, pars vero ut pars non habet esse nisi in potentia secumdum Philosophum in 7 physic...... Secundo, quia ipsum esse partis, quale habet, dependet ab esse totius. Pars enim extra totum existens non est pars, sicut prius dicebatur, dum esset in toto. Manus enim abscissa non est manus nisi aequivoce*:' 'First, indeed because the whole has more existence than the part. For

the whole is existent in actuality, but the part as part has no existence unless in potential, according to the Philosopher in 7 *Physics* ...... Secondly, because the very existence of the part such as it has, depends upon the existence of the whole. For the part existing outside the whole is not a part, as was said before seeing that it was in the whole. For a hand which is cut off is not a hand except equivocally.'

38. *Ibid.*, pp. 17–8: '*Totum enim prius necessarium est esse parte. Interempto enim toto, nec erit pes, neque manus nisi equivoce, velut si quis dicat lapideam: corrupta enim erit talis. Omnia enim opere diffinita sunt et virtute ...... Unde destructa civitate remanet civis lapideus aut depictus, quia scilicet caret virtute et operatione quam prius habebat ...... Ut qui erat civis Florentinus per destructionem Florentie iam non sit Florentinus dicendus, sed potius flerentinus. Et si non est civis non est homo, quia "homo est naturaliter animal civile," secundum Philosophum in 8 Eth. et in 1 Polit.*'
39. Aristotle, *Politics*, I. ii, 1253a1–2. Here and after I follow Barker's translation. E. Barker (trans.) *Politics*, rev. edn (Oxford: Oxford University Press, 1998).
40. *Ibid.*, III. xviii, 1288a37.
41. Remigius, '*De Bono Communi*,' p. 49: '*Et dicendum quod pars naturaliter diligit totum amore amicitie, sed quia in bono rei naturaliter amate includitur etiam bonum rei naturaliter ipsam amantis inde est quod pars etiam dicitur amare totum propter bonum proprium non quod ordinet bonum totius ad bonum proprium, sed potius e contrario ordinat bonum proprium ad bonum totius.*'
42. Biblioteca Nazionale, Florence, Cod. 940 C. 4 Conv. Soppr. f. 355r: '*Ferte sententiam et in commune decernite quod facto opus sit (Iud. xix); istud verbum vos hortatur ad quatuor officio vestro valde necessaria...tertio, ad Communis promotionem, quia 'quod facto opus est in commune' idest pro bono Communis, scilicet utili delectabili et honorabili, non pro bono huius persone vel domus, vel illius, nec pro bono horum vel illorum, sed, sicut estis facti et positi in officio per Commune, ita laboretis pro communi bono.*' I owe the Latin text to L. Minio-Paluello, "Remigio Girolami's *De Bono Communi*: Florence at the Time of Dante's Banishment and the Philosopher's Answer to the Crisis," *Italian Studies*, XI (1956), p. 58.
43. Cf. Viroli, *From Politics to Reason of State*, p. 47. In contrast to Remigius' concern with people's virtue, Viroli holds that the theorists of city-rule of the thirteenth century focused on the virtues of the ruler. We can take Aquinas, John of Paris and Gile of Rome as those thinkers in favour of monarchy.
44. Remigius, '*De Bono Communi*,' p. 5: '*Scilicet multis quasi dicatur: quanto bonum est communius tanto est magis amandum scilicet bonum civitatis magis quam bonum unius civis et bonum provincie que multas continet civitates magis quam bonum unius civitatis. Unde et per consequens bonum regni magis amandum est quam bonum unius provincie et bonum universalis ecclesie magis quam bonum unius regni.*'
45. *Ibid.*
46. Biblioteca Nazionale, Florence, Cod. 940 C. 4 Conv. Soppr. f. 355v: '*Concordia, que nichil aliud est quam unio vel coniunctio cordium, idest voluntatum ad idem volendum, sit summum bonum civitatis:*' 'Harmony which is nothing other than oneness or union of hearts, that is, of wills to desire the same thing, is the highest good of a city.' Cited in Minio-Paluello, "Remigio Girolami's *De Bono Communi*," p. 59.

47. *Ibid.*: '*Potestas et terror apud eum est qui facit concordiam in sublimibus (Iob xxxv). Instinctu diabolico vel divino iudicio maxima videtur esse discordia in hac civitate; de quo summe gemendum est nobis, quia cum discordia nullum potest esse bonum in civitate*:' 'Power and terror belong to the one who makes harmony in the highest (Iob xxxv). Through the devil's prompting or divine judgement discord in this city seems to be very great; about which we should groan greatly, because with discord there cannot be any good in a city.'
48. *Ibid.*: '*Sine iustitia nulla civitas potest bene vel in concordia regi, sicut domus non potest sine ruitione diu subsistere que male fundata est... .et ideo omnis iniustitia removenda est a statutis civitatis*:' 'Without justice no city can be ruled well or in harmony, just as a house cannot subsist for a long time without falling which has bad foundations...... and therefore every injustice has to be removed from the statutes of a city.'
49. Aristotle, *Nicomachean Ethics*, X. ix, 1180a22.
50. Aristotle, *Politics*, III. xi, 1282b1.
51. Aristotle, *Nicomachean Ethics*, X. ix, 1180a4.
52. Biblioteca Nazionale, Florence, Cod. 940 C. 4 Conv. Soppr. ff. 106^{v}–109^{r}. The tract *De Bono Pacis* is also contained in Davis, "Remigio de' Girolami and Dante," pp. 123–36.
53. Remigius, '*De Bono Pacis*,' p. 132.
54. *Ibid.*, p. 133.
55. Biblioteca Nazionale, Florence, Cod. 940 C. 4 Conv. Soppr. f. 355^{v}: '*Deus est pax nostra, qui fecit utraque, idest magnos et populum, unum, idest unius velle, ut dicitur ad Eph. ii.*:' 'God is our peace, who makes both, that is, the nobility (*magnos*) and people (*populum*), one, that is, of one will, as is said ad Eph. ii.' Cited in Minio-Paluello, "Remigio Girolami's *De Bono Communi*," p. 59.
56. Remigius, '*De Bono Pacis*,' p. 126: '*Bonum enim Dei prefertur bono cuiuscumque creati. Sed pax est bonum Dei et ad Deum pertinens. Huiusmodi autem temporalia sunt bonum pertinens ad homines. Ergo pro bono pacis assequendo sustineri debent dampna in bonis temporalibus.*'
57. *Ibid.*, p. 127: '*Et dicendum quod predictum verbum Domini intelligendum est quando prelati ecclesie concordant cum Christo, maxime quantum ad intentionem, sicut qui audit nuntium audit dominum mictentem, et qui audit vicarium audit dominum principalem, ubi nuntius et vicarius concordant cum domino mictente et principali. Ubi enim discordarent ab eo, audiendo eos non audirent dominum.*'
58. *Ibid.*, p. 126: '*Et dicendum quod pax potest accipi proprie et vere, et sic semper summitur in bono sicut et ordo, quia pax includit in se ordinem, ut dicit Augustinus in libro 19 de Civitate Dei.*'
59. *Ibid.*, p. 124: '*Philosophus dicit in primo Ethicorum quod bonum gentis et civitatis et multitudinis est preferendum bono unius solius persone tanquam divinius et melius. Sed summum bonum multitudinis et finis eius est pax, sicut dicit Philosophus in tertio Ethicorum, sicut sanitas est summum bonum totius corporis, ut dicit. Unde, sicut propter sanitatem totius corporis negligitur bonum unius membri quod interdum etiam preciditur, ita propter pacem civitatis debet negligi bonum unius particularis hominis.*'
60. Remigius' conception of health seems to be borrowed from Aquinas. For it, see Aquinas, ST, 2a2ae q. 64 a. 2.
61. Remigius, '*De Bono Pacis*,' p. 128: '*Bonum enim mundi consistit in pace, idest in ordinata tranquillitate ad invicem, sicut enim dicit Augustinus in libro 19 de Civitate Dei: Pax corporis est*

ordinata temperatura partium, et pax omnium rerum est tranquillitas ordinis. Et in hoc ordine consistit bonum mundi, secundum Philosophum in 12 Metaphysice. Unde dicit quod omnia coordinata sunt aliqualiter. Sed bonum totius prefertur bono partis. Ergo pro bono pacis pretermictendum est temporale bonum particularium personarum.'

62. Augustine, *The City of God*, XIX. xi and xvii.
63. Ptolemy of Lucca, '*De Regimine Principum*,' in *Thomae Aquinatis Opuscula Omnia* (Paris: P. Lethielleux, 1949), Vol. I, pp. 221–426.
64. Ptolemy, *De Regimine*, IV. ii. 178: '*Necessitudo autem apparet primo quidem considerata humana indigentia, per quam cogitur homo in societate vivere quia, ut in Job scribitur: 'Homo natus de muliere brevi vivens tempore, repletus multis miseriis,' id est necessitatibus vitae in quibus miseria manifestatur: unde secundum naturam est animal sociale sive politicum, ut Philosophus probat in I Polit., et inde concluditur communitatem civitatis esse necessariam pro necessariis humanae vitae:*' 'The necessity is clear when human need has first been considered, through which a human being is compelled to live in a society because, as it is written in Job—'man born of woman has a short life, being full of misery'—, that is the necessities of life in which misery is manifested: hence by nature he is a social or political animal, as Aristotle shows in I *Politics*. and so it is concluded that the communality of the city is necessary because of the necessities of human life.'
65. See *ibid.*, IV. iii. 183; IV. xxiii. 242.
66. *Ibid.*, IV. ii. 180: '*Ex quibus omnibus concluditur civitatem esse necessariam homini constituendam propter communitatem multitudinis sine qua homo vivere decenter non potest, et tanto magis de civitate quam de castro vel quamque villa quanto in ea plures sunt artes et artifices ad sufficientiam humanae vitae, ex quibus civitas constituitur. Sic enim Augustinus definit eam in I De Civ. Dei quod* <*est multitudo hominum in uno societatis vinculo colligata*>': 'From all these things, it is concluded that it is necessary for a human being for a city to be established because of community of the multitude without which a human being cannot live properly. All the more so for the city than for the fort or village, since there are in it more arts and craftsmen for the sufficiency of human life, from which the city is constituted. Thus Augustine defines it in I *De Civ. Dei* as <a multitude of human beings assembled in one bond of society>.' See also *ibid.*, IV. xxiii. 243.
67. *Ibid.*, IV. xxiii. 244.
68. Aristotle, *Politics*, III. vi.
69. *Ibid.*, III. vi–vii.
70. On the other hand, the corresponding deviations are as follows: "for tyranny is the rule of one for the benefit of the monarch, oligarchy for the benefit of the men of means, democracy for the benefit of the men without means. None of the three aims to be of profit to the common interest." *Ibid.*, III. vii, 1279b4–10.
71. See Ptolemy, *De Regimine*, IV. i. 174–5.
72. *Ibid.*, IV. i. 176: '*in ipsorum pectore sunt leges reconditae ...... et pro lege habetur quod principi placet, sicut iura gentium tradunt.*' See also *ibid.*, III. xx.
73. This raises the question of the authorship of *De Regimine*. While Book I of *De Regimine* is devoted to arguing that monarchy is the best form of government, Books II–IV do not maintain this. This is one of main arguments for the claim that the former is written by Aquinas, the latter by Ptolemy. On the authorship of *De Regimine*, see A. O'Rahilly, "Notes

on St. Thomas: IV. *De Regimine Principium*" and "Notes on St. Thomas: V. Tholomeo of Lucca, Continuator of the *De Regimine Principium*," *Irish Ecclesiastical Record*, 31 (1929), pp. 396–410 and pp. 606–14. Cf. More recently, Black, *Political Thought in Europe*, p. 22; James M. Blythe (trans.), *On the Government of Rulers* (Philadelphia: University of Pennsylvania Press, 1997), pp. 3–5.

74. Ptolemy, *De Regimine*, IV. i. 175; IV. viii. 201.
75. *Ibid.*, IV. ii. 178: '*Et quia regimen politicum maxime consistit in civitatibus, ut ex supradictis apparet, provinciæ enim magis ad regale pertinere videntur ut in pluribus reperitur, excepta Urbe Romana quæ per consules et tribunos ac senatores gubernabat orbem ...... et quibusdam aliis Italiae civitatibus quæ licet dominentur provinciis reguntur tamen politice, ideo de ipsius constitutione nunc est agendum*': 'Because political rule particularly exists in cities, as it appears from the above-mentioned, provinces seem to belong more to the rule of a king, as we see in many cases, except the city of Rome which governed the world through consuls, tribunes and senators......and except certain other Italian cities which, although they rule provinces, are however governed in a political way, therefore we must deal with the constitution of the city-state itself.'
76. *Ibid.*, IV. i. 175.
77. See *ibid.*: '*quia si tale regimen gubernatur......per multos, veluti per consules, dictatores et tribunos, sicut in processu temporis in eadem contigit Urbe, postea vero senatores, ut historiæ narrant, tale regimen politiam appellant a polis quod est pluralitas sive civitas, quia hoc regimen proprie ad civitates pertinet, ut in partibus Italiae maxime videmus et olim viguit apud Athenas post mortem Codri*': 'namely if such a regime is governed......by many people, as by consuls, dictators and tribunes, just as in the process of time happened in the same city, and thereafter senators, as histories narrate, they name such a rule political from polis which is pluralitas or city, because this rule properly extends to cities, as we see in parts of Italy especially and it formerly flourished in Athens after the death of Codrus.' Cf. Davis, "Ptolemy of Lucca and the Roman Republic," in *Dante's Italy and Other Essays* (Philadelphia: University of Pennsylvania Press, 1984), p. 287.
78. Ptolemy, *De Regimine*, IV. i. 174–5.
79. Viroli, *From Politics to Reason of State*, p. 44. Viroli mentions that such Aristotelians are Aquinas and Giles. Cf. Nicolai Rubinstein who argues that Ptolemy's republican theme was clarified by Aquinas and Giles of Rome. Rubinstein, "Marsilius and Italian Political Thought of His Time," in *Europe in the Later Middle Ages*, ed. by J. R. Hale (London: Faber & Faber, 1965), pp. 52–4 and pp. 59–60.
80. Ptolemy, *De Regimine*, IV. viii. 201: '*Assumendi igitur sunt rectores vicissim in politia, sive consules, sive magistratus vocentur, sive quocumque alio nomine.*' Also see *ibid.*, IV. i. 174.
81. Skinner, *Foundations of Modern Political Thought* I, pp. 54–5. Cf. Davis, "Ptolemy of Lucca," which shows Ptolemy's combination of theological monarchism and political republicanism.
82. Ptolemy, *De Regimine*, II. ix. 75.
83. *Ibid.*, IV. i. 176. Actually, when Ptolemy differentiates three kinds of lordship—political, imperial and regal lordship—, theoretically speaking, he does not show a negative attitude towards the imperial rule. Ptolemy identifies the characteristics of imperial rule by making a comparison with political and regal rule. First, imperial rule accords with political rule in

terms of how to choose the ruler, that is election, the various origins of the emperor (the elected), and the non-inheritance of emperorship. On the other hand, imperial rule has similarities to regal lordship in the respects of the mode of governing, of being crowned and the exercise of arbitrary power. See *ibid.*, III. xx.

84. *Ibid.*, III. xi. 133–4.
85. *Ibid.*, II. ix: '*Est autem hic advertendum quod principatus despoticus dicitur qui est domini ad servum, quod quidem nomen graecum est. Unde quidam domini illius provinciae adhuc hodie despoti vocantur, quem principatum ad regalem possumus reducere, ut ex sacra liquet Scriptura...... Ad cujus dubii declarationem sciendum est quod ex duplici parte regimen politicum regali praeponitur: Primo quidem, si referamus dominium ad statum integrum humanae naturae, qui status innocentiae appellatur, in quo non fuisset regale regimen sed politicum...... Unde apud sapientes et homines virtuosos, ut fuerunt antiqui Romani, secundum imitationem talis naturae regimen politicum ejus fuit. Sed quia perversi difficile corriguntur, et stultorum infinitus est numerus, ut dicitur in Ecclesiastico, in natura corrupta regimen regale est fructuosius; quia oportet ipsam naturam humanam sic dispositam quasi ad sui fluxum limitibus refrenare. Hoc autem facit regale fastigium...... Ergo quantum ad hoc excellit regale dominium. Patet igitur qua consideratione politiam regno et regale dominium politiae praeponimus*:' 'It is here to be noticed that what is called despotic lordship is that of master to slave, the term (despot) being Greek. Whence certain lords of those provinces today are still called despots, which lordship we can reduce to royal, as is clear from sacred Scripture. To clarify this dubious point, one should know that political rule is superior to royal for two reasons. First, if we refer the lordship to the original state of human nature, which is called the state of innocence, in which there was no royal rule but political instead...... Hence among wise and virtuous men, such as the ancient Romans, according to their imitation of this nature, its rule was political. But because perverse men are corrected with difficulty, and the number of fools is infinite, as is said in *Ecclesiasticus*, royal rule is more effective in corrupt nature, because, since human nature is so disposed, it is necessary to check it with boundaries to its flows. Royal power does this...... Therefore royal authority is superior in this respect...... Therefore it is clear for what reasons we prefer a polity to a kingdom and royal power to political.'

Part III

1. Nederman, "Knowledge, Consent and the Critique of Political Representation in Marsiglio of Padua's *Defensor Pacis*," *Political Studies*, XXXIX (1991), pp. 20–1.
2. *Ibid.*, p. 20.
3. *Ibid.*, p. 34.
4. For an example, see Quillet, "Community, Counsel and Representation," in *CHMPT*, p. 554.
5. On this view, see Conal Condren, "Democracy and the *Defensor Pacis*: on the English Language Tradition of Marsilian Interpretation," *Il Pensiero Politico*, 3 (1980), pp. 301–15.
6. Nederman, "Knowledge, Consent and the Critique of Political Representation," p. 28.
7. *Ibid.*, p. 33.

Chapter 7

1. It is also the main concern of contemporary writers in Marsilius' period, although they did not share his views about how to maintain peace in the city. It reflects the chaos in Italy at that time. For an overall view, see Skinner, *Foundations of Modern Political Thought* I, pp. 53–8.
2. Marsilius differentiates a number of definitions of the term *regnum*: 'i) a number of cities (*civitatum*) or provinces contained under one regime, in which sense *regnum* does not differ from a city with respect to species of polity. ii) a certain species of temperate polity or regime, which Aristotle calls "temperate monarchy," in which sense a state may consist in a single city as well as in many cities. iii) a combination of the first and the second, that is a royal monarchy composed of a number of cities. iv) something common to every species of temperate regime, whether in a single city or in many.' See *DP*, I. ii. 2. It is the fourth sense that Marsilius means when he talks about civil states in general. At the same time, Marsilius' sense of *regnum* sometimes implies the first sense, in particular when he mentions the *regnum Italicum*. Marsilius uses *civitas* or *regnum* interchangeably to indicate the civil community in general.

   Gewirth usually translates Marsilius' terms *civitas*, *civilitas* and *regnum* as 'state.' However, this is not a proper term for the Marsilian *regnum*. The above terms have different nuances according to contexts. It could mean a *polis* (as in the case of Barker's translation of Aristotle's *Politics*) or a political community (B. Jowett's translation) or a political association or sharing. Here for convenience I usually use the term 'political association' for *regnum* because the term 'state' has misleading modern connotations. In order to be faithful to the 'contextual approach' on which my work is in part based, I often use Marsilius' term in Latin, *regnum*, *civitas* and so on. When I use the term 'state,' this connotes the same meaning as 'political association' and only indicates a customary usage of civic community without any connotation of its distinctive modern meaning.
3. It should be remembered that Marsilius uses the older chapter-divisions of the *Politics*. For convenience, I follow Marsilius' use.
4. Aristotle, *Politics*, I. ii, 1252b27.
5. *DP*, I. iii. 4.
6. *DP*, I. iv. 5.
7. *DP*, I. ii. 3; I. iii. 5.
8. *DP*, I. xii. 7.
9. Cf. *DP*, I. iii. 4.
10. *DP*, I. i. 1.
11. Wilks, "Corporation and Representation in the *Defensor Pacis*," *Studia Gratiana*, 15 (1972), p. 260; *DP*, I. ii. 3; I. iii. 4.
12. *DP*, I. xii.
13. *DP*, II. xii. 8. Cf. *DP*, I. x. 3. For the discussion of Marsilius' understanding of nature, see this Chapter, Section 2.
14. Marsilius only mentions Aristotle's phrase (*Politics*, I. ii. 1253a 29) about the naturalness of civil association. See *DP*, I. iv. 3.
15. *DP*, I. i. 7.

16. *DP*, I. v. 5.
17. *DP*, I. iv. 5.
18. Aristotle, *Politics*, VII. vii.
19. *DP*, I. xiii. 4.
20. Marsilius did not interpret the term *honorabilitas* in the same sense as Aristotle. That is, Marsilius' term *honorabilitas* means the quality of being 'honourable' rather than owning 'assessed property.' Gewirth points out that it is because Marsilius and other Aristotelians were misled by William of Moerbeke's translation of the Greek. See Gewirth, *Marsilius of Padua*, Vol. I, p. 199 and p. 180, n. 7.
21. Aristotle, *Politics*, III. i.
22. *DP*, I. v. 11.
23. *DP*, I. ii. 3.
24. *DP*, I. ii. 3.
25. *DP*, I. i. 2.
26. *DP*, I. i. 3 and 7; I. xix. 1 and 3.
27. *DP*, III. iii. 1.
28. *DP*, I. iv. 3.
29. *DP*, I. xi. 1.
30. *DP*, I. xi. 1.
31. *DP*, II. xii. 7.
32. *DP*, I. xi. 1 and 6.
33. For law and sufficiency, see *DP*, I. xii. 7–8; II. xxii. 15.
34. For it, see *DP*, I. x. 3.
35. Cf. Nederman, *Community and Consent*, pp. 81–2. For the relation between Marsilian natural law and the Ciceronian conception, see Nederman, "Nature, Justice, and Duty in the *Defensor Pacis*," pp. 628–32.
36. See *DP*, II. xii. 7–8. Marsilius used the term *ius naturale* instead of *lex naturalis*. For Aquinas' notion of *ius naturale*, see *ST*, 2a2ae q. 57 a. 2.
37. *DP*, I. xii. 8.
38. Cf. Carr who argues that Marsilian natural law is non-rational; but he gives no convincing reasons for his conclusion. David R. Carr, "Marsilius of Padua and the Role of Law," *Italian Quarterly*, 108 (1987), p. 10.
39. For Marsilius, there are two kinds of human law: one is natural law (*ius naturale*), the other civil law (*ius civile*). *DP*, II. xii. 7. This division of human law in Marsilius comes from Aristotle who, unlike Aquinas, understands that natural law is not prepolitical. See Aristotle, *Nichomachean Ethics*, V, trans. by J. A. K. Thomson, rev. edn (Harmondsworth: Penguin Books, 1976), pp. 188–90.
40. *DP*, I. v. 3–5.
41. Aquinas, *ST*, 1a2ae, q. 93. Cf. Gewirth, *Marsilius*, Vol. I, p. 133 n. 7. According to Gewirth, whereas Aquinas' eternal law refers to an *examplar rerum artificiatarum* to illustrate analogically the divine creation and governance of the universe, Marsilius uses the same phrase literally to indicate a measure or pattern of objects made by human art. But Gewirth seems to miss a point that for Marsilius in the Middle Ages divine law is an inevitable criterion of the measurement of human acts. For it, see *DP*, II. xii. 9: "what is lawful and what unlawful

in an absolute sense must be viewed according to divine law rather than human law, when these disagree in their command, prohibitions, or permission."

42. Cf. Carr, "Marsilius and the Rule of Law," p. 10.
43. *DP*, I. x. 3.
44. *DP*, II. viii. 4.
45. *DP*, II. xii. 9.
46. *DP*, I. x. 3.
47. *DP*, I. x. 4.
48. *Ibid.*
49. *DP*, I. xii. 2.
50. *DP*, I. x. 5.
51. In contrast, Lewis argues that Marsilius found the essence of law in its coerciveness rather than in its justice. E. Lewis, "The 'Positivism' of Marsiglio of Padua," *Speculum*, 38 (1963), pp. 541–82.
52. For the various senses of *jus*, see *DP*, II. xii. 6–12.
53. *DP*, II. xii. 10.
54. *DP*, I. xii. 5. Marsilius differentiates three kinds of 'judge' in this world. First, the 'judge' is anyone who discerns or knows, especially in accordance with some theoretical or practical habit: e.g. the geometer, the physician and the house builder. In another sense, the 'judge' means the man who possesses the science of political or civil law, and who is usually called an advocate. In a third sense, 'judge' means the ruler who has the authority to judge concerning the just and beneficial in accordance with the laws or customs, and to command and execute through coercive force the sentences made by him (*DP*, II. iii. 8). Only the judge in the third sense, that is the legislator, has secular coercive jurisdiction, to which all men must be subject. See *DP*, II. viii. 8.
55. *DP*, I. xii. 6.
56. *DP*, III. ii. 9–10.
57. *DP*, I. xiii. 2.
58. Aristotle, *Nicomachean Ethics*, VIII. i. See also *Politics*, III. xi.
59. Aristotle supposed that the ideally best form of government was kingship or aristocracy, but the practically best rule was the mixed constitution.
60. *DP*, I. xiii. 1; II. xxii. 15.
61. *DP*, I. xi. 3.
62. *DP*, I. xiii. 2.
63. Cf. Carr, "Marsilius and the Role of Law," p, 24.
64. *DP*, I. xiii. 3.
65. *DP*, I. xi. 3.
66. *DP*, I. xiii. 8.
67. *DP*, I. v. 5–7.
68. *DP*, I. xiii. 5.
69. *DP*, I. xii. 8.
70. *DP*, I. xii. 6.
71. *DP*, I. xiii. 3.
72. *DP*, I. xii. 5.

73. *DP*, I. xiii. 8.
74. See *DP*, I. xii. 2.

Chapter 8

1. Rousseau criticises the idea of political representation on the grounds that representation is subversive of liberty and political identity. In Rousseau's view, when the supreme authority in a state, which means nothing other than the general will, is represented, the sovereign authority no longer expresses the general will but that of a particular individual because the artificial collective being that the general will sustains dissolves into a multiplicity of individuals who find themselves subject to the will of another. See J. J. Rousseau, *The Social Contract and Discourse* (London: J. M. Dent & Sons, 1973), p. 176 and pp. 182–5.
2. *DP*, I. xiii. 8.
3. *DP*, I. viii. 1.
4. See Aristotle, *Politics*, III. i and vii.
5. *DP*, I. xii. 4.
6. *DP*, I. xiii. 4.
7. *DP*, I. xii. 4.
8. See Aristotle, *Politics*, III. ii, 1281b26.
9. For it, see *DP*, I. viii. 3; I. xii. 4. Cf. Aristotle's *Politics*, III. i.
10. *DP*, I. xiii. 4.
11. Cf. Nederman, "Knowledge, Consent and Representation," p. 33.
12. Gewirth, *Marsilius of Padua*, Vol. I, pp. 182–99.
13. Wilks, "Corporation and Representation," p. 277 and pp. 279–89; Quillet, *La Philosophie Politique de Marsile de Padoue*, pp. 93–9; Lagarde, *La Naissance de l'Esprit Laïque*, Vol. III, pp. 141–5.
14. Quillet, "Community, Counsel and Representation," pp. 560–1.
15. *Ibid.*, p. 571.
16. Wilks, *The Problem of Sovereignty*, pp. 195–6 and p. 479.
17. *DP*, I. xiii. 2.
18. See *DP*, II. xxvi. 5.
19. *DP*, II. xxvi. 5.
20. *DP*, I. xii. 5.
21. See Nederman, "Knowledge, Consent and Representation," p, 24.
22. The translation 'weightier' was originally suggested by Previté-Orton. See his edition of the *DP* (Cambridge: Cambridge University Press, 1928), p. xvi; Previté-Orton, "Marsiglio of Padua, Doctrines," p. 8. It has been adopted as the best term available in English to render the complex variety of qualitative and quantitative features embodied in Marsilius' term. Cf. Allen, "Marsiglio of Padua and Medieval Secularism," p. 181; McIlwain, *The Growth of Political Thought*, pp. 301–3.
23. *DP*, I. xii. 3. The words '*et qualitate*' were omitted in several manuscripts. See Gewirth, *Marsilius of Padua*, Vol. I. p. 183.
24. *DP*, I. xii. 4. For it, see also *DP*, I. xii. 5 and 8; I. xiii. 1–3.

25. Gierke, *Political Theories of the Middle Ages*, p. 62.
26. d'Entrèves, *The Medieval Contribution*, p. 56; Gewirth, *Marsilius of Padua*, Vol. I, p. 183. For Marsilius' statement of it, see also *DP*, I. xii. 3.
27. *DP*, I. xiv. 8.
28. This division is based on the actual experience of the Italian communes: the *vulgus* and the *honorabilitas* take the place of the various groups of the *popolani* on the other hand, and *magnati* and clergy on the other. For a detailed account of these divisions, see Philip Jones, *The Italian City-State, From Commune to Signoria* (Oxford: Clarendon Press, 1997), Ch. 3–4, which include rich bibliographical materials.
29. *DP*, I. xiii. 2.
30. *DP*, I. xiii. 4.
31. Gewirth, *Marsilius of Padua*, Vol. I, p. 199.
32. *DP*, I. xiii. 4.
33. *DP*, I. xiii. 2.
34. *DP*, I. xiii. 2.
35. *DP*, I. xii. 5.
36. *DP*, I. xiii. 4.
37. *DP*, I. xiii. 3.
38. *DP*, I. xii. 6.
39. *DP*, I. xii. 2.
40. *DP*, I. xiii. 4. According to Wilks, Marsilius' *prudentes* are specially endowed by nature to be more politically minded than the rest and to act as natural leaders of the nascent community. In addition, they are more active politically by virtue of their greater natural rationality or right-mindedness, and their greater expertise in legal and civil matters. See Wilks, "Corporation and Representation," pp. 273–4. I doubt that this is in fact Marsilius' view of the *prudentes*.
41. *DP*, I. vii. 1.
42. Marsilius says that nature initiated the differentiation and produced some who in their natural dispositions were apt for farming, others for military pursuits, others for judicial roles and so on, that is, different men are suited to different works. Out of the diversity of the natural inclinations in all men, nature perfected what was necessary for the diverse parts of the political association (see *DP*, I. vii. 1). But we cannot find him affirming that the diversity is based on the natural differentiation in terms of quality in the sense of merit or worth.
43. When Marsilius is saying this, it indicates a deformed nature of some men. But the passage implies in part that men can be innocently ignorant of other things on which they do not work, due to their different functions in a civil community. For this, see *DP*, I. xii. 5.
44. *DP*, I. xiv. 3 and 5.
45. *DP*, I. xv. 4.
46. *DP*, I. xv. 11.
47. Aristotle, *Nicomachean Ethics*, V. vi, 1134b1. See *DP*, I. xiv. 2. Adapting Aquinas' translation of this passage, Marsilius says that "*est autem princeps custos iusti*." However, in the next chapter, we shall see the difference between *princeps* and *pars principans* in Marsilius.
48. *DP*, I. xv. 14.

49. *DP*, I. xv. 6.
50. *DP*, I. xv. 4.
51. *DP*, I. xii. 3.
52. *DP*, I. xiii. 8; I. xiv. 9.
53. For Marsilius, election by the whole body of citizens is a concrete method of exercising its authority to establish the offices of government. Lacking the authority of election, a person cannot be a ruler. Election by the whole body of citizens or the whole community is the means to give actual acknowledgement of the legality of rulers. Thus, election is the certain standard of government and the proper way to recognise the ruler. See *DP*, I. ix. 9; I. xiv. 9.
54. *DP*, I. xv. 6 and 10.
55. *DP*, I. xv. 8 and 10; I. xvii. 7.
56. *DP*, I. xix. 3.
57. *DP*, I. xv. 14.
58. *DP*, I. xi. 1.
59. Rousseau, *The Social Contract and Discourse*, p. 184.
60. *DP*, I. xi. 6.
61. *DP*, I. xviii. 3.
62. Nederman, "Knowledge, Consent and Representation," pp. 33–4.
63. Cf. *ibid.*, p. 35.

Chapter 9

1. *DP*, I. xiii. 8.
2. Marsilius, *Defensor Minor*, ed. by C. Kenneth Brampton (Birmingham, 1922); *Œuvres Mineures: Defensor Minor and De Translatione Imperii*, ed. by Colette Jeudy and Jeannine Quillet (Paris: Editions du Centre National de la Recherche Scientifique, 1979); *Writings on the Empire: Defensor Minor and De Translatione Imperii*, trans. by Cary J. Nederman (Cambridge: Cambridge University Press, 1993). While Gewirth, Wilks and Quillet agree that *DM* is a work in favour of the Roman empire or the rule of the emperor, Nederman challenges the view of *DM* as a work of imperial political theory. Nederman argues that *DM* is an extension and application of the principles of *DP* that the community is the legitimate source of political authority. See Gewirth, *Marsilius of Padua*, p. 131; Wilks, *The Problem of Sovereignty*, p. 111; Quillet, *La Philosophie Politique*, p. 265; Nederman, "From *Defensor Pacis* to *Defensor Minor*: The Problem of Empire in Marsiglio of Padua," *History of Political Thought*, XVI (1995), pp. 313–29.
3. *DP*, I. xv. 6–7; *DM*, xiv. 3; xv. 3.
4. *DP*, II. xvii. 9 and 15–18; II. xxi. 5–8; *DM*, i. 5. Hereafter, while Gewirth translates '*principans ipsius auctoritate*' as 'the ruler by its authority,' I translate it as 'the ruler by the authority of the legislator' for the clarification of the meaning. Marsilius uses *ipsius* as an indirect reflexive modifying *legislator* in order to avoid ambiguity over whose authority is meant. If he had meant to indicate that the *auctoritas* belonged to the *principans*, he would have written *sua*. This grammatical distinction supports our populist interpretation of the

legislator in Marsilius. That is, insofar as the ruler is authorised by the people, the power of the ruler is given by the people, not by himself.

5. *DM*, xiii. 9 (see both Quillet's and Brampton's edition of *DM*). For more, see *DP*, II. xxi. 2; II. xxii. 10; *DM*, xvi. 4; i. 7: iii. 7. Usually, I cite English translations of Marsilius' texts, but here I leave this passage in Latin. I have two reasons for doing so. One is to show Marsilius' populist position on the legislator again. As seen in the quotation above, the Quillet edition of *DM* says '*summus imperator vocatus*,' while in the Brampton edition, '*summus*' is replaced by '*humanus*.' Referring to the Quillet edition, which is the modern standard edition of *DM*, Nederman translates these words as 'the supreme Roman ruler who is called emperor,' which implies the absolutist theory of the emperor. By contrast, given that the Roman ruler is the equivalent of the legislator (the whole body of citizens) in historical context, not the sole sovereign legislator, it is interesting to know the Brampton edition about the passage. Second, I cite this passage in Latin for consistency in terminology. Nederman translates '*civium universitas* or *eius par valentior*' as 'the community of citizens or their greater part,' while Gewirth translates it as 'the whole body of citizens' or 'its weightier part' in *DP*.
6. For example, see *DM*, xiii. 7 ('*Alius vero iudex est principans proprie vocatus, cui tradita est auctoritas et data coactiva potestas ad transgressores legum per poenas arcendos*').
7. *DP*, I. xv. 5.
8. Cf. Wilks' view which interprets the emperor as the *pars principans*. See his *The Problem of Sovereignty*, pp. 110–1.
9. *DP*, I. xviii. 1–3; II. xxviii. 14–5. In particular, Marsilius uses the term *princeps* often in the context in which he argues for the ruler's coercive jurisdiction over the pope. See *DM*, viii. 3; x. 6; xvi. 3. For Marsilius' mixed use of the terms *princeps* or *principans*, see *DP*, II. viii. 9; II. xxx. 5; *DM*, 13. vii.
10. See *DM*, iii. 1. For the conception of the weightier part in Marsilius, see my Ch. 8, pp. 117–122.
11. For some, inconsistency between Discourse I and II of *DP* raises the question of the authorship of the *DP*: was *DP* co-written with John of Jandun? On this point, d'Entrèves and Gewirth argue for attributing the authorship of the whole work to Marsilius alone (d'Entrèves, *Medieval Contribution*, p. 67; Gewirth, "John of Jandun and the *Defensor Pacis*," *Speculum*, XXIII (1948), pp. 267–72). By contrast, Previte-Orton says that John of Jandun is not a sharer in the composition of *DP* but an auxiliary to the real author. Previté-Orton, "Marsilius of Padua," *The Proceedings of the British Academy*, XXI (1935), p. 142.
12. According to Nederman, Marsilius' secular political theory is 'generic' in character and he does not want to specify a particular political unit which he prefers. By using terms of *civitas* and *regnum* interchangeably, Marsilius leaves the term for political units vague. Nederman considers this ambiguity to be deliberate. See Nederman, "The Problem of Empire," p. 317.
13. *DM*, xii. 1.
14. *DP*, II. xxvi. 5. For the constitution of the electors, see *TI*, Ch. 11 and *DP*, II. xxvi. 9.
15. See *DP*, II. xxx. 8.
16. Cf. Barraclough who points out very succinctly that the empire was Roman in the sense that a German empire was not established independent of Rome, but in substance was German in the sense that its establishment reflected the ascendancy of the German monarchy.

Geoffrey Barraclough, *The Medieval Empire: Idea and Reality* (London: The Historical Association, 1969), p. 15.

17. *DP*, I. xvii. 1.
18. *DP*, I. xvii. 6.
19. *DP*, I. xvii. 3 and 5.
20. *DP*, I. xvii. 2.
21. *DP*, I. xvii. 11.
22. *DP*, I. xvii. 2–6.
23. *DP*, I. i. 3.
24. Rubinstein, "Marsilius of Padua and Italian Political Thought," pp. 44–5.
25. *Ibid.*, p. 46. Cf. Wilks, *The Problem of Sovereignty*, p. 111.
26. Rubinstein, "Marsilius of Padua and Italian Political Thought," pp. 72–3.
27. *Ibid.*, pp. 56–7.
28. Gewirth, *Marsilius of Padua*, Vol. I, p. 128.
29. *DP*, II. xxviii. 15.
30. Wilks, *The Problem of Sovereignty*, p. 110. For Marsilius' opinion which Wilks cites, see *DP*, I. i. 6. Cf. Rubinstein who says that the original purpose of the book was not to formulate an imperial doctrine in answer to the papalist claims of plenitude of power, and it was not until much later, after years of service with Louis of Bavaria, that Marsilius used some of the conclusions he had reached in the *DP* to substantiate a theory of universal empire. Rubinstein, "Marsilius and Italian Political Thought," p. 44.
31. See Bartolus, *Comment. on Dig, Nov.* 49.15.24. § 7, pp. 983–4. Cf. Wilks, *The Problem of Sovereignty*, p. 113 and p. 239.
32. Folz, *The Concept of Empire*, p. 6.
33. *Ibid.*, p. 23.
34. Marsilius, *TI*, Ch. 1. Historically speaking, the deposition of Romulus Augustulus by Odovaca in 476 signified the end of the Western Roman empire, but the concept of the Roman empire as a synonym for the empire survived. Folz and Bryce see that it is caused by the tradition of the universal rule of Rome politically and religiously. Folz, *The Concept of Empire*, pp. 4–5; J. Bryce, *The Holy Roman Empire* (London: Macmillan, 1928), pp. 375–7.
35. Cf. Wilks, *The Problem of Sovereignty*, p. 112.
36. See Charles T. Davis, *Dante and the Idea of Rome* (Oxford: Clarendon Press, 1957), p, 18.
37. Barraclough, *The Medieval Empire*, p. 24.
38. Dante, *Monarchy*, trans. by Prue Shaw (Cambridge: Cambridge University Press, 1996), III. xvi, p. 91.
39. The title 'Roman empire' appeared under Conrad II (1034); 'holy' was added by Frederick Barbarossa in 1157 as a counterpart to 'holy Catholic church.' See Bryce, *The Holy Roman Empire*, pp. 199–201; Barraclough, *The Medieval Empire*, p. 4.
40. Quillet, *La Philosophie de Marsile*, pp. 75–7.
41. *Ibid.*, p. 87.
42. *Ibid.*, p. 47. For the emperor as the titular ruler of the Italian city-states after the peace of Constance between Frederick I and the Lombard league, see *CMH*, V, Ch. 5 and 13.
43. Quillet, *La Philosophie de Marsile*, p. 89.

44. Cf. Nederman, "The Problem of Empire," p. 315.
45. See *DP*, II. xxv–vi; II. xxx. 7–8.
46. For them, see Ch. 4 of this book.
47. McIlwain maintains that the *DP* was the first book in the whole controversy which denied to the clergy coercive authority of any kind whatever, spiritual or temporal. McIlwain, *The Growth of Political Thought*, p. 313. See also d'Entrèves, *Medieval Contribution*, p. 73. Cf. Gewirth, *Marsilius of Padua*, Vol. I, p. 9.
48. Recognising that the senses of plenitude of power are various according to its use, Marsilius differentiates the meanings of *plenitudo potestatis* as follows: 'i) the unlimited power to perform every possible act and to do anything at will. ii) any voluntarily controlled act upon any other man and upon any external thing. iii) the power of supreme coercive jurisdiction over all the governments, peoples, communities, groups, and individuals in the world. iv) the jurisdictional power over all clergy only, including the power to appoint them to church offices, to deprive them or depose them, and to distribute ecclesiastical temporal goods or benefices. v) the power whereby priests can in every way bind and loose men from guilt and punishment, and excommunicate them, lay them under interdict, and reconcile them to the church. vi) the power of the priests to lay their hands on all men, and the power to bestow or prohibit ecclesiastical sacraments. vii) the power to interpret the meaning of Scripture, and the power to distinguish the true meanings from the false, the sound from the unsound: the power to regulate all church ritual, and to make a general coercive command ordering the observance of such regulations under penalty of anathematization. viii) a general pastoral cure of souls, extending to all peoples and provinces in the world.' *DP*, II. xxiii. 3.
49. See my Ch. 3, pp. 49–57.
50. *DP*, II. xvi. 12; II. vi. 3; II. xxiii. 5.
51. *DP*, II. x. 2.
52. *DP*, II. iv.
53. *DP*, II. v.
54. *DP*, I. x; II. x. 8.
55. *DP*, II. iv. 8.
56. *DP*, I. iv. 5; I. v. 1.
57. See Gewirth, *Marsilius of Padua*, Vol. I, pp. 92–3.
58. d'Entrèves and Gewirth find the novelty (or modernity) of Marsilius' position in its complete absorption of the church into the state, in the sense that it was the reversal of the normal approach to the problem of the relation between church and state. d'Entrèves, *Medieval Contribution*, pp. 46, p. 73 and p. 82; Gewirth, *Marsilius of Padua*, Vol. I, pp. 9–10.
59. d'Entrèves, *Medieval Contribution*, p. 69.
60. *DP*, II. ix. 9.
61. On the powers, see my Ch. 3, pp. 49–57.
62. That is, they indicate the persons whom the apostles ordained (i.e. Timothy and Titus). See *DP*, I. xix. 5.
63. *DP*, II. vi. 2: II. xv. 6.
64. *DP*, II. vi. 3–4; II. viii. 1.
65. *DP*, II. ix. 1–3.

66. *DP*, I. xix. 6. Marsilius points out that nevertheless, the popes occupied the temporalities of provinces, estates and other possessions belonging to the empire (see *DP*, II. xxv. 14). In particular, the bishops' desire for temporal goods was the primary source of the conflict between the emperors and the Roman pontiffs. *DP*, II. xxv. 10–13.
67. *DP*, I. xv and xix; II. ix. 2.
68. *DP*, II. vii. 4.
69. *DP*, II. x. 1.
70. *DP*, II. x. 3 and 9.
71. See my Ch. 3, Section 1.
72. *DP*, II. vi. 12. Marsilius' assertion of the priests' non-coercive power is also shown in his treatment of the conflict between the divine law and the human law. For example, to commit fornication is to sin against divine law, but it does not sin against human law and therefore is not punished in this world. But if somebody's sins against divine law are those which human law also prohibits, he is punished in this world as a sinner against human law. See *DP*, II. x. 8.
73. *DP*, II. xxii. 4–5.
74. For Marsilius' description of it in terms of historical explanation, see *DP*, II. xv. 5–6; II. xvi. 8.
75. *DP*, II. xviii. 5; II. xxii. 8 and 16.
76. *DP*, II. xxviii. 13 and 21.
77. See my Ch. 3, Section 3.
78. *DP*, II. xxii. 10; II. xviii. 5.
79. *DP*, II. xviii. 7; II. xi. 8.
80. For Marsilius' statement about this, see *TI*, Ch. 2.
81. *DP*, II. iii. 14.
82. For the electors of the emperor, see *TI*, Ch. 11: *DP*, II. xxvi. 9.
83. *TI*. Ch. 12. In fact, Marsilius argued that without being confirmed by John XXII, the election of Louis by the princes was enough to certify that he was the emperor. See *DP*, II. xxvi. 11.
84. *DP*, II. xxvi. 3.
85. *DP*, II. xxvi. 5–7.
86. *DP*, II. xxiv. 15.
87. *DP*, II. xv. 7–8.
88. See *DP*, II. xv. 6.
89. I suggest that for Marsilius the whole body of the believers (*universitas fidelium*) in the ecclesiastical domain is almost identical with the whole body of citizens (*universitas civium*) in a temporal community. In other words, the scope of citizen in a civil community includes that of the whole body of the believers. It is, first, so in respect of their membership. In the medieval context (of both time and place) in which Marsilius was writing, the Christian community and the civil society were almost coterminous, because the members of the civil society actually consisted of all those who obeyed the church. More importantly, it is so in respect of their role as the supreme judge in the two domains. For the historical overlap of the two terms with reference to the Italian city-states, see Woolf, *Bartolus*, p. 196 and p. 99. Cf. Lagarde, who differentiates *universitas civium* from *universitas fidelium*

in the presumption that in Marsilius, the church is not a proper society, but an aspect of the civil community. See Lagarde, *La Naissance de l'Esprit Laïque*, Vol. III, pp. 219–21.

90. *DP*, II. xvii. 8–9; II. xvi. 1.
91. See *DP*, II. xxv. 9.
92. *DP*, II. v. 8; II. ix. 8.
93. Tierney, *Foundations*, p. 4 and pp. 12–3.
94. *DP*, II. xxiv. 2.
95. *DP*, II. ii. 3.
96. To make the meaning of the term 'church' clear, Marsilius distinguished various senses of 'church' which had been used in historical contexts. First, the term 'church' is a word used by the Greeks, signifying an assembly of people contained under one regime. Second, among the Latins, this word means a temple or house in which the believers worship together and most frequently invoke God. Third, 'church' is defined as clergymen (all the priests, bishops and deacons) and others who minister in the temple or the church. Fourth, it means those ministers, priests or bishops and deacons, who minister in and preside over the metropolitan or principal church. *DP*, II. ii. 2–3.
97. *DP*, II. ii. 3.
98. *DP*, II. iv. 2.
99. As mentioned above, for Marsilius, the whole body of the believers is the ecclesiastical equivalent of the whole body of citizens. In effect, Marsilius uses these terms according to context. That is, when he discusses the people's power in the temporal domain, he adopts the term the whole body of citizens. By contrast, in talking about the people's power at ecclesiastical level, he substitutes the term the whole body of believers or faithful more often for that of the citizens. See *DP*, II. xvii. 9; II. xxv.
100. *DP*, II. xviii. 8; II. xxi. 1
101. *DP*, II. xxi. 4.
102. *DP*, II. xvii. 11.
103. *DP*, II. xvii. 11–15.
104. *DP*, II. xxii. 9.
105. *DP*, II. xxii. 11. For more about the co-possessors of coercive power in the church, see *DP*, II. xvii. 15; II. xxi. 6; III. ii. 25 and 33.
106. *DP*, II. xxv. 4 and 6.
107. *DP*, II. ix. 2–3.
108. *DP*, II. v. 9. For more passages, see *DP*, II. xxii. 4; II. vi. 13; III. ii. 16 and 18.
109. *DP*, II. vi. 12.
110. *DP*, II. xxii. 5.
111. The fourth Lateran council summoned by Innocent III was an embodiment of the representative principle in action on a large scale. It included some 400 bishops, over 800 abbots from all parts of Christendom, representatives of cathedral chapters, other collegiate churches and Christian lay rulers from cities and kingdoms (see Clarke, *Medieval Representation and Consent*, p. 236; Tierney, "The Idea of Representation in the Medieval Councils of the West," p. 27). Even though Marsilius did not mention the Lateran council, its representative nature would have differed from what he thought proper. For Marsilius, all Christians or the whole body of believers should be the constitutive members of the

general council. Marsilius did not talk about the technical or practical composition of the general council, but his view on it is very comprehensive: the general council should be inclusive of all Christians, so non-priests properly participate in the deliberations of the council and help to formulate its decrees. *DP*, II. xx. 13. On Marsilius' description of the procedure of electing the general council, see *DP*, II. xx. 2.

112. For the properties of the general council, see *DP*, II. xviii. 8. It belongs to the general council to appoint and remove ecclesiastical officials, to distribute or bestow on their behalf ecclesiastical temporal goods and to define doubtful meanings and sentences of divine law. *DP*, II. xxi. 10.

113. *DP*, II. xix. 3; II. xxi. 9. For the history of the doctrine of papal infallibility in the Middle Ages, see Tierney, *Origins of Papal Infallibility 1150–1350: A Study on the Concepts of Infallibility, Sovereignty and Tradition in the Middle Ages* (Leiden: E. J. Brill, 1972). Tierney mentions that the transition from the idea of a shared superiority of pope-council to that of a superiority of the council over the pope is one of the most important developments in conciliar theory in the period from the twelfth century to the fourteenth century (Tierney, *Foundations*, p. 55). In this aspect, Marsilius was an influential figure on conciliarism at its early stages, but he went too far to be accepted by later conciliarists. see Black, "Conciliar Movement," in *CHMPT*, pp. 577–8.

114. *DP*, II. xxviii. 21. For the view that the general council is an example of delegation, see Nederman, *Community and Consent*, pp. 57–8. Cf. Quillet "Community, Counsel and Representation," p. 561.

115. *DP*, II. xvii. 14.

116. *DP*, II. xxi. 3.

Conclusion

1. McIlwain, *The Growth of Political Thought*, p. 307. For a similar evaluation of Marsilius' thought, see Lagarde, *La Naissance de l'Esprit Laïque*, Vol. I, p. 188; d'Entrèves, *The Medieval Contribution*, pp. 54–7; Wilks, *The Problem of Sovereignty*, p. 196.
2. Poole, *Illustrations of the History of Medieval Thought*, p. 240. See also, Previté-Orton, "Marsiglio of Padua," p. 2; Morrall, *Political Thought in Medieval Times*, pp. 112–3.
3. On this, see my Introduction.
4. James H. Burns' remark that to embark without restraint on a search for 'origins and development' would be to undertake a virtually endless task is accurate enough. See Burns, *Lordship, Kingship and Empire* (Oxford: Clarendon Press, 1992), p. 16. But, the more important key which may explain this difficulty and evade anachronistic conclusions lies in the fact that the existence of a form does not necessarily guarantee the identity of its content and nature. For example, the democratic form existed in Greece, Rome and the Italian city-states. However, without examining the theoretical presumptions, the constitutional order and other values in a society which support democratic rule as a state form, the appearance of a democratic form does not allow us to say that Greece, Rome and Italy had the same kind of democracy, not to mention that of ours today. Likewise, even though a concept is referred to by later thinkers, in order to identify the influence and continuity of the concept

which has passed through conceptual changes and has had various political ramifications, a more general and historical account of it is demanded. See J. Dunn, *Democracy: The Unfinished Journey 508 BC to AD 1993* (Oxford: Oxford University Press, 1993); Black, "Political Languages in Later Medieval Europe," in *The Church and Sovereignty c. 590–1918*, ed. by Diana Wood (Oxford: Basil Blackwell, 1991), pp. 313–28.

5. However, while for Aristotle, democracy is a deviation, a bad regime, Marsilius, like Ptolemy his contemporary Aristotelian, believes the rule of the people (polity) to be the best regime based on the superiority of people as a collectivity.
6. See Gewirth, "Republicanism and Absolutism in the Thought of Marsilius of Padua," in *Medievo: Rivista di Storia Della Filosofia Medievale*, V (1979), p. 34.
7. *DP*, I. viii. 3.
8. On this, see my Ch. 1, pp. 28–31 and Ch. 8, pp. 128–132.
9. The common good in Marsilius' thought does not always have the same meaning as the public interest in the modern theories of political representation, because as mentioned above, the latter includes more or less the utilitarian understanding of interest. But in the sense that both of them indicate the well-being of the people in a state, I use them without differentiation.
10. On a political division of labour in modern states, see Dunn, "Trust and Political Agency," in *Interpreting Political Responsibility*, p. 42; *ibid.*, *Democracy*, pp. 262–3; P. Pasquino, "The Constitutional Republicanism of Emmanuel Siéyès," in *The Invention of the Modern Republic*, ed. by B. Fontana (Cambridge: Cambridge University Press, 1994), p. 111.
11. On this, see Dunn, "Capitalism, Socialism and Democracy: Compatibilities and Contradictions," in *The Economic Limits to Modern Politics*, ed. by Dunn (Cambridge: Cambridge University Press, 1990); Adam Przeworski, *Capitalism and Social Democracy* (Cambridge, Cambridge University Press, 1985).

BIBLIOGRAPHY

The Works of Marsilius of Padua

Marsilius of Padua, *Defensor Pacis*, ed. by C. W. Previté-Orton (Cambridge: Cambridge University Press, 1928).

Marsilius of Padua, *Defensor Pacis*, trans. by A. Gewirth (New York: Columbia University Press, 1956).

Marsilius of Padua, *The Defender of the Peace*, ed. and trans. by A. Brett (Cambridge: Cambridge University Press, 2005).

Marsilius of Padua, *Le Défenseur de la Paix*, trans. by J. Quillet (Paris: Librairie Philosophique J. Vrin, 1968).

Marsilius of Padua, *Defensor Minor*, ed. by C. K. Brampton (Birmingham: Cornish Brothers Ltd., 1922).

Marsilius of Padua, *Oeuvres Mineures*: *Defensor Minor and De Translatione Imperii*, ed. by Colette Jeudy and Jeannine Quillet (Paris: Editions du Centre National de la Recherche Scientifique, 1979).

Marsilius of Padua, *Writings on the Empire: Defensor Minor and De Translatione Imperii*, trans. by Cary J. Nederman (Cambridge: Cambridge University Press, 1993).

Primary Sources

Albertus Magnus, *Commentary on Nicomachean Ethics* (*Opera Omnia*, Vol. IV) (Lyon, 1651).

Albertus Magnus, *Commentary on Politics* (*Opera Omnia*, Vol. IV) (Lyon, 1651).

Aquinas, T. '*Summa Theologiae*' in *Opera Omnia Iussu Impensaque Leonis XIII Edita*, Vol. V, VII and VIII (Rome, 1882).

Aquinas, T. '*De Regimine Principum Ad Regem Cypri*,' in *Thomae Aquinatis Opuscula Omnia Necnon Opera Minora*, ed. by J. Perrier, Vol. I (Paris: P. Lethielleux, 1949).
Aristotle, *Nicomachean Ethics*, trans. by J. A. Thomson, rev. edn (Harmondsworth: Penguin Books, 1976).
Aristotle, *Politics*, trans. by E. Barker, rev. edn (Oxford: Oxford University Press, 1998).
Aristotle, *Politics*, trans. by B. Jowett (Oxford: Clarendon Press, 1931).
Augustine, *The City of God against the Pagans*, ed. and trans. by R. W. Dyson (Cambridge: Cambridge University Press, 1998).
Azo, *Summa super Codicem* (Pavia, 1506; repr. Augustae Taurinorum, 1966).
Azo, *Lectura super Codicem* (Paris, 1577; repr. Augustae Taurinorum, 1966).
Bartolus, *Commentaria on Digestum Vetus* (Basileæ, 1562).
Bartolus, *Commentaria on Digestum Novum* (Basileæ, 1562).
Bartolus, *Commentaria on Infortiatum* (Basileæ, 1562).
Bartolus, *Commentaria on Codex* (Basileæ, 1562).
Bartolus, '*Tractatus de Regimine Civitatis*,' in *Politica e Diritto nel Trecento Italiano: il 'De Tyranno' di Bartolo da Sassoferrato (1314–1357): con l'Edizione Critica dei Trattati 'De Guelphis et Gebellinis,' 'De Regimine Civitatis' e 'De Tyranno'*, ed. by D. Quaglioni, *Il Pensiero Politico Bibliotaeca* 11 (Firenze: Olschki, 1983), pp. 149–69.
Bentham, J. 'Constitutional Code,' in *The Collected Works of Jeremy Bentham*, ed. by F. Rosen and J. H. Burns (Oxford: Clarendon Press, 1983).
Bentham, J. *First Principles Preparatory to Constitutional Code*, ed. by P. Schofield (Oxford: Clarendon Press, 1989).
Bentham, J. *An Introduction to the Principles of Morals and Legislation*, ed. by J. Burns and H. L. A. Hart (Oxford: Clarendon Press, 1996).
Blickle, P. (ed.) *Resistance, Representation, and Community* (Oxford: Clarendon Press, 1997).
Burke, E. *The Works of the Right Honourable Edmund Burke*, new edn. ed. by W. King and F. Laurence (London: Rivington, 1826–7).
Burke, E. *Writings and Speeches*, ed. by L. G. Mitchell, Vol. 8 (Oxford: Clarendon Press, 1989).
Corpus Iuris Canonici, I: *Decretum Gratiani*, II: *Decretalium Collectiones*, ed. by A. Friedberg (Leipzig, 1881; repr. Graz, 1959).
Corpus Iuris Civilis—Digest, Latin text ed. by Theodor Mommsen; English translation ed. by Alan Watson (Philadelphia: University of Pennsylvania Press), 1985. *Institutes*, ed. by Paul Krueger (Frankfurt, 1970) and *Codex*, ed. by Krueger (Frankfurt, 1970).
Dante, *Monarchy*, trans. by Prue Shaw (Cambridge: Cambridge University Press, 1996).
Innocent IV, *Apparatus super Quinque Libris Decretalium* (Augustae Taurinorum, 1581).
Irnerius, *Summa Codicis des Irnerius*, ed. by H. Fitting (Berlin: J. Guttentag Verlagsbuchhandlung, 1894).
James of Viterbo, *On Christian Government*, trans. by R. W. Dyson (Woodbridge: The Boydell Press, 1995).
John of Paris, *On Royal and Papal Power*, trans. by J. A. Watt (Toronto: Pontifical Institute of Medieval Studies, 1971).
John of Paris, *On Royal and Papal Power*, trans. by A. P. Monahan (New York; Columbia University Press, 1974).
Mill, J. S. 'Considerations on Representative Government,' in *Collected Works of J. S. Mill*, ed. by J. M. Robson, Vol. XIX (Toronto: University of Toronto Press, 1977).
Mill, J. S. *Collected Works of J. S. Mill*, Vol. XVIII: Essays Politics and Society.
'Peace of Constance,' in MGH, *Constitutiones et Acta Publica Imperatorum et Regum*, I (Hanover, 1893), pp. 411–8.

Placentinus, *Summa Codicis* (Mainz, 1536; repr. Torino, 1962).
Ptolemy of Lucca, '*De Regimine Principium ad Regem Cypri*,' in *Thomae Aquinatis Opuscula Omnia*, ed. by J. Perrier, Vol. I (Paris: P. Lethielleux, 1949), pp. 221–426.
Ptolemy of Lucca, *On the Government of Rulers*, trans. by James M. Blythe (Philadelphia: University of Pennsylvania Press, 1997).
Remigius de Girolami, '*De Bono Communi*,' in *La Teologia Politica Communale di Remigio de' Girolami*, ed. by Maria C. De Matteis (Bologna: Pàtron Editore, 1977).
Rousseau, J. J. *The Social Contract and Discourse* (London: J. M. Dent & Sons, 1973).

Secondary Sources

Allen, J. W. "Marsiglio of Padua and Medieval Secularism," in *The Social and Political Ideas of Some Great Medieval Thinkers*, ed. by F. J. C. Hearnshaw (London: Harrap, 1923), pp. 167–91.
Ball, Terence, "Reappraising Political Theory," in *Reappraising Political Theory* (Oxford: Clarendon Press, 1995), pp. 3–38.
Barker, E. *Essays on Government* (Oxford: Clarendon Press, 1951).
Barker, E. "The Concept of Empire," in *The Legacy of Rome*, ed. by Cycil Bailey (Oxford: Clarendon Press, 1957), pp. 45–89.
Barraclough, Geoffrey, *The Medieval Empire: Idea and Reality* (London: The Historical Association, 1969).
Beard, C. H. and Lewis J. D. "Representative Government in Evolution," *American Political Science Review*, 26 (1932), pp. 223–40.
Benson, Robert L. *The Bishop-Elect, A Study in Medieval Ecclesiastical Office* (Princeton: Princeton University Press, 1968).
Benson, Robert L. "Political Renovatio: Two Models from Roman Antiquity," in *Renaissance and Renewal in the Twelfth Century*, ed. by Benson and G. Constable (Oxford: Clarendon Press, 1982), pp. 339–86.
Berger, Adolf. *Encyclopedic Dictionary of Roman Law* (Philadelphia: American Philosophical Society, 1953).
Berger, Suzanne D. (ed.) *Organising Interests in Western Europe: Pluralism, Corporatism, and the Transformation of Politics* (Cambridge: Cambridge University Press, 1981).
Birch, A. H. *Representative and Responsible Government* (London: Allen & Unwin, 1964).
Birch, A. H. *Representation* (London: Pall Mall Press, 1971).
Black, A. *Council and Commune: The Conciliar Movement and the Fifteenth Century Heritage* (London: Burnes and Oates, 1979).
Black, A. "The Conciliar Movement," in *CHMPT*, ed by J. H. Burns (Cambridge: Cambridge University Press, 1988), pp. 573–87.
Black, A. "Political Languages in Later Medieval Europe," in *The Church and Sovereignty c. 590–1918*, ed. by Diana Wood (Oxford: Basil Blackwell, 1991), pp. 313–28.
Black, A. *Political Thought in Europe 1250–1450* (Cambridge: Cambridge University Press, 1992).
Bloom, A. "Leo Strauss," *Political Theory*, 2 (1974), pp. 372–92.
Blythe, J. M. *Ideal Government and the Mixed Constitution in the Middle Ages*, (Princeton: Princeton University Press, 1992).
Bryce, J. *The Holy Roman Empire* (London: Macmillan, 1928).

Brynteson, W. E. "Roman Law and Legislation in the Middle Ages," *Speculum*, 41 (1966), pp. 420–37.

Burns, J. H. (ed.) *The Cambridge History of Medieval Political Thought c. 350–c. 1450* (Cambridge: Cambridge University Press, 1988).

Burns, J. H. *Lordship, Kingship and Empire* (Oxford: Clarendon Press, 1992).

Cam, H. M. *Liberties and Communities* (Cambridge: Cambridge University Press, 1944)

Cam, H. M. "Medieval Representation in Theory and Practice," *Speculum*, 29 (1954), pp. 347–55.

Canning, J. P. "Ideas of the State in Thirteenth and Fourteenth-Century Commentators on the Roman Law," in *TRHS*, 5th ser., 33(1983), pp. 1–27.

Canning, J. P. *The Political Thought of Baldus de Ubaldis* (Cambridge: Cambridge University Press, 1987).

Canning, J. P. "Introduction: Politics, Institutions and Ideas," in *CHMPT*, pp. 341–66.

Canning, J. P. "Law, Sovereignty and Corporation Theory, 1300–1450," in *CHMPT*, pp. 454–76.

Canning, J. P. *A History of Medieval Political Thought 300–1450* (London: Routledge, 1996).

Canning, J. P. "The Role of Power in the Political Thought of Marsilius of Padua," in *History of Political Thought*, XX (1999), pp. 21–34.

Carlyle, R. W. and A. J. *A History of Medieval Political Theory in the West*, Vols. 6 (London: William Blackwood & Sons Ltd., 1903–36).

Carr, David R. "The Prince and the City: Ideology and Reality in the Thought of Marsilius of Padua," in *Medievo: Rivista di Storia Della Filosofia Medievale*, pp. 279–91.

Carr, David R. "Marsilius of Padua and the Role of Law," in *Italian Quarterly*, 108 (1987), pp. 5–25.

Chodorow, S. *Christian Political Theory and Church Politics in the Mid-Twelfth Century: The Ecclesiology of Gratian's Decretium* (Berkeley: University of California Press, 1972).

Chrimes, S. *English Constitutional Ideas in the Fifteenth Century* (Cambridge: Cambridge University Press, 1936).

Clarke, M. V. *Medieval Representation and Consent* (London: Longmans, Green & Co. 1936).

Coleman, C. B. *Constantine the Great and Christianity* (New York: Columbia University Press, 1914).

Coleman, J. "The Dominican Political Theory of John of Paris in its Context," in *The Church and Sovereignty c. 590–1918*, pp. 187–223.

Collingwood, R. G. *Autobiography* (Oxford: Oxford University Press, 1939).

Condren, C. "Democracy and the *Defensor Pacis*: on the English Language Tradition of Marsilian Interpretation," *Il Pensiero Politico*, 3 (1980), pp. 301–16.

Congar, M. J. "*Quod Omnes Tangit, ab Omnibus Tractari et Approbari Debet*," *Revue Historique de Droit Français et Étranger*, 4th ser., 36 (1958), pp. 210–59.

Davis, C. T. *Dante and the Idea of Rome* (Oxford: Clarendon Press, 1957).

Davis, C. T. "Remigio de' Girolami and Dante: A Comparison of their Conceptions of Peace," *Studi Danteschi*, 36 (1959), pp. 105–36.

Davis, C. T. "Ptolemy of Lucca and the Roman Republic," in *Dante's Italy and Other Essays* (Philadelphia: University of Pennsylvania Press, 1984), pp. 254–89.

Dunbabin, J. (1982), "The Reception and Interpretation of Aristotle's *Politics*," in *CHLMP*, ed. by N. Kretzmann, A. Kenny and J. Pinborg (Cambridge: Cambridge University Press, 1982), pp. 723–37.

Dunn, J. "The Identity of the History of Ideas," *Philosophy*, 43 (1968), pp. 85–116.

Dunn, J. *Interpreting Political Responsibility* (Cambridge: Polity Press, 1990).

Dunn, J. "Capitalism, Socialism and Democracy: Compatibilities and Contradictions," in *The Economic Limits to Modern Politics*, ed. by Dunn (Cambridge: Cambridge University Press, 1990), pp. 195–219.

Dunn, J. *Democracy: The Unfinished Journey 508 BC to AD 1993* (Oxford: Oxford University Press, 1993).

Dunn, J. "The Identity of the Bourgeois Liberal Republic," in *The Invention of the Modern Republic*, ed. by B. Fontana (Cambridge: Cambridge University Press, 1994), pp. 206–25.

Dunn, J. "The History of Political Theory," in *The History of Political Theory and Other Essays* (Cambridge: Cambridge University Press, 1996), pp. 11–38.

Edwards, J. G. "The *Plena Potestas* of English Parliament Representatives," in *Oxford Essays in Medieval History Presented to H. E. Salter*, ed. by Jolliffe, J. A. (Oxford: Oxford University Press, 1934), pp. 141–54.

Egenter, R. "Die Soziale Leitidee im '*Tractatus de Bono Communi*' des Fr. Remigius von Florenz," *Scholastik* 9 (1934), pp. 79–92.

Emerton, E. *The Defensor Pacis of Marsiglio of Padua: A Critical Study* (Harvard Theological Studies 8) (Cambridge, Mass., 1920).

Entrèves, A. P. de. *The Medieval Contribution to Political Thought* (New York: Humanities Press, 1959).

Finer, S. E. *The History of Government from the Earliest Times*, Vol. II (Oxford: Oxford University Press, 1997).

Folz, R. *The Concept of Empire in the Western Europe from the Fifth to the Fourteenth Centuries* (London: Edward Arnold, 1969).

Ford, H. J. *Representative Government* (New York: Henry Holt & Company, 1924).

Gewirth, A. *Marsilius of Padua and Medieval Political Philosophy*, Vol. I (New York: Columbia University Press, 1951).

Gewirth, A. "John of Jandun and *Defensor Pacis*," *Speculum*, XXIII(1948), pp. 267–72.

Gewirth, A. "Republicanism and Absolutism in the Thought of Marsilius of Padua," in *Medievo: Rivista di Storia della Filosofia Medievale*, V (1979), pp. 23–48.

Gierke, O. *The Development of Political Theory*, trans. by B. Freyd (London: George Allen & Unwin, 1939).

Gierke, O. *Political Theories of the Middle Ages*, trans. by F. W. Maitland (Cambridge: Cambridge University Press, 1987).

Gouron, A. "Coutume contra Loi chez les Premiers Glossateurs," in *Renaissance du Pouvoir Législatif et Genèse de L'État* (Montpellier: Société d'Histoire du Droit et des Institutions des Anciens Pays de Droit Écrit, 1988), pp. 117–30.

Griffiths, A. P. "How Can One Person Represent Another?" *Aristotelian Society, Supplementary*, 34 (1960), pp. 187–224.

Grignaschi, M. "La Definition du 'Civis' dans la Scolastique," in *Anciens Pays et Assemblées d'État*, 35 (1966), pp. 71–88.

Harrison, R. *Bentham* (London: Routledge & Kegan Paul, 1983).

Henderson, E. F. (ed.) *Select Historical Documents of the Middle Ages* (London: Bell, 1903).

Hirst, P. *Representative Democracy and Its Limits* (Cambridge: Polity Press, 1990).

Hume, L. J. *Bentham and Bureaucracy* (Cambridge: Cambridge University Press, 1981).

Hyde, J. K. *Society and Politics in Medieval Italy: the Evolution of the Civil Life, 1000–1350* (London: Macmillan, 1973).

Jolowicz, H. F. *Historical Introduction to the Study of Roman Law* (Cambridge: Cambridge University Press, 1972).

Jones, P. *The Italian City-State, From Commune to Signoria* (Oxford: Clarendon Press, 1997).
Kantorowicz, E. H. *The King's Two Bodies: A Study in Medieval Political Theory* (Princeton: Princeton University Press, 1957).
Kantorowicz, H. (with the collaboration of W. W. Buckland) *Studies in the Glossators of the Roman Law* (Cambridge: Cambridge University Press, 1938).
Keen, M. H. "The Political Thought of the Fourteenth Century Civilians," in *Trends in Medieval Political Thought*, ed. by Beryl Smalley (Oxford: Basil Blackwell, 1965), pp. 105–26.
Kelley, Donald R. *Foundations of Modern Historical Scholarship* (New York: Columbia University Press, 1970).
Kelley, Donald R. *The Human Measure: Social Thought in the Western Legal Tradition* (London: Harvard University Press, 1990).
Kelly, J. M. A *Short History of Western Legal Theory* (Oxford: Clarendon Press, 1992).
Kern, F. *Kingship and Law in the Middle Ages*, trans. by S. B. Chrimes (Oxford: Basil Blackwell, 1939).
Kristeller, Paul O. *Renaissance Thought and Its Sources* (New York: Columbia University Press, 1979).
Lagarde, G. de. "L'idèe de Représentation dans les Œuvres de Guillaume d'Ockham," *International Committee of the Historical Sciences, Bulletin*, XI (1937), pp. 425–51.
Lagarde, G. de. *La Naissance de l'Esprit Laïque au Déclin du Moyen Age, Vol. I: Bilan de XIII Siècle*, 3rd edn (Louvain: Éditions E. Nauwelaerts, 1956).
Lagarde, G. de. *La Nassaince de l'Esprit Laïque au Déclin du Moyen Age, Vol. III: Le Defensor Pacis* (Louvain: Éditions Nauwelaerts, 1970).
Laski, H. J. "Political Theory in the Later Middle Ages," in *CMH*, ed. by H. M. Gwatkin and J. P. Whitney (Cambridge: Cambridge University Press, 1911–36), VIII, pp. 620–45.
Lewis, E. "The 'Positivism' of Marsiglio of Padua," *Speculum*, 38 (1963), pp. 541–82.
Lewis, E. *Medieval Ideas* (New York: Cooper Square Publisher Inc., 1974).
Lockwood, S. "Marsilius of Padua and the Case for the Royal Ecclesiastical Supremacy," *TRHS*, 6 ser., I (1991), pp. 89–119.
Lord, R. H. "The Parliaments of the Middle Ages and the Early Modern Period," *Catholic Historical Review*, XVI (1930), pp. 125–44.
Macpherson, C. B. *The Political Theory of Possessive Individualism* (Oxford: Clarendon Press, 1962).
Macpherson, C. B. *Burke* (Oxford: Clarendon Press, 1980).
Maffei, D. *La Donazione di Costantino nei Giuristi Medievali* (Milan: Dott. A. Giuffrè Editore, 1964).
Manin, B. *The Principles of Representative Government* (Cambridge: Cambridge University Press, 1997).
Mansfield, H. C. Jr. "Modern and Medieval Representation," in *Nomos X: Representation*, ed. by J. R. Pennock and J. W. Chapman (New York: Atherton, 1968), pp. 55–82.
Marongiu, A. "The Theory of Democracy and Consent in the Fourteenth Century," in *Lordship and Community in Medieval Europe*, ed. by F. L. Cheyette (New York: Holt, Rinehart and Winston, 1968), pp. 404–21.
Marongiu, A. *Medieval Parliaments, A Comparative Study*, trans. by S. J. Woolf (London: Eyre & Spottiswoode, 1968).
McIlwain, C. H. *The Growth of Political Thought in West: From the Greeks to the End of the Middle Ages* (New York: Macmillan, 1932).
McIlwain, C. H. "Medieval Estates," in *CMH*, VII, pp. 664–715.
Merkl, Peter H. *Political Continuity and Change* (New York: Harper and Row, 1967).

Minio-Paluello, L. "Remigio Girolami's *De Bono Communi*: Florence at the Time of Dante's Banishment and the Philosopher's Answer to the Crisis," *Italian Studies*, XI (1956), pp. 56–71.

Monahan, A. P. *Consent, Coercion and Limit: The Medieval Origins of Parliamentary Democracy* (Kingston: McGill-Queens University Press, 1987).

Morrall, J. B. and Ehler, S. Z. (ed.) *Church and State Through the Centuries* (London: Burns & Oates, 1954).

Morrall, J. B. *Political Thought in Medieval Times*, 3rd edn (London: Hutchison University Library, 1971).

Nederman, C. J. "Nature, Justice, and Duty in the *Defensor Pacis*: Marsiglio of Padua's Ciceronian Impulse," *Political Theory*, 18 (1990), pp. 615–37.

Nederman, C. J. "Knowledge, Consent and the Critique of Political Representation in Marsiglio of Padua's *Defensor Pacis*," *Political Studies*, 39 (1991), pp. 19–35.

Nederman, C. J. *Community and Consent: the Secular Political Theory of Marsiglio of Padua's Defensor Pacis* (Lanham, Md.: Rowman & Littlefield, 1995).

Nederman, C. J. "From *Defensor Pacis* to *Defensor Minor*: The Problem of Empire in Marsiglio of Padua," *History of Political Thought*, 26 (1995), pp. 313–29.

Nederman, C. J. *Medieval Aristotelianism and Its Limits: Classical Traditions in Moral and Political Philosophy, 12th–15th Centuries* (Aldershot: Variorum, 1997).

Nelson, L. "What is the History of Philosophy?" *Ratio*, 4 (1962), pp. 22–35.

Oakley, F. *Natural Law, Conciliarism and Consent in the Later Middle Ages* (London: Variorum, 1984).

Offler, H. S. "Empire and Papacy: the Last Struggle," *TRHS*, 5th ser., 6 (1956), pp. 21–47.

O'Rahilly, A. "Notes on St. Thomas: IV. *De Regimine Principium*" and "Notes on St. Thomas: V. Tholomeo of Lucca, Continuator of the *De Regimine Principium*," *Irish Ecclesiastical Record*, 31 (1929), pp. 396–410 and pp. 606–14.

Pacaut, M. "L'autorité Pontificale selon Innocent IV," *Le Moyen Age*, 66 (1960), pp. 85–119.

Pasquino, P. "The Constitutional Republicanism of Emmanuel Sieyes," in *The Invention of the Modern Republic*, pp. 107–17.

Pennington, K. "Pope Innocent III's Views on Church and State: A Gloss to *Per Venerabilem*," in *Law, Church and Society: Essays in Honor of Stephen Kuttner*, ed. by Pennington and R. Somerville (Philadelphia: Pennsylvania University Press, 1977), pp. 49–67.

Pennington, K. "Law, Legislative Authority and Theories of Government, 1150–1300," in *CHMPT*, pp. 424–53.

Pennington, K. *The Prince and the Law 1200–1600: Sovereignty and Rights in the Western Legal Tradition* (Berkeley: University of California, 1993).

Pennock, J. R. and Chapman, J. W. (ed.) *Representation, Nomos X* (New York: Atherton, 1968).

Pitkin, H. F. *The Concept of Representation* (Berkeley: University of California Press, 1967).

Pizzorno, A. "Interests and Parties in Pluralism," in *Organising Interests in Western Europe: Pluralism, Corporatism, and the Transformation of Politics*, pp. 247–84.

Plucknett, T. F. T. "Parliament," in *The English Government at Work, 1327–1336*, Vol. I, ed. by J. F. Willard and W. A. Morris (Cambridge, Mass.: The Medieval Academy of America, 1940), pp. 82–128.

Pocock, J. G. A. "The Concept of a Language and the *Mètier d'Historien*: Some Considerations on Practice," in *The Languages of Political Theory in Early-Modern Europe*, ed. by A. Pagden (Cambridge: Cambridge University Press, 1987), pp. 19–38.

Pocock, J. G. A. "The History of Political Thought: A Methodological Enquiry," in *Philosophy, Politics, and Society*, ed. by P. Laslett and W. G. Runciman, 2nd ser. (Oxford: Basil Blackwell, 1962), pp. 183–202.

Pollard, A. F. *The Evolution of Parliament* (London: Longman, Green & Co. 1926).

Poole, R. L. *Illustrations of the History of Medieval Thought and Learning* (London: S. P. C. K., 1932).

Post, G. *Studies in Medieval Legal Thought: Public Law and State 1100–1322* (Princeton: Princeton University Press, 1964).

Previté-Orton, C. W. "Marsiglio of Padua, Doctrines," in *EHR*, 38 (1923), pp. 1–18.

Previté-Orton, C. W. "Marsilius of Padua," in *the Proceedings of the British Academy*, 21 (1935), pp. 137–83.

Przeworski, A. *Capitalism and Social Democracy* (Cambridge: Cambridge University Press, 1985).

Quillet, J. *La Philosophie Politique de Marsile de Padoue* (Paris; Librairie Philosophique J. Vrin, 1970).

Quillet, J. "*Universitas Populi* et Reprèsentation au XIV Siècle," in *Der Begriff des Repræsentatio im Mittelalter, Miscellanea Mediaevalia* 8 (Berlin: Walter De Gruyter & CO., 1971), pp. 186–201.

Quillet, J. "Community, Counsel and Representation," in *CHMPT*, pp. 520–72.

Riley, P. "How Coherent is the Social Contract Tradition?" in *Journal of the History of Ideas*, 34 (1975), pp. 543–62.

Rosen, F. *Jeremy Bentham and Representative Democracy* (Oxford: Clarendon Press, 1983)

Rubinstein, N. "The Beginnings of Political Thought in Florence," in *Journal of the Warburg and Courtauid Institutes*, 5 (1942), pp. 198–227.

Rubinstein, N. "Marsilius of Padua and Italian Political Thought of His Time," in *Europe in the Later Middle Ages*, ed. by J. R. Hale (London: Faber & Faber, 1965), pp. 44–75.

Schiller, A. A. *Roman Law: Mechanism of Development* (The Hague: Mouton, 1978).

Sibley, Mulford Q. "The Place of Classical Theory in the Study of Politics," in *Approaches to the Study of Politics*, ed. by R. Young (Chicago: University of Chicago Press, 1958), pp. 125–48.

Skinner, Q. "Meaning and Understanding in the History of Ideas," in *History and Theory*, 8 (1969), pp. 3–53.

Skinner, Q. *The Foundations of Modern Political Thought*, Vol. I, II (Cambridge: Cambridge University Press, 1978).

Skinner, Q. "Political Philosophy," in *CHRP*, ed. by C. B. Schmitt, E. Kessler and Skinner (Cambridge: Cambridge University Press, 1988), pp. 389–451.

Skinner, Q. *Liberty before Liberalism* (Cambridge: Cambridge University Press, 1998).

Stein, P. *The Character and Influence of the Roman Civil Law* (London: The Hambledon Press, 1988).

Stein, P. "Roman Law," in *CHMPT*, pp. 37–47.

Strauss, L. "Marsilius of Padua," in *The History of Political Philosophy*, ed. by L. Strauss and J. Cropsey (Chicago: Chicago University Press, 1964), pp. 235–38.

Thompson, D. F. *John Stuart Mill and Representative Government* (Princeton: Princeton University Press, 1976).

Tierney, B. *Foundations of the Conciliar Theory: the Contribution of the Medieval Canonists from Gratian to the Great Schism* (Cambridge: Cambridge University Press, 1956).

Tierney, B. *The Crisis of Church and State 1050–1300* (Englewood Cliffs, N. J.: Prentice-Hall, 1964).

Tierney, B. *Origins of Papal Infallibility 1150–1350* (Leiden: E. J. Brill, 1972).

Tierney, B. *Religion, Law and the Growth of Constitutional Thought 1150–1650* (Cambridge: Cambridge University Press, 1982).

Tierney, B. "The Idea of Representation in the Medieval Council of the West," *Concilium*, 187 (1983), pp. 25–30.

Tierney, B. "'The Prince is not Bound by the Laws': Accursius and the Origins of the Modern State," *Comparative Studies in Society and History*, 5 (1963), pp. 378–400.

Tuck, R. "History of Political Thought," in *New Perspectives on Historical Writings*, ed. by P. Burke (Cambridge: Polity Press, 1991), pp. 193–205.

Tuck, R. "Contribution of History," in *A Companion to Contemporary Political Philosophy*, ed. by R. E. Goodin and P. Pettit (Oxford: Blackwell, 1993), pp. 72–89.

Tully, James, *Meaning and Context: Quentin Skinner and His Critics* (Princeton: Princeton University Press, 1988).

Ullmann, W. *The Medieval Idea of Law, as Represented by Lucas de Penna: A Study in Fourteenth-Century Legal Scholarship* (London: Methuen, 1946).

Ullmann, W. "The Development of the Medieval Idea of Sovereignty," in *EHR*, CCL (1949), pp. 1–33.

Ullmann, W. "Some Reflections on the Opposition of Frederick II to the Papacy," *Archivio Storico Pugliese* 13(1960), pp. 3–26.

Ullmann, W. "*De Bartoli Sententia: Concilium Repraesentat Mentem Populi*," in *Bartolo Da Sassoferrato; Studi e Documenti per ILVI Centenario II* (Milan, 1962), pp. 707–33.

Ullmann, W. *Medieval Political Thought* (Harmondsworth: Penguin Books Ltd., 1975).

Ullmann, W. *Law and Politics in the Middle Ages* (London: The Sources of History Limited, 1975).

Ullmann, W. *Principles of Government and Politics in the Middle Ages*, 4th edn (London: Methuen, 1978).

Ullmann, W. "Personality and Territoriality in the *Defensor Pacis*: The Problem of Political Humanism," in *Medioevo; Rivista di Storia della Filosofia Mediovale*, VI (1980), pp. 397–410.

Vinogradoff, P. *Roman Law in Medieval Europe*, 3rd edn (Oxford: Clarendon Press, 1961).

Viroli, M. *From Politics to Reason of State: The Acquisition and Transformation of the Language of Politics 1250–1600* (Cambridge: Cambridge University Press, 1992).

Waelkens, L. *La Théorie de la Coutume chez Jacques de Révigny* (Leiden: E. J. Brill: Universitaire Pers Leiden, 1984).

Waley, D. *The Italian City Republics*, 3rd edn (London; Longman, 1988).

Watkins, M. "Political Theory as a Datum of Political Science," in *Approaches to the Study of Politics*, ed. by R. Young (Chicago: University of Chicago Press, 1958), pp. 148–55.

Watt, J. A. *The Theory of Papal Monarchy in the Thirteenth Century: The Contribution of the Canonists* (London: Burns & Oates, 1965).

Waugh, W. T. "Germany: Lewis the Bavarian," in *CMH*, VII, pp. 113–36.

Wieland, G. "The Reception and Interpretation of Aristotle's Ethics," in *CHLMP*, ed. by N. Kretzmann, A. Kenny and J. Pinborg (Cambridge: Cambridge University Press, 1982), pp. 657–72.

Wilks, M. "*Papa est Nomen Jurisdictionis*: Augustinus Triumphus and the Papal Vicariate of Christ, Part I," in *Journal of Theological Studies*, N.S. 8 (1957), pp. 71–91.

Wilks, M. *The Problem of Sovereignty in the Later Middle Ages* (Cambridge: Cambridge University Press, 1963).

Wilks, M. "Corporation and Representation in the *Defensor Pacis*," *Studia Gratiana*, 15 (1972), pp. 253–92.

Woolf, C. N. S. *Bartolus of Sassoferrato: His Position in the History of Medieval Political Thought* (Cambridge: Cambridge University Press, 1913).

Zinkeisen, F. "The Donation of Constantine as Applied by the Roman Church," *EHR*, 9 (1894), pp. 625–32.

INDEX